Do-It-Yourself Marketing
For the Professional Practice

Laura Sachs

Wishing you success!

Laura Sachs

Prentice-Hall, Inc.
Englewood Cliffs, New Jersey

Prentice-Hall International, Inc., *London*
Prentice-Hall of Australia, Pty. Ltd., *Sydney*
Prentice-Hall Canada, Inc., *Toronto*
Prentice-Hall of India Private Ltd., *New Delhi*
Prentice-Hall of Japan, Inc., *Tokyo*
Prentice-Hall of Southeast Asia Pte. Ltd., *Singapore*
Whitehall Books, Ltd., Wellington, *New Zealand*
Editora Prentice-Hall do Brasil Ltda., *Rio de Janeiro*
Prentice-Hall Hispanoamericana, S.A., *Mexico*

© 1986 *by*

PRENTICE-HALL, INC.
Englewood Cliffs, N.J.

10   9   8   7   6   5

Library of Congress Cataloging-in-Publication Data

Sachs, Laura.
    Do-it-yourself marketing for the professional practice.

    Bibliography: p.
    Includes index.
    1. Medicine — Practice.   2. Medical care — Marketing.
I. Title.
R728.S23   1986   610′.68′8   85-30168

ISBN   0-13-216201-6

Printed in the United States of America

With love to my husband, Bob Sachs

Acknowledgments

Special thanks are due to Bob Crawford, publisher of Professional Communications Inc. (Procom), who introduced me to this subject and suggested that I write a book. My gratitude for reading the manuscript and offering your helpful suggestions, Bob, and for your unending words of encouragement.

Sincere thanks to Rick Pereira, president of the management consulting firm Pereira & Associates, for your contributions and suggestions for Chapter 6.

My thanks to Tod Swormstedt, editor of *Sign of the Times* magazine, for teaching me about sign design and construction.

Sincere thanks, also, to the many professionals and consultants who shared their marketing experiences, materials, ideas, and enthusiasm. In particular, thank you to those individuals who allowed me to reproduce their marketing materials in Appendix D, and to those who provided me with review quotations.

A special thank you to my parents, David and Janice Kirschenbaum. I love you both.

And finally, to my husband and best friend, Bob Sachs, thank you for all the support and sacrifice during the years of this effort, and for your many contributions. Without you there would be no book.

About the Author

Laura Sachs is the president of Laura Sachs Consultations, a State College, Pennsylvania-based marketing, communications, and management firm for professionals in private practice. She consults with individual practitioners throughout the country to develop practice-tailored marketing programs and unique marketing tools, including practice logos, brochures, client newsletters, press releases, practice-building letters, and special events.

Ms. Sachs is best known for her no-nonsense, how-to-do-it marketing and management articles that appear in newsletters, magazines, and tabloids for private-practice professionals. Notably, she is the executive editor of Procom, publisher of *Practice Marketing and Management, Dental Care Marketing, Patient Pleasers,* and *Update* newsletters.

A popular public speaker for professional groups, Ms. Sachs conducts lectures, seminars, and workshops on marketing, communications, and management topics. The former Laura Kirschenbaum, she graduated with honors from Rutgers College and is a member of Phi Beta Kappa.

Foreword

Before Laura Sachs began the arduous task of planning and writing this *Guide,* we talked at length about the need for a source of guidance by the many professionals who want to do something to fend off competition and develop their practices, but who also would be uncomfortable with media advertising. In this *Guide* she amply demonstrates that you can do many effective things to build your practice without being overtly commercial.

Let me emphasize, however, that it's most important in today's economic environment to do something *now.* Almost every profession has its own story of an oversupply of graduates, newly aggressive and price-smart clientele, and waning growth among practitioners. The much-debated question of the ethicality of marketing, while still capable of raising voices and blood pressures among otherwise good friends and colleagues at local professional society meetings, is far from the point. To survive in today's economic environment, one *must* be a marketer. The question is not "should we?" but rather "how can we do it well?" Those professionals who do it well will thrive and prosper. The rest will stagnate or fail.

As the author shows, marketing is not engaging in bragging, puffery, or misrepresenting one's self or services. Effective marketing means providing information to the potential client so that the client will find out about you and acknowledge a need for your services. Truthful, factual information, well told, will be the engine of your marketing plan.

I urge you to recognize that your success depends as much or more on the nature and quality of the information you provide about yourself, your practice, and your services as it does on the quality of the service itself. The fact is that, regardless of the excellence of your technical ability, your potential client has never had a reliable way to make the informed choices that will lead him to your door. And with increasing competition among practitioners in many professions, his choices are even harder to make.

Regarding advertising, the good news is that you most likely don't have to advertise to succeed. Advertising is just one form of marketing, and not always a very effective one for most traditional private practices. Oh yes, it can "bring in the bodies," but as Ms. Sachs points out it doesn't produce long-term loyalty and repeat referrals. And advertising done poorly or without adequate preparation by the entire practice to handle increased leads and inquiries can actually do serious harm to both your image and your profits.

So start now. Start slowly if that's your style and learn as you go. Get your whole staff involved from the start; you'll find you won't be able to do it alone. And besides, marketing is more fun when you can share your successes. We wish you good luck and all the prosperity you desire.

Bob Crawford
Professional Communications, Inc.

What This Guide Will Do for You

This *Guide* contains a wealth of proven nonadvertising practice-building ideas, ranging from the most traditional, low-key projects to the most radical. These ideas are not merely suggested and mentioned in passing; each one is presented with all the complete, how-to-do-it instruction you will need to carry it out to completion. In addition, this *Guide* offers practical suggestions for scheduling, delegating, budgeting, and goal setting so that you will formulate your own specific three-year marketing game plan, tailored to the special needs and circumstances of your practice.

Armed with the information in this *Guide,* you can make informed decisions about your practice and the direction of its marketing activities. You will learn the specific marketing options available to you to make your practice prosper in today's competitive environment — and you will see that you can do it on your own terms. If you wish to advertise your professional services, you may certainly do so, but many practitioners today would prefer not to advertise. Some who do advertise wonder what else they should, could, or might be doing. Others advertise reluctantly. Still others see themselves heading that way with no options.

Do-It-Yourself Marketing for the Professional Practice shows you many options. It provides a great variety of tasteful, affordable marketing techniques that have worked for others — techniques that can be employed in addition to, before, or instead of advertising. Read on to learn about these imaginative options in detail, how others have used them, and how you can adapt them to your situation. This *Guide* will help you make your own decisions about the future of your practice. It is based on the firm belief that calling your own shots is one of the greatest advantages, privileges, and joys of being in practice for yourself.

Using the marketing projects and strategies in this *Guide,* practices of varying sizes, professions, resources, personalities, and geographic areas have developed more clients, a strong referral base, greater name recognition, a motivated staff, and increased profits. Here are some of the special features of this *Guide* that will help you build your practice to its full potential.

This *Guide:*

• **Presents scores of practical ideas that have worked for others.** The table of contents should whet any practitioner's appetite for the extensive menu of marketing projects unfolded in the pages that follow. In all, well over sixty individual projects are given. (A complete listing of the *Guide's* projects appears in Chapter 18.)

• **Provides all the how-to-do-it, step-by-step instruction you need to take any project from concept to reality.** You've come to the wrong place if you're looking for academic marketing theory, with lots of vague, abstract discussion. This *Guide* concentrates only on practical marketing as it applies to professional practices — what works, what doesn't work. It is chock full of the nitty-gritty detail, the "this-is-how-you-do-it" instruction you need, and that you won't get from other marketing books. It cuts through the theory and gets right to the heart of what you'll need to know — whether it is about graphic design, printing, publicity, promotion, writing, speaking, managing, or motivating.

• **Gives numerous examples and inspiring success stories.** When you are considering or undertaking a marketing project, it is invaluable to see successful examples of how others tackled the same project. The *Guide* is laced with numerous successful applications. In addition, Appendix D provides reproductions of the actual marketing materials others are using to build their practices.

• **Alerts you to potential problems and errors.** This *Guide* will save you a great deal of time, money, and aggravation by pointing out the mistakes others have made in their marketing efforts. Use this *Guide* to put the experiences of others to work for you.

• **Helps you analyze your current situation.** Every practitioner needs a clear, accurate assessment of his or her marketing potential to develop a successful marketing plan. You will be shown how to analyze your situation objectively. This *Guide* will help you define your current and potential clients, your competitors, and referral sources, using practical market research techniques that are simple and affordable. It will teach you how to use the information you gather about your market to develop the correct image. It will show you how to convey that image uniformly in your marketing projects.

• **Guides you in planning your marketing strategy, budget, and goals.** You are given specific recommendations about the money you should spend on marketing your practice. This *Guide* will help you develop your marketing plan with a logical, step-by-step system, supported with a series of questions and hands-on worksheets.

• **Develops your practice management systems and techniques so you can execute your marketing plan.** Many of the marketing projects, especially those in Part 2, will help strengthen your practice management systems and skills. Employing the systems described will lead to better telephone procedures, appointment scheduling, staff recruitment, staff motivation, financial arrangements, recall, fee setting, insurance processing, and case consultations.

- **Uses no-nonsense, down-to-earth, concise style.** Much of the instruction in this *Guide* has been boiled down to easy-to-follow, step-by-step checklists. It purposely uses simple, clean, everyday language and is written in supertight style. You will not waste any time or effort trying to decipher instructions or ideas.

- **Organizes the material in a logical, easy-to-follow format designed for quick reference as projects are executed.** Each chapter is organized logically and is supported with many descriptive subheadings. This will make it easy to retrieve information later as you are working on marketing projects.

Do-It-Yourself Marketing for the Professional Practice will be an invaluable aid to any practitioner in any profession — and to any staff member involved in marketing. It takes the mystery out of a complex, often bewildering subject.

To Advertise or Not to Advertise?
That Is NOT the Question

How does a professional develop and maintain the kind of practice that he or she truly wants?

Despite all the hoopla over the 1977 Supreme Court decision allowing lawyers to advertise, and the array of ads that followed, I have observed that professional advertising is at best only a small part of any successful marketing effort. In fact, I've met some incredibly successful practitioners who will go to their graves (and leave sizable estates) without ever having run as much as the smallest Yellow Pages or newspaper ad.

Whether you choose to advertise your practice is up to you. There is no one path to success, but be warned that advertising alone will not guarantee your success. The reason is simple: *You* are the essential ingredient in your success. A good ad may attract new clients but it cannot keep them. *You* can. And if you put into action the ideas in this *Guide* as hundreds of practitioners already have, I am confident that *you will*.

In the pages that follow I will share with you scores of affordable, tasteful alternatives or supplements to advertising that have helped others attract new clients from inside and outside their practices. More important (and here is where advertising alone is weak), the many ideas in this book have helped others develop and maintain a loyal client base. Established, loyal clients are the foundation of any healthy practice. Sure, you can keep looking for new clients to take the place of those you lose — but most successful practitioners usually don't lose a lot of clients. They keep them loyal to the practice and encourage them to invite *more* clients through referral.

A loyal client base does not depend on an ad, no matter how slick and appealing it is. It depends on you, your staff, your policies, and the quality of the services you provide. In short, a loyal client base depends on your clients' total experience of your practice. Most practitioners want to give clients a positive experience in their practices. The question is — how? Providing quality services, while essential, is usually not enough. Unfortunately, most clients are not in a position to judge the quality of the professional services they receive. Nevertheless, they will form an opinion — and probably voice it.

The answer to providing a positive experience for clients is in *marketing*. Good marketing has two facets.

1.   Marketing makes your practice exceptional by treating clients positively on a *personal* level. Usually, an exceptional practice does more for clients than is expected.

2.   Marketing makes current clients and the public aware of how exceptional your practice is.

Advertising may be one way to accomplish the second facet of marketing, and in truth advertising is one aspect of marketing. However, there are plenty of other things you can do in addition to or instead of advertising to make clients and the public aware of your exceptional practice. These marketing projects are described in this *Guide*. Advertising's shortcoming is that it alone cannot accomplish the first facet of marketing; it cannot make your practice exceptional — and yet, many of the marketing projects in this *Guide* can and have done so for others.

Thus, to advertise or not to advertise is *not* the most important question today. What is important is to decide what type of practice you truly want. Once you know what you want, the way to get it is by providing top-quality professional services and by marketing — making your practice *exceptional* and telling people about it.

A CONSISTENT IMAGE UNIFIES YOUR MARKETING PROGRAM

Clients experience your practice in so many ways: they call for appointments or information, they see your office from outside and in, they interact with you and your staff, they receive (and, you hope, pay) your bills. Your marketing efforts must make positive *all* aspects of clients' experiences.

Given the diversity of this interaction, your message to clients must be clear and consistent to have maximum impact. Without one consistent image to unify your marketing efforts, you can end up being your own worst enemy, leaving contradictions and confusion in your wake.

Your professional image is the overall impression people have of you and your practice. It is by its very nature somewhat intangible. Yet it pervades your relationship with each of your clients. Just as we all know some people we like but never quite understand exactly why, many clients will rave about their physician, lawyer, dentist, or accountant without being able to list particular attributes. These practitioners have succeeded in creating a positive image.

Many different professional images can be positive. All positive images share certain characteristics: thoroughness, intelligence, honesty, integrity, and professional concern, to name a few. In other areas there are many ranges of acceptable variation. These include costliness, formality, rigidity, and sense of humor. Let's see how variations in these areas can be positive for different practitioners:

- *Costliness:* Part of a professional image is how clients perceive fees and services provided. *K* mart and Bloomingdale's both have satisfied customers who think their money is well spent. A professional can also convey an image ranging from utmost economy to lavish services, and can succeed, as long as the chosen image is carried through consistently and is appropriate to that professional's style and the expectations of his or her clients.

- *Formality:* Do you introduce yourself by your first name or will clients of thirty years still call you Mr., or Ms., or Dr. Smith? This is an aspect of formality. Professionals can (within obvious limits) decide for themselves how formally or informally they choose to deal with both staff and clients.

- *Rigidity:* Some practitioners convey the image that they run a very tight ship. Others meet equal success by seeming less rigid and rolling with the punches. Either extreme or some compromise can work as long as you are usually on time for appointments and have control of your practice.

- *Sense of humor:* Barring offensive jokes or excessive buffoonery, making clients laugh is usually an asset, but if you lack this skill or are uncomfortable using it in your practice, there is no reason you can't succeed.

As a rule, the wisest course in choosing your image is to remain true to your basic personality. Build on your own strengths. Do not attempt major personality overhauls but rather polish those skills you already have.

Another factor in image selection is current and potential clients' expectations and desires. Using client feedback studies, client file analyses and other market research techniques described in Chapters 1 and 2, you should be able to guess which kinds of images clients will respond to. For example, if you wish to draw clients from a high-income, class-conscious community, a total economy image may drive clients away. If you practice in a low-income area, an image of total luxury may be out of the question.

Finally, once you've decided on your image, let it permeate your practice. If you opt for an informal image, let everything about your practice and marketing projects reinforce this message. Design your personal office with an informal seating arrangement for meetings with clients. Decorate your reception area comfortably and informally. Train your receptionist to encourage an informal atmosphere by appearance and manner of greeting clients. Your business cards and other stationery should not be "wedding-invitation" formal, but should again convey your basic message. Choose reception area reading material, exterior signs, your own manner of dress, tone of oral and written communication — even the name and location of your practice — so they don't contradict your informal image.

As we study each marketing project in Parts 2 and 3 of this *Guide,* and as you later formulate your own three-year marketing plan, your image will be the unifying theme that helps tie these efforts together. Your image will help you make decisions about the kinds of projects to undertake and how to implement them. If you consciously choose one image for your practice, each marketing effort will enhance all the others. Your successful image will feed upon itself and shine throughout your practice.

HOW TO GET THE MOST FROM THIS GUIDE

Marketing your practice requires many steps: goal-setting, planning, budgeting, selection, assignment and coordination of tasks, monitoring of progress, and goal reassessment. Many of the individual projects you may undertake demand skills or knowledge not within your normal repertoire. I have written this *Guide* to help you overcome these obstacles. The chapters that describe individual marketing projects include complete how-to-do-it instruction, advice about pitfalls and common mistakes to avoid, and examples of actual practitioners who have used them to make their practices successful. These chapters may be skimmed on first reading and studied more carefully when you are ready to undertake those projects.

Good, sound ideas and the step-by-step instructions for carrying them out successfully are very valuable, but I've seen many practitioners take a piecemeal approach to marketing and be disappointed. Some projects are naturally prerequisites for others; some are of a higher priority than others; some are more expensive; some are more time consuming; some are better suited to your personality and practice.

In Chapter 18, you will be creating a three-year marketing plan designed specifically for your practice. A plan will enable you to implement a coherent, coordinated marketing program that will achieve your particular goals. It will help you develop a successful image for your practice and choose from the many good marketing ideas and projects in this *Guide,* giving each a concrete timeframe, budget, and tool to measure its success.

In Part 1, you will learn how to assess your current practice and potential market. A client feedback study, a file analysis, a nonclient survey, and other practical, affordable market research techniques will be described in detail.

Parts 2 and 3 of this *Guide* are devoted to internal and external marketing, respectively. Internal marketing refers to projects aimed primarily at the clients already *within* your practice. Internal marketing projects will help you provide a positive experience for your clients by making your practice exceptional. Part 3 covers external marketing, which is everything you can do to attract new clients from *outside* your practice. These projects are the nonadvertising ways to make the public aware of how exceptional your practice is. Part 4 will help you develop and implement your marketing plan for the next three years. For the sake of continuity, I have separated from the text numerous guidelines, samples, and examples of marketing materials. These appear in the four appendixes.

I urge you not to read this *Guide,* put it on the shelf, and say, "Yes, those are some great ideas. Maybe I'll try some of them — someday." These marketing projects have worked for others and they can work for you. I hope you will develop your three-year marketing plan and carry it out.

Successful marketing has many rewards, financial and otherwise. I look forward to including *your* success stories in one of my future books.

Instant Finder Chart of Marketing Idea Generators

Problem Area and/or Issue	Alternative Solutions/ Idea Generator	Chapter References and Subsections
1. What are the most practical, affordable and reliable ways to gather my own market research data about current clients, potential clients, competitors and referral sources?	1A. Conduct a client feedback study, either by personal interview, written in-office survey, telephone, or mail.	1. Getting Started in Market Research 1. Why and How to Conduct Client Feedback Studies
	1B. Conduct a client file study to determine where your clients live and work, their ages, sex, most common reasons for seeking your services, how they heard about you, and related factual information.	1. Client File Studies Reveal Valuable Factual Information 1. Case Histories: How Four Practitioners Used Client File Studies
	1C. Record and track clients' complaints to pinpoint weaknesses of your practice.	1. How to Use Clients' Complaints to Strengthen Your Practice 7. 40: Start a Complaint Record
	1D. Use meetings to gather marketing information from your staff.	1. Staff: An Untapped Source of Vital Marketing Information
	1E. Establish a lay advisory panel to gather marketing insights from representative clients.	1. How to Get More Marketing Mileage from Your Clients 7. 38: Lay Advisors
	1F. Check with government agencies and publishers to see what they already know about your market.	2. How to Get a Free Ride on Someone Else's Market Research

Instant Finder Chart of Marketing Idea Generators

Problem Area and/or Issue	Alternative Solutions/ Idea Generator	Chapter References and Subsections
1. (continued)	1G. Survey potential clients to learn how your market thinks or what it already knows.	2. Surveying Potential Clients; Some Reservations before You Begin 2. The Best Do-It-Yourself Method for Surveying Potential Clients
	1H. Identify competitors and use Yellow Pages, newspapers and other sources to gather marketing information about them.	2. Five Reliable Ways to Learn about Competitors
	1I. Develop referral sources through colleagues and other professionals, and in the community.	17. Proven Techniques for Building and Tracking Referrals 17. Acknowledging and Rewarding Referrals
2. What can I do to make my practice physically attractive so it makes a positive first impression on new clients?	2A. Name your practice in a positive, memorable and appropriate way.	4. What's in a Name? Almost Always an Important Marketing Message
	2B. Develop a tasteful practice slogan to convey your message.	4. Slogans Aren't for Big Companies Only
	2C. Choose an office location with market appeal.	4. The Three Top Priorities for Office Real Estate: Location, Location, Location
	2D. Make your office and the people in it physically attractive.	4. Projecting Your Image through Your Own Appearance 4. Designing Your Office to Appeal to Clients 5. Establish a Code of Dress for Your Practice 7. 44: Look at Your Office through Your Clients' Eyes

Instant Finder Chart of Marketing Idea Generators

Problem Area and/or Issue	Alternative Solutions/ Idea Generator	Chapter References and Subsections
4. How should I structure my office policies so they attract and keep clients?	4A. Establish client-centered telephone policies about fee quotes, interruptions, absentee coverage, and staff evaluation.	6. Policy Area 1: The Telephone
	4B. Make appointment scheduling convenient for clients. Offer a choice of appointments, limit advance appointment scheduling, save premium appointments for clients who need them most, screen and handle emergencies, and plan appointments well.	6. Policy Area 2: Appointment Scheduling 7. 27: Have a Plan for Schedule Delays
	4C. Learn to conduct case consultations that make clients want to accept your recommendations.	6. Policy Area 3: Case Consultations
	4D. Arrange your fees competitively so they appeal to clients.	6. Policy Area 4: Fees
	4E. Offer and publicize payment options and make fair, firm financial arrangements with clients who need them.	6. Policy Area 5: Financial Arrangements
	4F. Make your practice attractive to patients who have insurance coverage.	6. Policy Area 6: Insurance
	4G. Perfect your recall system so clients remain active in your practice and will refer others.	6. Policy Area 7: Recall
	4H. Develop a system for seeking and rewarding client referrals	6. Policy Area 8: Follow-Up and Referrals

5. How can I project a positive, appropriate marketing message with written materials?	5A. Develop a one-of-a-kind practice logo that projects your image and makes you easy to identify and remember.	8. How to Design a One-of-a-Kind Logo for Your Practice
	5B. Use your logo consistently on all practice stationery and office signs.	9. Designing Stationery and Office Signs with Your New Logo
	5C. Create a practice brochure to describe your fine services and make a strong first impression.	10. How to Write, Produce, and Distribute a Practice Brochure
	5D. Publish a regular client newsletter to stay in contact with current and potential clients and referral sources.	11. How to Write, Produce, and Distribute a Client Newsletter
6. How can I get my local newspapers to publish stories about me?	6A. Recognize what's newsworthy in your practice. Send editors press releases with news value.	12. How to Be Successful with Publicity and Promotion Projects
		13. How to Get Publicity for Your Practice with Press Releases
		13. Look for the News in Your Practice
		13. Write an Attention-Grabbing Lead
		13. Prepare Releases the Way Editors Want Them
	6B. Submit journalistic, high-quality publicity photos to newspapers.	13. Submit Interesting Photos to Publication Editors

Instant Finder Chart of Marketing Idea Generators

Problem Area and/or Issue	Alternative Solutions/ Idea Generator	Chapter References and Subsections
6. *(continued)*	6C. Look for other opportunities to appeal to editors, such as feature stories, fillers, letters to the editor, and public service announcements.	13. Modify Releases for Broadcast Journalists
		14. Ten More Projects that Get Publicity for a Practice
	6D. Develop good relationships with media editors.	13. Be Courteous to Editors — Always
		13. Be Careful after Your Release Is Published or Aired
7. How can I use public speaking to build my practice?	7A. Learn as much as you can about the group you want to address.	15. Do Your Homework about Your Audience
	7B. Practice until you can give your speech with confidence and ease.	15. Outline Your Speech According to Its Purpose
		15. Prepare Your Speech
		15. Don't Be a Slave to Your Visual Aids
		15. How to Make Your Notes Foolproof
		15. Rehearse Your Physical Presentation, Not Only Your Words
		15. Keep Your Cool When You Give Your Speech — 10 Tips
	7C. Seek publicity for all public speaking engagements, both before and afterwards.	15. Get Advance Publicity for Your Speech
		15. Milk Your Speech for All It's Worth

Instant Finder Chart of Marketing Idea Generators

Problem Area and/or Issue	Alternative Solutions/ Idea Generator	Chapter References and Subsections
9. Who can help me carry out marketing projects?	9A. Every member of your staff can be actively involved in marketing projects.	5. The Role of Your Staff in Marketing
	9B. Consider hiring a full- or part-time marketing coordinator.	5. Take the Ultimate Step: Hire a Marketing Coordinator
	9C. A graphic artist can design your practice logo and other written marketing tools.	8. Getting a Top-Notch Logo Designed in Ten Easy Steps 10. Work with Your Artist to Design a Quality Brochure 11. Designing Your Newsletter with a Graphic Artist App. A. Employing Others to Carry Out Marketing Projects
	9D. Free-lance photographers, writers, interior designers, and others are a good choice.	App. A. Employing Others to Carry Out Marketing Projects
10. Which marketing projects should I tackle first?	10A. Every practice is different. You'll need to develop a marketing plan tailored to your situation.	18. How to Develop Your Three-Year Marketing Plan
	10B. The first thing you'll need to do is analyze your current situation.	18. Assess Your Current Practice
	10C. Next, be honest with yourself and write down your personal goals for yourself and your practice.	18. Determine Your Long-Term Personal Goals

10D. Then create a specific plan to help you attain your goals, choosing from the many marketing projects described in this *Guide*.	18. Narrow Your Choice of Projects 18. Evaluate Individual Projects with an Analysis Worksheet 18. Establish Annual Budgets for Time and Money 18. Eleven Down-To-Earth Tips for Reconciling Your Budget and Projects 18. Map Out a Three-Year Plan 18. How to Put Your Plan into Action 18. Some Final Thoughts about Marketing 3. Make Internal Marketing a Top Priority
11. What are some good, inexpensive and tasteful ways to show my clients that I appreciate them? 11A. Do more for your clients than they expect you to do.	4. How to Create a Favorable First Impression for Your Practice 6. How to Use Office Policies as Marketing Tools 7. Fifty Ways to Roll Out the Red Carpet for Clients
11B. Organize special events for your clients: open houses, tours, client appreciation day, contests.	16. How to Organize Open Houses, Tours, and Other Special Events to Promote Your Practice

Instant Finder Chart of Marketing Idea Generators

Problem Area and/or Issue	Alternative Solutions/ Idea Generator	Chapter References and Subsections
11. *(continued)*	11C. Write and call patients whenever possible to communicate your care and concern.	7. 41: Write to Children 7. 42: Write to Adults App. B. 1: New Client Welcome Letter App. B. 2, 3: Appreciation Letter to an Established Client App. B. 4: Thanksgiving Appreciation Letter to an Established Client App. B. 5: Appreciation Letter to a Long-Term Client App. B. 7: Handwritten Appreciation Note to a Client Completing a Treatment/Service App. B. 8: Letter to Parents of a Teenage Client App. B. 9: Handwritten Note to a New Child Client
12. Is it possible to publish your own client newsletter if you have a small budget?	12A. First determine what it is you want your newsletter to accomplish. Identify your readers and define your specific editorial goals.	11. How to Write, Produce, and Distribute a Client Newsletter 11. The Four Questions You Must Answer First
	12B. Next, design the look of your newsletter. Make your masthead attention-getting and easy to identify.	11. Preliminary Design Decisions 11. Designing Your Newsletter with a Graphic Artist
	12C. Learn the professionals' secrets for writing good newsletter articles	11. Eight Secrets for Writing Superb Newsletter Articles

Instant Finder Chart of Marketing Idea Generators

Problem Area and/or Issue	Alternative Solutions/ Idea Generator	Chapter References and Subsections
13. *(continued)*		App. B. 32: Letter to the Personnel Manager of an Area Employer, with Brochure
		App. B. 33: Letter to a Pharmacist, Health Food Store, Recreation Center or Other Potential Source of New Clients, with Brochure
14. How much should I spend on marketing my practice?	14A. A good rule of thumb is to spend from 4 percent to 6 percent of your annual gross income.	18. How to Develop Your Three-Year Marketing Plan
	14B. With that figure in mind, establish a concrete marketing plan, with specific goals, priorities, and timeframes.	18. Create a Plan to Help You Attain Your Goals
		18. Establish Annual Budgets for Time and Money
		18. Eleven Down-to-Earth Tips for Reconciling Your Budget and Projects
15. What can I do to make my practice unique?	15A. Do special things for your clients that other practices don't do.	4. Expanding Your Practice with Specialization and Special Services
		4. Your Hours: Are You There When Clients Need You?
		4. Designing Your Office to Appeal to Clients
		7. Fifty Ways to Roll Out the Red Carpet for Your Clients
		16. Unusual Office Decor and Attractions

15B. Develop a unique practice name and slogan.	4. What's in a Name? An Important Marketing Message 4. Slogans Aren't for Big Companies Only
15C. Design unique written materials, all held together with a one-of-a-kind practice logo.	8. How to Design a One-of-a-Kind Logo for Your Practice 9. Designing Stationery and Signs with Your New Logo 10. How to Write, Produce, and Distribute a Practice Brochure 11. How to Write, Produce, and Distribute a Client Newsletter
15D. Hold unusual special events for clients and your community.	15. How to Become a Popular Public Speaker in Your Community 16. How to Organize Open Houses, Tours, and Other Special Events to Promote Your Practice
15E. Get publicity for unique things you do in your practice.	13. How to Get Publicity for Your Practice with Press Releases 14. Ten More Projects that Get Publicity for a Practice

Instant Finder Chart of Marketing Idea Generators

Problem Area and/or Issue	Alternative Solutions/ Idea Generator	Chapter References and Subsections
16. What are the biggest mistakes professionals make when trying to market their practices?	16A. They lack clear goals.	Intro. To Advertise or Not to Advertise? That Is Not the Question 18. How to Develop Your Three-Year Marketing Plan
	16B. They don't assess their current situation: who their clients are now, who they could be, where referrals come from, who are the competitors.	1. Practical Internal Market Research Techniques for Evaluating Your Own Clients 2. Practical External Market Research Techniques for Evaluating Potential Clients and Competitors
	16C. They fail to define and project a specific, market-tailored professional image.	Intro. A Consistent Image Unifies Your Marketing Program
	16D. They dive into one marketing project or another, without a specific plan, budget, and timeframe.	18. How to Develop Your Three-Year Marketing Plan
	16E. They concentrate on external marketing projects only, and do little to develop client loyalty with internal marketing. Thus, they attract new clients, but have trouble keeping them.	3. How Internal Marketing Builds a Professional Practice 3. Make Internal Marketing a Top Priority
	16F. They try to take on too much of the work themselves.	5. The Role Of Your Staff in Marketing App. A. Employing Others to Carry Out Marketing Projects

16G. They design a practice brochure or client newsletter before they have a practice logo. The result: They have unrelated printed pieces that project different, sometimes contradictory, images.	8. How to Design a One-of-a-Kind Logo for Your Practice
16H. They expect too much from a single marketing project. To be successful, marketing must be a process, not a one-time effort.	Intro. To Advertise or Not to Advertise? That Is Not the Question 12. Be Realistic about What One External Marketing Project Can Do
17. What is the difference between the terms *marketing, advertising, publicity,* and *promotion?*	
17A. Marketing makes your practice exceptional by treating clients positively on a personal level. It makes current clients and the public aware of how exceptional your practice is.	Intro. To Advertise or Not to Advertise? That Is Not the Question
17B. Advertising is one way to accomplish the second facet of marketing. However, there are plenty of other things you can do in addition to or instead of advertising to make clients and the public aware of your exceptional practice. These are all the activities described in Parts 2 and 3 of this *Guide.*	Intro. To Advertise or Not to Advertise? That is Not the Question

Instant Finder Chart of Marketing Idea Generators

Problem Area and/or Issue	Alternative Solutions/ Idea Generator	Chapter References and Subsections
17. *(continued)*	17C. Publicity is another marketing tool. It occurs when you supply true, interesting, and newsworthy information to media not controlled by you and the media use it.	12. How External Marketing Builds a Practice 13. How to Get Publicity for Your Practice with Press Releases 14. Ten More Projects that Get Publicity for a Practice
	17D. Promotion, on the other hand, includes all marketing activities that do allow you to control your message. Media advertising is a form of promotion, as are speeches, posters, special events, and direct mail.	15. How to Become a Popular Public Speaker in Your Community 16. How to Organize Open Houses, Tours, and Other Special Events to Promote Your Practice

Table of Contents

P·A·R·T   1

Techniques for Assessing Your Current Practice and Client Potential

Practical Internal Market Research Techniques for Evaluating Your Own Clients

Market research is any activity that helps you learn about your market: current clients, potential clients, and competitors. You will find market research data useful when planning your marketing activities and projects, and market research is usually an excellent tool for monitoring and measuring your marketing plan's effectiveness over time.

Most market research plans are not created for the professional practice. They tend to be on a grand scale, suitable for the budget, staffing levels, and needs of big corporations. Yet a practitioner has neither the time, the financial resources, nor the need for the kinds of market research programs undertaken by Procter and Gamble, IBM, or General Motors.

Therefore, the market research techniques described in Chapters 1 and 2 may not sound quite like a typical marketing textbook approach. This is not to suggest that they don't work. To the contrary, these market research programs have worked quite successfully for many professionals. They are utterly consistent with the size, scope, and resources of even the smallest professional practice.

GETTING STARTED IN MARKET RESEARCH

Several points are essential before you undertake any market research project:

1. Start market research early: Suppose you're wondering whether to spend your marketing budget remodeling your reception area or developing a practice brochure. It is useless to discover through market research that the brochure was the better choice after you've hired an interior decorator to design a new reception area for you. Likewise, it's too late to survey a community's population after you've opened a pediatric practice in a new community. That is no time to learn that there are few children in the area.

2. Know what you're looking for: Narrowing the scope of market research keeps it within your grasp. A narrow set of relevant topics will limit the time and money needed and enable you to determine if a marketing project is worthwhile.

3. Determine whether market research will affect your course of action: Research is wasteful if you have no alternatives. Good market research helps you make choices; for example, should you open a second practice, offer new services, undertake a client newsletter, relocate, or stay where you are? But if you're retiring in a year and there is no way you would relocate now, or if you know you won't ever want a second practice, why investigate these projects through market research?

4. Judge whether market research will be cost-effective: How much will the research cost? How much will you lose if you make a wrong decision? How much will you gain if you make the right one?

5. Decide whether you can handle the research yourself: The techniques you'll find in this *Guide* can be undertaken without much difficulty by most practitioners. But if you do not have the desire or inclination to carry out these programs yourself, or if you want to do more extensive market research, you may need to seek the outside help of an advertising or public relations agency (described in Appendix A). If so, be sure the market research is cost-effective for your practice.

WHAT IS INTERNAL AND EXTERNAL MARKET RESEARCH?

In this chapter, we will be exploring the best methods for conducting *internal* market research, that is, research that helps you learn about your current clients. Valuable marketing data can be obtained from your clients because they are the people with whom you've already had success. They can help you determine what you have been doing in your practice that is right, and they can point out things you can do to change your practice so it is even better. Also, an analysis of your current clients will help you learn which kinds of clients (market segments) are currently overserved or underserved by your practice and which might be rich untapped sources of new clients in your community.

The basic market research techniques covered in this chapter are client feedback surveys and client file studies. We will also explore briefly a few other practical internal market research techniques. Then in Chapter 2, you'll see how to conduct *external* market research — research on your community and competitors.

WHY AND HOW TO CONDUCT CLIENT FEEDBACK STUDIES

Clients' needs, satisfaction, and perceptions change over time. As a marketing practitioner, you will appreciate being able to spot changes in advance. You will also want to verify periodically that your present dealings with clients are indeed as they wish them to be, that clients perceive your image and their experiences in your practice the same way you do. One of the easiest and most direct ways to measure client needs and satisfaction is through client feedback surveys.

There are four methods for conducting client feedback surveys: Personal interview, written in-office survey, telephone, and mail surveys. We will be exploring each method in detail shortly. But first, let's consider survey techniques that apply to all four methods:

Which Kinds of Questions Work Best?

Two kinds of information can be obtained through client feedback surveys:

1. Quantifiable data come from questions that ask clients to rate services objectively on a numerical or multiple-choice scale. Such question formats make it easy for the client to respond. Consequently, surveys are most likely to be completed and returned, and quantifiable data are the easiest to tabulate.

2. Intangible (nonquantifiable) data can be obtained from responses to open-ended questions such as, "How satisfied are you with our appointment scheduling policies?" or "What would you most like to change about our practice?" Surveys made entirely of open-ended questions occasionally produce insightful responses. However, people have different levels of verbal skills and motivation. Thus some clients may not respond to a survey composed completely of open-ended questions for fear that they cannot put their ideas into words.

> **Hint:** The best format for client feedback survey questions is usually quantifiable. If you find it necessary or helpful to get some general answers, insert a few good open-ended questions *at the end* of a quantifiable survey. That way the client who doesn't respond to the open-ended questions will at least provide some other quantifiable information. (Sample quantifiable and open-ended questions appear later in this chapter.)

Anonymity

When you are developing written client feedback surveys, the question of anonymity always arises. Practitioners ask: Is it necessary to know who the respondent is? Will the client be more honest if he believes he is answering the questions anonymously? Generally, if your survey deals with noncontroversial issues such as which new hours or services your practice might offer, there is no need for anonymity. However, if the survey asks clients to reveal delicate, personal, or confidential information, their anonymity must be guaranteed.

Sample Size

How many clients should be surveyed? If you have 200 clients in your practice, you should be able to survey all of them without too much trouble. However, if you have more clients you'll need to do a random or selected sample with a goal of receiving 200 responses. Why 200? Any sample is not as accurate as an analysis of every client of record. However, in most practices, a sample of 200 is reliable enough to give a good picture of the practice and certainly, it is a much more manageable and affordable task. About sampling methods:

1.   A *random* sample might take perhaps every twentieth or thirtieth client in your records and survey only them. That way if your return rate is good (that is, if 30 to 60 percent of those surveyed respond), you may infer that those responses more or less represent the feelings of most clients.

2.   A *selected* sample is useful if your clients are greatly different. For instance, if a law firm serves both corporate and individual clients, it might take a random sample within each selected subgroup. If a practitioner draws clients from two very distinct communities, he or she might take a random sample within the clients from each community.

Five Tips for Conducting Better Feedback Surveys

Tip 1. Ask relevant questions: The best surveys are restricted to questions important to the practice and nothing more. Do not ask for the client's middle name, past employment history, career aspirations, or other similar responses unless this information is useful.

Tip 2. Keep it brief: Write your survey so it takes no more than three to five minutes to administer. If the survey is too long, clients may feel annoyed, overburdened, bored, or intimidated and not respond.

Tip 3. Set a deadline: Tell participants the deadline for all surveys.

Tip 4. Survey inactive clients too: Inactive clients from your "dead" file may reveal important information about the weaknesses of your practice. Bonus: If inactive clients are *not* dissatisfied, the survey may give them the push they need to renew their relationship with your practice.

Tip 5. Assign surveying tasks to one person: *You* will want to be involved in preparing the survey questions and determining which kind of survey to administer and to which clients — *you* will want to analyze your survey results. However, someone else should be responsible for administering the survey to clients and tallying their responses. Your marketing coordinator (Chapter 5) is the ideal person for this job. However if you don't have one, delegate the survey tasks to a staff member or hire someone outside your practice to conduct and tally the survey. A public relations or advertising agency will be able to write and administer a client feedback survey for you (see Appendix A). Alternatively, you can hire a part-time or temporary worker or college student to administer a survey you write.

Five Common Survey Pitfalls to Avoid

Pitfall 1. Oversurveying: Do not survey the same clients too often. Once or twice a year is enough. If you conduct surveys too frequently, clients are less likely to reply. If you need more frequent information, sample different clients in different months.

Pitfall 2. Ambiguities: Pretest all surveys before you administer them to see that your questions clearly ask what you want them to ask. Have a client you know well, a friend, or a staff member respond to the survey before you administer it to your entire sample.

Pitfall 3. Poor timing: Fridays, Saturdays, Sundays, and Mondays are usually the worst days for clients to receive surveys. They are most distracted on those days with work and weekend activities. Plan your survey schedule so you call clients (or they receive mail surveys) on a Tuesday, Wednesday, or Thursday. Do not administer surveys right before, on, or after holidays when clients will be too busy to answer them.

Pitfall 4. Bias: The pretest described under Pitfall 2 above is the best defense against biased survey questions. Beyond that, be sure that all surveys are administered identically. This is most challenging in a telephone or interview survey. Be sure your interviewer uses the same unbiased tone of voice to ask the same questions of all respondents.

Pitfall 5. Inconclusive response: As mentioned earlier, your goal should be to receive 200 responses from your survey. If you do not receive an adequate response, increase your sample and/or extend the deadline. An inadequate response is a poor measure of client trends. Don't let a small response mislead you.

The Four Methods of Conducting Client Feedback Surveys

Method 1. Personal interview: A personal interview or discussion may be fairly enlightening; however, it is the most time consuming of all survey methods and usually the most difficult. Interviews have a way of wandering from the main topic and providing data that are hard to quantify. Since interviews are usually administered to clients already in the office for scheduled appointments, they do not normally provide a good random sample of the clients. (The interviewer does not have an opportunity to administer the survey to inactive clients.) Another drawback of interviews is that some clients may not wish to participate or won't answer delicate questions truthfully because they cannot remain anonymous.

Despite these disadvantages, interviews may be put to good use as an informal barometer of your practice. To administer a personal interview survey

Delegate.   Assign the task to someone in your practice who clients already know and trust.

Ensure privacy.   Have the interviewer speak with each client in private, either in a conference room or private office. (The reception area is too public for a meaningful or confidential discussion.)

Be brief.   Limit each interview to no more than five minutes. Ask only a few key quantifiable and open-ended questions.

Vary questions.   If the interviewer asks too many "yes/no" questions, the client may feel as though he is being interrogated. Mix these questions with others that elicit more descriptive responses.

Report.   After meeting with the client, have the interviewer write a short report on what transpired.

Schedule.   Schedule several weeks to administer a personal interview survey. It usually takes at least two or three times as long to write up the report after the interview as it does to meet with the client.

Study results.   Don't be disappointed if you don't end up with a wealth of quantifiable data. Look for revealing comments, suggestions, and criticisms.

Method 2. Written in-office survey: Like the personal interview, the written in-office survey has the drawback that it provides a sampling only of active clients who are in your office for appointments. However, it is much less time consuming and less difficult to administer than an interview. If the questions you ask require clients to reveal confidential or delicate information, a written in-office survey can provide anonymity. To administer a written in-office survey

Invite participation. Have your receptionist invite the client to participate in the survey and hand him a pen and the questionnaire on a clipboard. This personal touch will encourage a better response than you're likely to get if you leave a pile of blank questionnaires and a sign in your reception area.

Keep it short. Keep the questionnaire a maximum of one $8\frac{1}{2} \times 11$-inch sheet of paper, both sides. Longer questionnaires can make clients feel overburdened and take too much time.

Collect surveys. Ask clients to put their completed surveys in a covered box designated for the purpose. If you ask them to hand the survey back to the receptionist when they are done, they may fear the receptionist will read it right away. This has been known to embarrass some clients and it discourages honest responses.

Consider this alternative: Administer a post-treatment questionnaire to clients after you have provided services for them. This is an excellent tool for determining how clients feel about the quality of your professional services. Types of questions you might ask: Are you pleased with the outcome? Did we proceed at a comfortable pace? Did you understand what we were doing for you at each step of your treatment or services?

Method 3. Telephone survey: Telephone surveys can be done relatively quickly; up to fifty can be surveyed in a day. The disadvantage, of course, is that many clients cannot be reached because they are unavailable when called. And, as with the personal interview, the phone survey allows no possibility for anonymity. To administer a telephone survey

Keep calls consistent. For the sake of continuity and avoiding bias, one person should make all the calls and use the same script each time.

Identify self. Your caller should give his or her name, identify your practice clearly, and state the purpose of your survey. Example: "Hello, Mr. Burke. This is John Angelo from the accounting firm of Michael Smith and Associates. I'm calling to find out if you have been satisfied with the services our firm has provided for you in the past year."

Respect the client's time. Your caller should ask the client, "Do you have a few minutes to answer a few questions?" or something similar, and find out when to call back if the client says he does not have time to talk at that moment.

Administer questions. Once the client has given the go-ahead, the caller should read each question clearly, with as little biasing emotion as possible, and record his responses on a survey response sheet.

Thank the client. Finally, the caller should thank the client for his participation at the end of the survey.

Method 4. Mail survey: The mail survey is the most popular method of gathering information from clients. It is usually easy and inexpensive to prepare mail surveys. (Postage and printing still cost less than hiring interviewers.) Mail surveys make it easy to provide anonymity if needed, and they can generate definitive, quantifiable data. The major drawback of mail surveys is that response rates are traditionally low, typically 25 to 40 percent. Thus, to obtain responses from 200 clients, most practitioners will need to mail as many as 800 surveys.

Regarding mail surveys, studies have shown that it can be advantageous to offer a premium or incentive to increase the rate of return. For instance, A. C. Nielsen sends a crisp one-dollar bill to all participants in its weekly television survey. While you need not go to this costly extreme, it might not be a bad idea to enclose a small gift with your survey such as an informative brochure or pen. Research has also shown that follow-up letters sent to clients who have not returned the survey also have some value. However, such letters should be sent no later than two weeks after the first mailing. To administer a mail survey

Send cover letter. Send a cover letter with your survey questionnaire, explaining its intent.

Motivate participation. Stress the need for client information in order for your practice to continue providing the best service.

Provide incentive. Mention any gift you have enclosed.

Stress deadline. Also mention your cutoff date. (You can expect most mail surveys to be returned in two weeks.)

Send return postage. Enclose a self-addressed stamped envelope with your survey. Clients are less likely to respond at their own expense. *Tip:* Use a stamp on the envelope, not a postage meter mark. Stamps seem more like money to some people. They may respond just so you don't waste your money.

Keep it short. Just like a written in-office survey, the mail survey should be no more than one $8\frac{1}{2} \times 11$-inch sheet, both sides. A longer survey will decrease your response rate.

Check sample size. Count your responses after two weeks. If they are inadequate, send a follow-up reminder letter to those who have not yet responded, giving them two more weeks and the opportunity to call your office for another survey if they have misplaced theirs. If the survey is anonymous, send a second letter to all the clients in your sample. Thank them if they have already sent in their surveys. Urge those who haven't to send theirs in within the next two weeks.

Sample Quantifiable Survey Questions in Four Formats

Format 1. True or false: The client is asked to check the True or False column for statements such as the following:

Statement	True	False	Comment
1. You are always available by phone when I need to speak with you.			
2. Your hours are convenient.			
3. You have ample parking facilities for clients.			
4. You are able to explain things to me clearly.			
5. You see me on time for my appointments.			
6. You are truly concerned about me as a person.			
7. You keep up with the latest developments in your field.			
8. Your reception area is pleasant and comfortable.			
9. You make me feel welcome in your office.			
10. I would recommend your practice to a friend.			

Format 2. Multiple choice: The client is asked to circle the answer he feels best completes statements like the following:

1. I usually have to wait _____ once I arrive for my appointment.

    A. 0–2 minutes

    B. 3–5 minutes

    C. 6–8 minutes

    D. 9–11 minutes

    E.   12 minutes or more

2. It's usually _____ to get appointments when I need them.

    A. very easy

    B. not a problem

    C. a bit difficult

    D. hard

    E. impossible

3. The office is _____

    A. spotlessly clean.

    B. very clean.

    C. adequately clean.

    D. not clean enough.

    E. filthy.

4. The practitioner _____ discusses fees with me before treatment or services begin.

    A. always

    B. usually

    C. sometimes

    D. rarely

    E. never

5. Overall, I am _____ with the care I receive.

    A. very pleased

    B. satisfied

    C. usually satisfied

    D. sometimes dissatisfied

    E. very dissatisfied

Format 3. Graded scale: (In this example, the scale is Always to Never.) The client should check the column he or she feels best completes statements such as the following:

Statement	Always	Usually	Sometimes	Rarely	Never
1. The practitioner _____ really listens to me.					
2. The members of the office staff are _____ friendly and courteous.					
3. The reception area is _____ neat and clean.					
4. The practitioner _____ remembers me from visit to visit.					
5. The practitioner _____ answers my questions well.					

Format 4. Choose one: The client is asked to circle the answer he feels completes statements like the following correctly. (These sample questions measure how much clients actually know about your policies and practice.)

1. Office policy is that clients must call the office (Choose One: twelve, forty-eight) hours before a scheduled appointment to cancel it.

2. Weekday office hours are (Choose One: 9:00 A.M. to 5:00 P.M., 8:00 A.M. to 8:30 P.M.).

3. Dr. Adams (Choose One: does, does not) fit contact lenses (or whatever service is appropriate to your profession).

4. Patients not experiencing problems should return for a periodic exam every (Choose One: six, twenty-four) months.

5. Mary Haskell, Dr. Adams' assistant, (Choose One: is, is not) a registered nurse.

Sample Open-Ended Survey Questions

1. What do you like most about the practice?

2. What do you most dislike about the practice?

3. What kinds of reading materials would you like to see in our reception area?

4. If you could change one thing about the practice, what would it be?

5. How can we make you feel more comfortable when you visit our office?

6. How do you feel about our receptionist?

7. What about our practice has encouraged you to be a loyal client these many years?

8. Why did you leave your former practitioner?

9. What are the most convenient hours for you to schedule your appointments?

10. Would you ever consider going to another practitioner? Why or why not?

CLIENT FILE STUDIES REVEAL VALUABLE FACTUAL INFORMATION

Ledger cards or computer files contain valuable information that you can use to assess strengths and weaknesses and to establish a marketing plan. A client file study is an easy, inexpensive form of market research that will help you obtain relevant marketing information about your current client population. For example, a file study can help you determine where your clients work and live, their ages and sex, their most common reasons for seeking your services, whether they have children, how they heard about you, whether they have insurance that covers all or part of your services — even personal information (if necessary to your field) such as race, ethnic group, marital status, or religion. Factual information about your clients will help you identify underserved market segments that may be a rich source of new clients for your practice.

Practitioners sometimes don't see the point of conducting a client file analysis. Many believe that they already know who their clients are. But almost without exception, a file study turns up some surprising findings that suggest new ways of attracting and pleasing clients. Four successful applications of client file studies are discussed on page 17. First, let's cover the steps involved in conducting a file study.

How to Conduct Your Own Client File Study: Seven Steps

Step 1. Choose characteristics to study: Determine which client characteristics you wish to study. In most practices, some or all of the following characteristics will be helpful: Age, sex, place of residence (by ZIP code), initial complaint, final diagnosis and treatment/services, frequency of various services used, place of employment, race, religion, ethnic group, number of other family members under your care, number of other family members not under your care, referral sources. Of course, the information you require will vary depending upon your profession and circumstances. For instance, an OBG specialist will certainly not need a breakdown by sex and a pediatrician will usually cut off age analysis at 21. The occupational breakdown of your clients will be influenced by the major sources of employment in your area, and some practitioners will think of additional kinds of information worth analyzing. (For example, a veterinarian would probably want a breakdown analysis of each type of animal treated.)

> **Hint:** A referral source analysis may be included in a client file study. However, most practitioners also find it helpful to study referrals according to the procedures outlined in Chapter 17.

Step 2. Prepare tally sheets: If your client records are computerized, it should be relatively easy to obtain and tabulate the information you want; however, if your records are not on a computer, you'll need to use a manual system for conducting a client file analysis. Start by having your marketing coordinator or an assistant prepare file study tally sheets, itemizing each of the characteristics you want studied. These worksheets should be large and have plenty of space for hatchmarks, totals, and percentages. Use the "Client File Analysis Tally Form" on page 16 as a guide.

Step 3. Pull your file sample: Ask the person doing your tallying (marketing coordinator, staff assistant, or outside temporary employee) to pull 200 client files at random; he or she will then pull every tenth chart if you have 2,000 clients, every twentieth chart if you have 4,000 and so on. A sample of 200 should provide a reasonably good measure of most practices.

Step 4. Enter data on tally sheets: Have your tallyer scan each client file and make the appropriate hatchmarks on your tally sheets next to the proper headings. Some practitioners have found it easier to have two assistants work together on this task — one reading the file, the other recording the data on the tally sheets.

> **Hint:** If a file is incomplete, do not let your tallyer return it to the file drawer and get another. Rather, instruct the tallyer to put a mark next to the "not recorded" category. This will be a valuable indicator of how complete or incomplete your files actually are. In the future, you can improve your new client get-acquainted form and fill in the information you are missing from current clients when they return for appointments.

Step 5. Tabulate entered data: When all the data from the files are entered, have your tallyer total the hatchmarks in each category and calculate percentages. (Use the sample tally form as a guide.)

Step 6. Return files: Be sure all pulled files are returned to their proper places.

Step 7. Use visual aids: Most of the tabulations on your tally sheet will tell their own stories. However, some visual aids may help you appreciate your data better. For example, a map of your community and its surrounding areas will give you a good visual representation of your ZIP code study. Get a detailed street map that shows the boundaries of each ZIP code area; your city planning commission, chamber of commerce, or public library should have one. If you have a computerized practice you can illustrate the results of your study with bar graphs and pie charts—a cinch if you've purchased a graphics package.

CLIENT FILE ANALYSIS TALLY FORM

DATE: ___2/7/86___   NUMBER IN SAMPLE: ___200___

I. BREAKDOWN OF CLIENTS BY RESIDENCE (ACCORDING TO ZIP CODE)

Zip Code	Clients	Total	Percent
16803	JHT JHT JHT JHT JHT JHT JHT JHT	40	20%
16823	JHT JHT	10	5%
16827	JHT JHT JHT JHT	20	10%
16828	JHT JHT	10	5%
16851	JHT JHT JHT JHT	20	10%
16865	JHT JHT	10	5%
16866	JHT JHT	10	5%
16873	JHT JHT	10	5%
16879	JHT JHT	10	5%
16884	JHT JHT	10	5%
16888	JHT JHT JHT JHT	20	10%
16890		0	0%
Other	JHT JHT JHT JHT	20	10%
Not Recorded	JHT JHT	10	5%

II. BREAKDOWN OF CLIENTS BY EMPLOYER

Employer	Clients	Total	Percent
State University	H̶H̶ H̶H̶ H̶H̶ H̶H̶ H̶H̶ H̶H̶	30	15%
HRB Singer	H̶H̶ H̶H̶ H̶H̶ H̶H̶ H̶H̶ H̶H̶	30	15%
School District	H̶H̶ H̶H̶ H̶H̶ H̶H̶	20	10%
City/Borough	H̶H̶ H̶H̶	10	5%
County	H̶H̶ H̶H̶	10	5%
Corning Glass	H̶H̶ H̶H̶	10	5%
Nittany Beverage	H̶H̶ H̶H̶	10	5%
People's Bank	H̶H̶ H̶H̶	10	5%
United Federal	H̶H̶ H̶H̶	10	5%
Telephone Company	H̶H̶ H̶H̶	10	5%
The *Times*	H̶H̶ H̶H̶	10	5%
Self-Employed	H̶H̶ H̶H̶	10	5%
Unemployed	H̶H̶ H̶H̶	10	5%
Other	H̶H̶ H̶H̶	10	5%
Not Recorded	H̶H̶ H̶H̶	10	5%

How Four Practitioners Used Client File Studies

Successful application 1: A suburban dermatologist practicing near a county line learned from his patient file study that nearly all of his patients lived in the county where he practiced. Almost no patients were coming to him from the adjoining county, even though the nearest dermatologist in that county was ten miles farther from the line than he was.

Plan of action: He sent a letter to all potential referring physicians in the adjoining county to remind them of his availability. He sent press releases to the adjoining county's newspapers to publicize an upcoming seminar he was giving. He also advertised in the same papers.

Bottom line: In just six months, he got fifteen to twenty new patients *a month* from over the county line.

Successful application 2: A one-year-old ophthalmology practice wasn't growing as quickly as the practitioner wished. The ophthalmologist's patient file study revealed that none of his patients worked for a certain corporation, the largest employer in the area.

Plan of action: He called that corporation's personnel office and learned that the health-care benefit package offered to the firm's employees was proving to be extremely popular. He signed up with the plan at once.

Bottom line: In the first two months a few dozen of the firm's employees became patients.

Successful application 3: A gastroenterologist was dissatisfied with his practice growth. His patient file study surprised him by revealing that 10 percent of his patients were children — a rather high percentage for his specialty. However, his referral source study also indicated that there was only one pediatrician's name among referring physicians.

Plan of action: He inferred that the parents of his child patients were seeking his services because they had heard about him mostly by nonpediatrician referral. He decided that children were clearly a good target market segment, both because he was already attracting so many of them and because he enjoyed working with them. He sent a letter to area pediatricians describing his interest in treating children, his expertise with difficult cases, and his willingness to refer patients to them.

Bottom line: In three months he got a dozen referrals from pediatricians.

Successful application 4: A general practitioner's patient file analysis revealed that more than a third of her clients had hypertension.

Plan of action: She developed a patient information booklet about high blood pressure, its causes, effects, and control. She scheduled and publicized a seminar on the subject.

Bottom line: The seminar had to be held in a hotel conference room, not in her office as originally planned, because so many of her patients wanted to bring friends (nonpatients) to the program. Many new patients resulted.

HOW TO USE CLIENTS' COMPLAINTS TO STRENGTHEN YOUR PRACTICE

Clients' complaints and suggestions often indicate a great deal about weaknesses of a practice. However, it is very difficult to obtain quantifiable data from complaints that are overheard or mentioned in passing. That is why it is a good idea to establish a system for recording and tracking clients' complaints and suggestions.

Establish a complaint record: In Chapter 7, you will see specifically how to set up and maintain a complaint record for your practice. As you review that record, keep alert to telling remarks that indicate problems in your practice.

Track complaints: If the complaints are numerous, consider doing an analysis of them, much like a client file study. Use tally sheets to track the number of complaints you received each month and the type of client who made them. Break down and tally the number of complaints by type (for example: complaints about staff, complaints about fees, complaints about office policies). If possible, analyze how many of the complaints were successfully rectified.

Repeat your analysis: When a complaint record study is repeated over time, you can track your progress (or lack of it) as you see the number and kinds of complaints increasing, remaining the same, or dwindling.

STAFF: AN UNTAPPED SOURCE OF VITAL MARKETING INFORMATION

Your staff has day-to-day contact with clients. Through this experience they probably already know a great deal about your clients' needs, complaints, and level of satisfaction. Small points they may not have thought necessary to pass on to you can sometimes have important marketing implications and consequences. Here's how to gather marketing information from your staff:

Meetings: Regular staff meetings are an important factor in the marketing success of any practice. Meetings are often the best way to disperse information about upcoming marketing projects and to involve staff in them. However, meetings are also a great opportunity for getting staff's perceptions of your practice's marketing strengths and weaknesses based upon their relationships and experiences with your clients.

Idea in action: You might ask each staff member to prepare a one-minute oral summary of perceptions of a specific aspect of your practice and then open the floor for discussion. Or introduce one area of marketing (such as your current appointment policies, facilities, or stationery) and ask for each staff member's perceptions in a round-robin fashion. Or simply ask: "Who do you think our typical client is and what are his views of our practice?" and then see what kinds of answers you get.

An alternative to staff meetings: If you have a large staff, brainstorming sessions such as these may be difficult to control. If so, solicit staff participation in writing. Have each staff member write a summary of perceptions by answering a survey questionnaire. Use survey highlights to focus discussions at staff meetings.

HOW TO GET MARKETING MILEAGE FROM YOUR CLIENTS

Clients who are willing to share their opinions of your practice with you are a great source of marketing information. One way to solicit marketing data from clients is the client feedback survey already described in this chapter, but there are other ways clients may share their insights.

Passing remarks: Informal conversations with clients during their appointments can be revealing. Don't miss the opportunity to ask clients good open-ended questions about how you are doing. Questions like, "Do you think my reception area is comfortable?" "How do you like my new practice brochure?" and "Do I explain things clearly?" may not be the most scientific form of market research, but they are still valuable ways of gathering information and can be tremendous goodwill builders.

Lay advisory panel: The marketing insights and suggestions of a lay advisory panel are often extremely valuable (see Chapter 7).

C·H·A·P·T·E·R 2

Practical External Market Research Techniques for Evaluating Potential Clients and Competitors

O nce you have studied your own clients fully, it's time to move on and see what other relevant marketing information is available. External market research helps you learn about the market *outside* your current practice— potential clients and competitors.

The data you obtain from external market research can be used many ways. Statistical data about potential clients (age, sex, income, level of education, career, place of residence) can help you make decisions about marketing projects. For example, such information may influence decisions about a practice image, location, facility, areas of specialization, new services, hours, and external marketing projects.

Beyond hard statistical data, other types of external market research information can provide insights into how people in your community think, and what they already know about your services, practice, and profession. External market surveys can answer questions such as what image the public now holds of you, how people in your community choose their practitioners, how much knowledge of you and your profession they already have, and which kinds of people in your community are currently going without any professional care. This kind if information can help you make intelligent guesses about the kinds of marketing projects that will succeed with your external market.

Competition is also a part of market research. You'll need to know about competitors and what they are doing so you can distinguish your practice from theirs. (For example, you'll want an image, name, and location for your practice that is not easily confused with another.) You'll want to know what competitors are *not* doing so you can choose marketing activities that will make your practice unique. If you find that a competitor is extremely successful with certain marketing projects, this too can influence your marketing plan.

THREE SECRETS OF EXTERNAL MARKET RESEARCH

When it comes to conducting external market research, there are three very simple secrets.

1. Don't reinvent the wheel: It's a waste of time and money to gather your own information about your market if someone else has already done it. Chances are that a lot of the information you want has been researched by other organizations. These groups are often willing to share information.

2. Don't get carried away: External market research can easily get out of hand. Your market of potential clients is huge and you can spend years and a king's ransom trying to learn about it. Draw the line about how much you really need to know. Generally, you should be able to find sufficient market data about your potential clients without too much trouble or expense. Don't go beyond the research techniques described in this chapter unless you have a compelling reason to do so.

3. Don't use stale data: The whole point of learning about potential clients and competitors is to use the information to create marketing plans that will succeed *now*. What good will it do to base your plan on data that do not reflect the current market? Market research data are useful only while they are still timely.

HOW TO GET A FREE RIDE ON SOMEONE ELSE'S MARKET RESEARCH

Following is a list of sources that may provide good timely market research data at little or no cost. Check with these sources to see what they already know about your market before undertaking any external market research on your own:

1. U.S. Census Bureau: Some census data may be available at your public library. In larger cities, the bureau's local offices employ staff who can ferret out useful information such as population size, age, racial or ethnic distribution, employment and income statistics, sales trends, and the number of businesses of a certain type in an area. How valuable census information is depends on how recent it is. Newly gathered data will be more useful than statistics that have had years to gather dust. The census of population and the census of housing are carried out every ten years in years ending in zero. A census of business is done every five years in years ending in two and seven. Detailed information is published by state.

2. Chamber of commerce: Your local chamber of commerce may have already gathered and digested worthwhile information about your community from piles of census data and other materials.

3. Library sources: In addition to census data, your public library will contain many publications chock-full of useful market research data. Ask your librarian for suggestions and look into these sources:

The Dun and Bradstreet publications *Million Dollar Directory* and *Middle Market Directory* contain valuable information about local industry. Benefit: You can learn how many people are employed by each major company in your area.

The *Reader's Guide to Periodical Literature* and *Business Periodical Index* (both published by the H. W. Wilson Company, Bronx, N.Y.) can direct you to articles on general business trends and often to more specific information in your area.

Moody's manuals supply information about industries, public utilities, banking, and finance. They cover only the very largest corporations in the country.

The *Statistical Abstract of the United States* assembles statistics from almost every government agency. It can help you pinpoint useful data from the mass of all available government statistics.

4. The U.S. Commerce Department: The staff may be able to provide a list of helpful publications. Call or visit your local office.

5. State and local sources: Your state's commerce department or your city's economic planning commission may be good sources of marketing data, especially if you are looking for a published study.

6. Your advertising or public relations agency: Get in touch with your agency if you have one—even if it doesn't have a market research department. Someone at the agency may know sources of marketing information about your community. (These agencies are described in Appendix A.)

7. Media: Local newspapers, television, and radio stations that sell advertising are well aware of the local market. They use data about their readers', viewers', or listeners' ages, incomes, sex, and level of education to sell advertising space. Call the ad departments of local media to see what marketing data they have. They will certainly share their materials if you are considering placing an ad with them.

8. Your own professional associations: Find out if they have done market studies that tell what you want to know about potential clients and fellow practitioners. Also keep up with professional tabloids, journals, independent magazines, and newsletters for your profession. These are often excellent sources of up-to-the-minute market research data.

9. A computerized data base operation: If you lack the time to do library research or contact various agencies and media, try one of these operations. They use computers to store and access large amounts of market research data. One such New York firm charges a minimum fee of $150 for an answer to a question. Other firms charge by the hour. To find a data base operation, check your Yellow Pages under "Market Research" or "Information."

SURVEYING POTENTIAL CLIENTS

Some Reservations Before You Begin

Statistics from the sources listed above usually describe factual, quantifiable information about potential clients. They rarely tell you how a market *thinks* or what it *knows*. To get that kind of information you're usually going to have to do a survey of potential clients. Before we consider the steps for conducting a potential client survey, however, keep in mind the following reservations:

Reservation 1. Reliability

There are two ways to get a reliable sample of a potential market: (1) survey a significant fraction of that market or (2) select a smaller sample according to statistical sampling techniques. In either case, getting a reliable sample of a large market is costly and usually requires the help of experts such as a public relations or advertising agency. Otherwise, survey results could be wrong or unrepresentative.

Reservation 2. Usefulness

Even if survey data are reliable, some do not indicate which course of action is wisest.

Idea in action: Suppose you learn through research that a huge fraction of the people in your community have never used the services of your profession. How useful is that information in and of itself? It still doesn't give you a clue as to whether you'd be most successful trying to attract those people to your practice or if you'd be better off going after the segment that uses the services of your profession infrequently, or even regularly.

Reservation 3. Budget

Most of you will probably not be able to spend a great deal of time or money on original external market research — and those without budget constraints may still decide not to. It may be a smarter move to hire a marketing coordinator or to renovate a run-down office than to use the same money for extensive external market surveys. These are the kinds of priorities that you will be establishing as you devise your three-year marketing plan in Chapter 18.

What to do? Despite these reservations, I don't think you should cross off the possibility of surveying your potential market. If you're lucky, your survey will turn up interesting data. Some responses might spark a worthwhile idea. Although not *bona fide* scientific market research, small informal surveys can sometimes be as useful.

Idea in action: If you and your staff have a hunch that a location on the west side of town would draw many new clients, you may feel more confident about relocating when your hunch is confirmed by an informal survey. Do the best survey of your potential market that is reasonable within your marketing budget and needs. If market research data are very important to you and you can afford it, hire an expert to help you. If the data are not that important and you don't want to spend a large part of a limited marketing budget on research, consider doing some surveying of your potential market on your own. Just be sure that if you opt for this approach, you take your survey results with a grain — make that a whole shaker — of salt.

The Best Do-It-Yourself Method for Surveying Potential Clients

Almost everything covered in the last chapter about surveying your own clients applies to external market surveys:

Length. Keep survey questionnaires brief, no more than one $8\frac{1}{2} \times 11$-inch sheet of paper, both sides.

Questions. Restrict the survey to quantifiable questions with perhaps a few good open-ended questions at the end.

Pretests. Pretest potential client surveys for ambiguities and bias.

Sample size. I've already suggested that you will not have a reliable survey unless you survey a significant fraction of your market or let an expert help you choose your sample scientifically. If cost and priorities do not allow for either of these approaches, do the largest sample you can manage reasonably. A survey of 10 people is probably going to tell you less than a survey of 100 people (provided that neither sample is chosen scientifically).

Tallying. Tallying of external market surveys will be very much like the manual system for tallying client surveys. Use the sample tally sheets in Chapter 1 as a guide.

Delegating. Your marketing coordinator, staff member or temporary help should conduct all the surveys identically.

Format. You cannot usually conduct a survey of nonclients easily in your office. However, you can use a telephone or mail survey choosing names at random from the phone book. You may also try an on-site personal interview survey. These interviews are usually conducted door-to-door, in shopping centers, busy downtown locations, and schools. If you decide to conduct interviews in these locations, stop the people who are passing by and ask for their participation. Get permission to do this — a permit is often required.

Participation. The best way your surveyer can invite participation in a survey of potential clients is with an introductory statement along these lines: "I'm collecting information about health care (accounting services, legal services) in the greater Springfield area. Would you take a few moments to answer a few questions for me? Your participation in this survey (interview) is completely voluntary. If you want to stop the survey (interview) at any time, please let me know and we will stop."

To get maximum participation, avoid sensitive or personal questions such as those about income or marital status. You can usually get that kind of information about your potential market from other sources anyway.

Anonymity. If possible, allow external market surveys to be anonymous. Stick with questions that help you determine what people already know and think about you, your practice, your competitors, and your profession.

Sample question formats. Five sample quantifiable multiple-choice questions that a dentist might use in a survey of potential clients are shown below:

SAMPLE QUESTIONS FOR SURVEYS OF POTENTIAL CLIENTS

Please circle the answer that best completes each of the following statements:

1. I visit the dentist . . ? . .
   A. every three or four months.
   B. every six months.
   C. every twelve months.
   D. every eighteen months.
   E. every two years.
   F. less often than every two years.
2. I *should* visit the dentist . . ? . .
   A. every three or four months.
   B. every six months.
   C. every twelve months.

    D. every eighteen months.
    E. every two years.
    F. less often than every two years.
3. How important is location in choosing a dentist?
    A. very important.
    B. somewhat important.
    C. not important.
4. Which location for a dental office is most appealing?
    A. Springfield Park Mall.
    B. Downtown Springfield office building.
    C. Springfield's East Side Medical Complex.
    D. The Simmons Park section of Springfield.
    E. Other: _____.
5. I would be interested if a dentist offered nonclinical services such as: (Check as many as you wish.)
    A. Child care services at the dental office.
    B. Nutrition counseling.
    C. Counseling to overcome dental fears.
    D. Classes on home hygiene.
    E. Hypnosis for pain control.
    F. Acupuncture for pain control.
    G. Special services for the physically handicapped.
    H. A dentist who speaks Spanish.
    I. Other: _____.

FIVE RELIABLE WAYS TO LEARN ABOUT COMPETITORS

1. Yellow Pages: The Yellow Pages can be mined for basic information about competitors: who they are, locations, phone numbers, areas of specialty —and often, slogans, logos, hours, and special facilities. You can also tell something about competitors who advertise in the Yellow Pages by the kind of appeal they make and the image they project.

2. Newspapers: Newspapers are also an excellent source of information about competitors. Make a point of reading local papers often (or have an assistant do so) and clip all ads and articles about competitors. Also scan the classified ads. You can sometimes learn important information about competitors by their classified ads for new staff.

3. File: Compile a file about competitors in which you keep their ads, articles, and other materials you obtain about them; for instance, you may be receiving a competitor's client newsletter or you may have a sample of a competitor's stationery. It makes sense to hang onto these for future reference. Also file notes about television and radio ads you see and hear about competitors, as well as any other impressions you have about their marketing efforts and success.

4. Location study: When you plan a special event for your practice or if you are considering relocating, it will be very important to know where your competitors' offices are in relation to yours. Use a map and colored pins to identify them.

5. The horse's mouth: The easiest way to learn about your competitors is to get them to volunteer their marketing information to you. The ideal situation exists when practitioners in a community have mutual cooperation and respect for each other. Use meetings and study groups with area practitioners as an opportunity to share marketing experiences. When it's in your interest, work together with competitors to undertake joint marketing projects that can benefit all. Some of the projects described in Parts 2 and 3 of this *Guide* can be undertaken together by several practitioners. Open houses, fairs, and other special events can sometimes have greater impact if practitioners work together. Several practitioners might also pool their resources to publish one client newsletter that can be used successfully in each practice.

An old business adage states, "It's good sense to know your clients well and your competitors even better." Internal and external market research will help you do both.

We will be talking about budgeting and developing a three-year marketing plan in Chapter 18. But first you'll need an idea of the kinds of marketing projects you can undertake within your plan and budget. That's what we'll be covering in the next two units.

Keep the image of your practice in mind as you read about each marketing project in Parts 2 and 3. As you go, note which projects fit best with that image, which appeal to you most, and which you think will have the greatest success with your current and potential clients. All the how-to instructions you'll need to implement every project are included. You may want to skim some of the nitty-gritty how-to information now and refer back to it when you're ready to put the project into action. Many examples of the projects are included in Appendixes B and D. Refer to these as you read and also take a look at them again when you are developing your own materials — you'll find them a valuable guide and inspiration.

Now let's get to the real heart of our subject. Read on and learn about all the do-it-yourself ways to market your professional practice.

P·A·R·T 2

Internal Marketing Projects: Developing Loyal Clients and a Strong Referral Base

How Internal Marketing Builds a Professional Practice

L ife would be so simple if top-quality professional services were all that a client would desire from a practitioner. Yet in reality, most clients cannot judge the quality of the professional services they receive. They form opinions of a practitioner based upon his or her skills in nonclinical areas: the way the staff speaks to them on the phone, policies, fees, reception area decor, signs, stationery, slogan, whether they can get appointments conveniently — even by the name of the practice and the practitioner's appearance.

In the next eight chapters we will be exploring internal marketing projects that will help you develop skills in these and related nonclinical areas. Throughout these chapters we will consider the kinds of personal treatment clients *expect* from you. More important, you will learn what you can do *beyond* clients' expectations to make your practice exceptional, and you will see ways in which other practitioners tell their clients how exceptional the practice is — without seeming conceited or unprofessional.

MAKE INTERNAL MARKETING YOUR TOP PRIORITY

Internal marketing is the most traditional kind of marketing. For many practitioners, it is also the most effective and least expensive. Several of the internal marketing projects in the following chapters — especially those involving office environment, staff, policies, and the ways you deal with your current clients on a *personal* level — should be top priorities for you. These are the projects that will make your practice exceptional. They should be tackled before all others, before the other internal marketing projects (logo, signs, brochure, and newsletter) and before the projects that are designed to attract potential clients from *outside* your practice. Here's why:

1. An exceptional practice makes current clients loyal: Clients who feel that your practice is exceptional will want to stay with you. Those who don't may look elsewhere. These days there are many other practitioners who are more than willing to serve one of your dissatisfied clients.

2. Enthusiastic clients make referrals: A client who is satisfied and feels that your practice is exceptional is likely to make referrals. One who is lukewarm about you won't recommend you wholeheartedly (or at all).

3. An exceptional practice keeps new clients: Why look outside your practice for new clients until you're sure you can hang onto them? Success in marketing depends not only on your ability to *attract* new clients but also on your ability to *keep* them. New clients are the least loyal of all clients because they have no relationship with you yet. However, if you can impress them right away with your exceptional practice, they will be more likely to remain with you. Studies have suggested that a new client who is impressed with the practice is one of the richest referral sources. People love to talk about how wonderful their new physician, dentist, accountant, or lawyer is.

DRAWING LINES BETWEEN INTERNAL AND EXTERNAL MARKETING

By our definitions, internal marketing is everything you and your staff can do *within* your practice to make it exceptional. The result: Current and new clients remain loyal and generate referrals. External marketing is what you can do to attract potential clients from *outside* your practice. The problem is that some marketing projects fall within both definitions.

1. Brochure: A practice brochure can be used for internal marketing when given to current clients. However, it can also be used externally when given to newspaper editors, participants in a community fair, or members of the audience when you deliver an informative speech to a local club or school.

2. Signs: Exterior office signs will help current clients find your office, develop an impression of the kind of office you run, and therefore have internal marketing value. However, signs also attract potential clients from outside your practice (external marketing) as they walk or drive by your building.

3. Staff: An exceptional staff is a powerful internal marketing tool. Current clients often form opinions of your practice based upon their contact with your staff. However, a staff can be encouraged to market externally by attracting potential clients to a practice.

Whether a project is internal marketing, external marketing or both will depend largely upon how you use it. The projects in this *Guide* have been classified as either internal or external marketing by virtue of their foremost use in actual practice. Keep in mind that you may use many of these marketing projects both ways, to make your practice exceptional for existing clients *and* to attract new clients from outside your practice.

C·H·A·P·T·E·R   4

How to Create a Favorable First Impression for Your Practice

Right or wrong, people often make judgments based on appearances and limited knowledge. Since clients will judge your practice by its name, location, and facilities, you should turn these to your advantage. When making decisions on these matters, always consider the messages they convey. Try to be objective and fresh as though you were a client making a snap judgment about your practice.

WHAT'S IN A NAME? AN IMPORTANT MARKETING MESSAGE

The way you choose to name your practice must be acceptable to your professional association. There are also other considerations.

Naming the Practice After You

Decide whether to name your practice with your own name, keeping in mind the following:

1. If your name is difficult to pronounce, you may be better off choosing a practice name that is easier for potential clients to remember.

2. Whenever you write your first name, do so in a way that is consistent with your image. If you have a formal image, use your full first name or initials only. If your image is informal, use your full name or an appropriate nickname such as Jim, Fred, or Frank.

3. Identify your profession in the way that is most easily remembered by clients. Many potential clients will not know that veterinarians are D.V.M.'s or that optometrists are O.D.'s. For easy identification, refer to yourself as Mary White, Doctor of Optometry rather than Mary White, O.D.

4. If your specialty is not well understood, explain it wherever it appears with your name — not only in less well-known fields such as *hematology* or *endocrinology;* many people don't know what *internal medicine* is, or *podiatry* or *osteopathy.*

5. Practitioners who are doctors: Refer to yourself as doctors only once in your name. Don't call yourself Dr. Joseph Adamson, Doctor of Veterinary Medicine. *Better alternatives:*

— Joseph Adamson, Doctor of Veterinary Medicine

— Joseph Adamson, Veterinarian

— Dr. Joseph Adamson, Veterinary Medicine

— Dr. Joseph Adamson, Practice of Veterinary Medicine

Naming the Practice Another Way

If you prefer not to use your name as the name of your practice, there are other possibilities.

1. Check your phone book and market research data to learn the names of all the other practices in your area. Don't choose the same name as that of another practice or one so close that it can be easily confused with it.

2. Consider the words commonly used in practice names. As you read through this list, decide which words best project your practice image.

- Services (Legal Services, Inc.)
- Center (Rochester Podiatry Center)
- Family (Family Chiropractic)
- Clinic (Little Rock Allergy Clinic)
- Associated (Associated Physicians)
- Associates (Associates in Adolescent Psychiatry)
- Group (Springfield Optometric Group)
- Practice (Family Practice Dentistry)
- Arts (Whole Health Medical Arts)

3. Be sure your practice name as a whole is consistent with your image. *Successful application:* An ophthalmologist with an informal, light image calls his practice "The Private Eye." An ophthalmologist with a more formal image might call the practice after himself or use a formal name like Madison Ophthalmic Group.

SLOGANS AREN'T FOR BIG COMPANIES ONLY

A good practice slogan can convey your image and make your practice more memorable. *Successful applications:* Consider these slogans used by dentists around the country.

- Concerned dentistry for everyone.
- Gentle dentistry.
- Helping *you* achieve total oral health.
- Dentistry for children and adults.
- Comprehensive dentistry.
- Expect something wonderful to happen.
- For your oral health.
- Dentistry for a healthier, happier life.
- Your smile can last a lifetime!
- We cater to cowards.
- Dentistry for everyone with care and concern.

Once you create a slogan for your practice, use it universally — in your logo; on stationery, brochures, and newsletters; on office signs; and on name tags, pens, and giveaways.

THE TOP THREE PRIORITIES FOR OFFICE REAL ESTATE: LOCATION, LOCATION, LOCATION

The location of your practice is crucial to your future growth and the satisfaction of your clients. If you're thinking about relocating or establishing a second practice, do a marketing analysis of the location you're considering. The external market research techniques described in Chapter 2 will help you obtain the information you need about competition and potential clients. To analyze a location

1.   Buy a large map of the area from your local city planning office.

2.   With your Yellow Pages in hand, use colored pins to mark all your potential competition on the map.

3.   Identify and mark underserved areas and areas for projected growth.

4.   Once you have selected several areas for the possible location of your practice, zero in on a specific office site. Consider the following:

Convenience.   Is the site convenient to clients? Is it near bus routes or other public transportation? Is ample parking available?

Potential clients.   Who are the people living and working near the site (median income, age, employment)? What are their needs for your services? What professional services do they now use? Do they need evening and week-end hours or flexible payment terms?

Growth potential.   Will the site grow with you? If you plan to expand your practice, is more office space available? If you will own the building, is there enough land for making an addition to the building and/or parking lot if you need more space?

Image.   Does the site project your image? If your image is one of high quality and serving a high-income market, a consistent site might be one at a prestige address. However, if the goal of your image is to serve low- to middle-income clients, that same prestige address might give clients the wrong impression about you.

EXPANDING YOUR PRACTICE WITH SPECIALIZATION AND SPECIAL SERVICES

The decision to enter into a professional specialty or to offer special services will depend largely upon your abilities and interests; however, it *can* be a marketing decision.

Successful application: A general dentist found his practice declining. Through market research he learned that more general dentists practiced in the area than were needed to serve the population but that the number of children in the community was increasing. Action: He took further training to become a pedodontist — a dentist for children. Being the only pedodontist in his area, he now has a competitive edge and his practice is growing.

Successful application: An optometrist was interested in working with deaf patients. After doing some market research, he and members of his staff studied sign language. He publicized this fact. Bottom line: Deaf patients come to his practice from far away. His is the only eye care practice in the area that can communicate in sign language.

Successful application: Many health care professionals are now making house calls to shut-in patients with the use of mobile offices in vans.

Suggestion: You will probably not become a specialist, learn sign language, or set up a mobile office in a van only as a means to gain new clients. However, if you have interest in learning new skills, use market research to consider which skills would help make you unique and draw an underserved market segment.

YOUR HOURS: ARE YOU THERE WHEN CLIENTS NEED YOU?

Offering hours when clients want them most is an excellent way to gain an edge over competitors who don't. Client feedback surveys and other market research data may indicate that a large segment of your potential market works 9:00 A.M. to 5:00 P.M. on weekdays. If so, expanded evening and weekend hours may help you attract more of them to your practice.

Successful application: One practitioner offers early morning hours — beginning at 7:00 two days a week. He has attracted many new clients who work during the day and don't want to tie up evenings and weekends in his office. Another works a split shift from 7:00 to 1:00 and from 4:00 to 9:00 to draw new clients.

PROJECTING YOUR IMAGE THROUGH YOUR OWN APPEARANCE

Your own appearance is an important part of marketing and should not be overlooked. It is impossible to tell you in this *Guide* specifically how to dress and wear your hair; that will depend on your personal situation. However, consider the following:

1. Comfort: Dress in your office so you're comfortable with your appearance. You can't project confidence to clients if your clothes make you feel awkward.

2. Staff suggestions: Would members of your staff feel confident enough to tell you that you have bad breath? Dandruff? Food caught in your teeth? A stain on your shirt? An open zipper? The majority of assistants at a recent professional meeting reported they would *not* tell their bosses these things. From a marketing point of view, you *must* have a relationship with staff members in which they feel they can tell you how to improve your appearance, or if something is wrong. It will be far better to learn these things from your staff than from a client (or worse yet, not to learn them at all). Tell your staff that you *expect* them to tell you when something is wrong with your appearance.

3. Staff appearance: Make sure your staff's appearance is consistent with your image and appearance.

Successful application: Some health care practices coordinate staff uniforms with the doctor's dispensing jacket or lab coat. Also worth considering are: coordinated name tags and practice emblems; using one color or color combination to tie together staff's uniforms, decor, logo, office signs, and stationery.

4. Image: Don't contradict your image. Would you think an overweight physician who smokes takes his own prevention advice seriously? Would you think an accountant who looks sloppy is trustworthy about details? Would you think that any professional who dresses as if he's on vacation takes his work seriously? On the other hand, would you think that a well-dressed attorney could represent you well in court and make a good impression on jurors? Would you think that a dentist who wears a sparkling clean dispensing jacket runs a clean office? Would you think that an optometrist who wears a wardrobe of great-looking eyeglasses would have a good selection of attractive frames in his dispensary?

DESIGNING YOUR OFFICE TO APPEAL TO CLIENTS

Your office design can tell clients, "I care about you and am concerned about your comfort," or it can say, "I *don't* care about you," "I'm a loser — I can't afford a decent chair for you to sit on," "I don't like to serve people like you," or "This practice is too expensive (economical, formal, informal, traditional, modern) for you." To design an office with client appeal:

1. Furnish your office at least as well as your clients furnish their homes: People like to feel that their physician, dentist, accountant, or lawyer is at least as successful as they are, if not more so.

2. Plan your office for the clients you serve: Practices that cater to children are usually furnished with durable upholstery, bright colors, and posters and signs at the child's eye level. Practices that attract primarily older clients usually use calm quiet colors and chairs with sturdy arms and firm backs that are easy to get in and out of.

3. Amuse your clients in interesting ways: Most offices stock popular magazines and these should not be overlooked. However, go beyond the obvious and make yourself special. A dozen good possibilities:

a.   Subscribe to *unusual* magazines on special topics — art, wildlife, music, science, gourmet foods, cars, photography, computers, and tennis. Choose topics that interest you; they may be a good springboard for conversations. Keep current issues only. It's usually a poor reflection on you to have issues more than a few months old in your office.

b.   Subscribe to newsletters. Waiting clients and other office visitors may enjoy reading newsletters because they are short and easily digested. There are newsletters on virtually every topic — tax avoidance, pets, collecting, antiques, literature, management, crafts, cooking, boating, skiing, scuba diving, public speaking. To find appropriate newsletters, see which ones are carried by your local library. Ask your librarian to suggest others. Buy ring binders in which to keep newsletter issues in your reception area.

c.   Picture books on subjects such as animals, cars, cities, movies, and celebrities can be read quickly and are often on sale at book stores. Why not start a picture book library, budgeting to buy two or three books every month? Many picture books cost no more than a few issues of a good magazine.

d.   Have you ever thought of subscribing to a foreign newspaper or periodical, or to one from another city in the United States?

e.   Some practices keep recipe books in their reception areas along with blank recipe cards and pens so clients can copy their favorites. If this idea fits your practice and image, consider setting up a box or card file for recipes. Encourage clients and staff to contribute their favorites.

Successful application: One practice published a book of clients' recipes and got outstanding recognition and enthusiasm for the practice. Alternative: Start a joke or riddle file to which clients may contribute. Ask clients to submit their jokes to your receptionist for filing so offensive jokes can be discarded. Offshoot: Post a "joke or riddle of the week" on your reception area bulletin board.

f.   Most novelty shops sell inexpensive brain teasers, puzzles, and hand-held games that can be kept in the reception area.

g.   Amusements for children: story books, coloring books, crayons, construction paper, safety scissors, puppets, building block sets, a giant stuffed animal.

h.   Change your bulletin board display often. Also keep a well-stocked display of client information brochures on relevant topics. Clients will appreciate reading about subjects that interest them. More important, the brochures will teach clients to regard you as a source of information.

i.   Do you frequently recommend books to clients? If so, stock several copies of the books you most often recommend in your reception area. Invite clients to sign out and borrow books from your office "lending library." (See Sample letter 18, Appendix B, which introduces the office library to clients.)

j.   Get a few large-print books and magazines for your reception area.

k.   Arrange for a local florist to deliver flowers to your office regularly. Invite every client to take a fresh flower from your vase as he leaves your office.

Encourage your clients to give the flower to a secretary, friend, or spouse — any of whom might be a potential new client.

l.   Offer beverages in your reception area.

4. Play music: Many studies suggest that playing soothing music in your reception area can help clients relax. Music also projects your image. Consider the different images that could be projected by an office that plays Bach and Mozart versus one that plays current popular music; an office that plays country and western versus one that plays jazz (folk versus rock; rhythm and blues versus show tunes). Whatever music you play:

a.   Play it softly as background music.

b.   Turn off your music from time to time to give everyone a rest.

c.   Consider letting clients choose their own music. Some practitioners offer waiting clients the opportunity to borrow a portable individual stereo cassette player (with headphones) and a choice of tapes from a large varied collection. This may be a good solution for a busy practice that serves many different kinds of people with broad musical preferences.

5. Design lighting to project your image:

a.   Use soft, warm incandescent lighting in areas where client comfort is crucial — the reception area, your private office.

b.   Use fluorescent lighting wherever strong light is needed — laboratory, work stations. It may seem colder than incandescent lighting, but it provides more uniform light.

c.   Combine fluorescent and incandescent lights in your business area. Use incandescent general lighting to give warmth to the area and fluorescent task lighting at work stations.

6. Use colors to improve staff productivity and client comfort: Some colors and combinations of colors make people feel good. Others depress or irritate. Use the psychological effects of color to your advantage in your office.

a.   The most successful office color scheme uses at least two colors and not more than four.

b.   Repeat one color or combination of colors throughout all the rooms in your office. This will make your office feel coordinated and harmonious.

c.   Choose low-maintenance colors. For walls, medium tones of any light color are easiest to keep looking clean. The hardest wall color to maintain is flat white; it scuffs and soils incredibly fast. Choose commercial quality carpet in multicolors such as tweeds or small patterns; they mask stains. Use tile for heavy traffic areas.

d.   Consider the emotions various colors elicit:

Blue: soothing, relaxing. Good for high-stress office areas such as treatment or examination rooms.

Red: warm, stimulating. Effective as an accent.

Yellow: uplifting, cheerful. Don't use too much yellow in your business area; overuse causes eye strain.

Orange: stimulates some people but depresses others. Best when combined with calm colors such as beige and brown.

Green: cheerful, cool. Caution: Some tones of green provoke negative reactions and should be avoided. Pale green may induce fear, as it is thought of as institutional, used in hospitals, schools, and government buildings. Olive drab makes some people tense because of associations with the military.

Brown: conservative. Overuse may depress clients. Best used with stimulating colors such as orange.

Purple: exciting. Often makes people feel you're creative and different.

Tan/Beige: calm, quiet. A versatile color that can project a formal, informal, traditional, or modern image, depending upon how you use it and with which other colors.

Gray: cool, quiet, urbane. Can seem austere if used alone. Good when combined with red, orange, purple, or other stimulating colors.

e.   Combinations of colors can have psychological effects:

Tan, brown, and rust: warm, soothing, contemporary.

Red, orange, and yellow: very stimulating.

Black, gray, and white: cool, sophisticated, modern.

Blue or turquoise and beige: calm.

Purple and pink: warm, stimulating, feminine.

Green and white: cheerful, cool.

Burgundy and white: regal, crisp, rich.

f.   Metals can also be colors. The silver-colored metals — chrome, stainless steel, and pewter — are "cool" colors. On the other hand, brass and copper are "warm" colors.

7. Go beyond basic creature comforts: The way your office looks is important, but it is not the only design consideration. Others are:

a.   Do you have good sound absorption? It can be quite unnerving for clients in the reception area to hear a child shrieking in a treatment room. Good sound absorbers are: carpet, draperies, acoustic tiles, textured walls, large plants, upholstered furniture.

b.   Do you have zoned temperature controls? Reception areas tend to heat up because of all the bodies. However, disrobed patients waiting on a physician's examining table may have chattering teeth. Set inside-room thermostats between 73 degrees and 78 degrees Fahrenheit.

c.   Have you established a smoking policy for your office? Present a no-smoking policy tactfully. "We ask that you do not smoke in our office" is much more tactful than, "No smoking allowed" or "You'll have to smoke that outside." If you do allow smoking, provide adequate ventilation, ashtrays, and — if possible — separate areas in your reception area for smokers and nonsmokers.

d.   Are *all* areas of your office fastidiously clean? Glass (no fingerprints)? Parking lot (no litter)? Bathrooms? Ceilings? Elevator? Grounds? Rooms clients don't normally see such as laboratories and staff break rooms?

e.   Have you removed office barriers for physically handicapped clients? Do you have a ramp into your building? Have you installed handrails in your bathroom and along corridors to make them more accessible to elderly and disabled clients?

f.   Do you have an adequate coat rack or closet for clients? An umbrella stand? Boot tray (in the snowbelt region)?

g.   Health care practitioners: Have you installed a shelf or hook in each of your treatment/examination rooms for patients' purses and attaché cases? Does your waste receptacle have a cover? There's nothing more chilling than to be sitting on the exam table staring at the previous patients' used bandages. Do you keep instruments out of sight? Some instruments that look perfectly familiar to you may look like torture devices to a patient. Keep instruments in a solid, not glass-fronted, cabinet. If patients disrobe, do you provide a private dressing area and a place to store clothes out of your sight? Many patients do not like to hang their clothes, especially undergarments, where you can see them.

h. Do you equip your bathroom with more than the bare essentials? Depending on the clients you serve, consider a lighted mirror, liquid soap, hand lotion, a baby's changing table.

i. Does your office smell good? If necessary, take steps to keep clinical smells from creeping into the reception area. Possibilities are: a stronger ventilation system, sweet-smelling flowers, fresh coffee brewing in the reception area, large plants, air fresheners.

8. Choose objects that convey your image in your private office: Five of the best are:

a. Your desk. A desk with a closed front is formal and establishes a position of authority and distance. A lighter, open-fronted desk is more informal. The large mahogany-paneled office with the monumental hand-carved mahogany desk conveys quite a different image from a small simple office that has a modest chrome-leg desk with a laminated walnut finish.

b. Chairs. If your chair is high, has arms and a high back and the ones for visitors are lower and smaller, they may view the encounter as a put-down, as though they are being made to feel inferior. On the other hand, similar chairs equalize your relationship.
Tip: If sitting behind your desk when talking with clients seems impractical or conveys too formal an image for you, think about a separate conference area. This may be a few comfortable chairs in front of your desk where you join clients for important conferences or it may be a small table and chairs separate from your desk.

c. Diplomas and Awards. Group together your diplomas, certificates and awards and hang them where clients can see them easily. Of all objects, these are best for instilling trust and peace-of-mind. Put them in a place of honor in your office.

d. Dramatic symbols. A few dramatic symbols of your science or profession displayed conspicuously in your office can illustrate to clients your knowledge of your field. Books, of course, are excellent for this and, like many professionals, you may want to display your books on shelves in your private office. Other objects to dramatize your professionalism are: models, equipment, microscope, charts, maps, a globe.

e. Personal possessions. Objects related to your family and personal interests can create conversation and help clients see that you do have another life. For some practitioners — especially those who are feared by their clients — this can be an effective way to help nervous clients relax. Examples of personal objects are: family photographs, a collection (inkwells, arrowheads, old instruments of your profession, or whatever you collect), pictures of a favorite pet or prized sailboat.

The Role of Your Staff in Marketing

A motivated, efficient, and caring staff is by far the strongest, most important marketing tool for any practice. Not only is the right staff the key to keeping established clients satisfied with and loyal to the practice, but each staff member can affect your own enthusiasm and be an excellent potential source of new clients.

HOW TO HIRE THE BEST PEOPLE FOR YOUR STAFF

The best people for the staff of a marketing practice are, simply, the best. They are the brightest, the most energetic, sensitive, outgoing, and diligent of all applicants. They are the ones with a contagious positive attitude that doesn't quit.

Unfortunately, these kinds of applicants are rare. You'll have to compete for them, not only with other practitioners in your community but often with area businesses as well.

1. Offer a competitive salary and benefits: Learn what colleagues pay their staffs, either by asking them directly or by gathering this information from your professional association or journals. Also learn what area businesses pay for comparable staff — receptionists, clerical workers, bookkeepers, and secretaries. A good place to find this information is your local newspaper's classified ads. Read them regularly to see what positions open up in your area as well as the salaries and benefits offered.

2. Provide opportunities for career development: Often the best people for your staff have ambitions for their own careers. You'll be best able to compete for them if you provide opportunities for promotions and further education.

Idea in action: Many practitioners pay for job-related courses and seminars. Others promise applicants more responsibilities and pay as they develop in their jobs and the practice grows.

3. Provide a pleasant work environment: We have already explored how to make your office pleasant for clients in Chapter 4. Most of those interior design ideas will also make your office attractive to staff and job applicants. (Of course, you also want your office to be attractive for *you*.) Have a good working relationship with your staff, be fair and encourage staff members to get along and work as a team. Do nice things for them from time to time.

Successful application: Many practitioners take their staffs to lunch once a month.

4. Write attractive classified ads: Recruitment specialists have found that on average, the most highly qualified individuals already have jobs and are not actively seeking change. Nevertheless, one survey found that 35 percent of these "cold prospects" read the classified want ads at least once a week. Your goal: Attract these top-achieving "skimmers" by making your ad stand out from the competition.

a. Write an attention-grabbing headline. As many as *five times* more people read a headline than read the rest of the typical classified ad. Arouse the reader's curiosity or present a challenge.

Successful applications: "Are You Motivated?" "Are You a People-Person?" "Do You Have What It Takes to Be My Assistant?" "Sally's Leaving — Can You Fill Her Shoes?"

b. Write a subhead to define the position further and screen out inappropriate applicants. *Good examples:* "Part-Time," "Downtown Office," "Pediatric Practice."

c. List specific job duties and skills.

Successful application: "Must have good people skills and be able to handle a busy client load while maintaining a sense of humor."

d. Personalize the ad by using the pronouns "you," "we," "us," and "our."

Successful application: "As *our* receptionist *you* will be the first contact many clients have with *our* office." This conveys a more human tone than, "Receptionist. Much client contact."

e. Describe the *benefits* of working in your office. If you have unusually good fringe benefits, pleasant surroundings, an incentive bonus program, a newly remodeled office or unusual decor, say so in your ad. Tell the reader every "plus" at your disposal to sell the position.

f.   Describe your practice. Are you a general practitioner or specialist? How many practitioners are in your office? Do you keep evening or weekend hours?

Idea in action: "We're a private, two-doctor practice specializing in dermatology."

g.   List the salary. Omitting salary leads to time-consuming contact with applicants beyond your salary, and fewer people respond to ads omitting salary.

Tip: If you don't want to quote a salary outright, give a salary *range* or provide a ceiling.

h.   End the ad with an invitation to action. Tell interested applicants how to apply and to whom: "Call Kathy at 555-1234 for more information or to apply."

Caution: Requests for a résumé could prevent "cold prospects" from applying. Ask only for a telephone contact or letter of interest, or give the applicant a choice of sending a letter or résumé.

Tip: If the position requires writing skills, ask for a letter; it will reveal a lot about the applicant's writing ability.

i.   Say who you are. Blind box ads have a lower response rate than ads that reveal the employer. One study found that even if it described their "dream" job, only 34 percent of workers surveyed would answer a blind ad. Many were afraid a blind ad could be from their own employers. An additional advantage of identifying yourself is that classified ads are a discreet way to get your name before the public. About 35 percent of the general population reads the want ads once a week (60 percent once a month). If these people see your practice name and associate it with a positive image, they may think of you the next time they need your services.

j.   Consider using a larger two-column display ad rather than a standard one-column ad. Studies show that larger ads often pay off in better and faster responses; and display ads allow for more interesting layouts and provide room for your logo. *Budget consideration:* Display ads cost more. You may want to use them only when trying to fill a more difficult position in your practice. Many practitioners run small classified ads to find a receptionist and larger display ads when seeking a more unusual skill (experience as a chairside assistant, paralegal, or laboratory aide).

k.   Schedule your ad optimally. Sunday is by far the best day to advertise in most daily newspapers. Suburban weekly newspapers are also considered good places to advertise since they often remain in the home all week.

Tips for running ads: Classified rate structures usually provide a discount for running an ad several days. Since most people read want ads sporadically, advertise a position at least two days. Sunday – Monday is usually a successful combination. *Do not* advertise on or just before a major holiday when people are less likely to read classified ads.

l.   Evaluate your results. Keep a file of all the classified ads you run, along with a list of the responses to each ad (number of applicants who responded and were interviewed). Also ask applicants which features of your ad drew them to your practice. Learn from mistakes and successes.

THIRTEEN WAYS TO GET YOUR STAFF TO MARKET YOUR PRACTICE

1. Establish financial incentives: Give your staff a reason to participate and succeed in your marketing projects, to make *your* goals *their* goals.

Successful applications: One practitioner structures a bonus program based on production and collections. Another links salary increases and promotions to how well staff members meet marketing goals. Another pays staff members a twenty-five-dollar bonus for every new client they refer to the practice. Another, a dentist, pays a cash bonus to his hygienist each time she persuades a patient to accept a dental treatment the doctor recommended but that the patient hasn't accepted. *Bottom line:* Last year this hygienist earned more than twice the amount that some hygienists earn. However, the doctor had more dentistry accepted than ever before and production increased dramatically.

Tip: Be sure the incentive you offer is valuable enough to your staff to motivate first-rate effort.

2. Keep your staff happy: Turnover is costly — on the average running at least $5,000 for each staff member you must replace (including classified advertising, lost production, screening, interviewing, and training). Frequent turnover also hurts your image. Clients may begin to ask what's wrong with you if too many people leave your employment. To keep your staff happy:

a.   Give them what they truly want. *Successful application:* One practitioner asks the staff what they want most and tries to give it to them. Over the years he has given paid uniforms, longer vacations, greater authority over projects, flexible hours, and longer maternity leaves. As a result, several extraordinary assistants have remained in the practice over eight years. Staff members are enthusiastic, motivated, and devoted to the practice.

b.   Share your success with them. *Successful applications:* One practitioner has rewarded his staff with fur coats, jewelry, and all expenses-paid vacations in Hawaii and Europe. Another developed a profit-sharing plan for employees who remain in the practice at least five years. Another takes his whole staff on an annual ski vacation. Another bought a condominium in a resort area for his staff to use during their annual vacations. Are these practitioners spoiling their staffs? No. They are all highly successful practitioners who believe their staffs deserve these things. They believe that if staff members contribute to your financial success, it's fair for them to share it with you.

c.   Treat staff with respect — always. Pay and treat your staff as well as you can. They will pay you back many times with hard work, in the ways they deal with your clients on your behalf and represent you in the community.

3. Delegate responsibility for many marketing projects to staff: One practitioner delegates the tasks of writing and producing her client newsletter to one staff member. The staff member does a fantastic job of it and loves it. Another practitioner devised a budget and goals for redecorating his reception area and turned the whole project over to his staff.

Bottom line: He ended up with a beautiful reception area within his budget. His staff is proud of it, clients love it, and it didn't take more than about an hour of his time. Another practitioner delegates to staff the task of screening job applicants for vacant positions. The staff chooses the three best candidates according to her guidelines, and she makes the final decision. *Result:* She spends far less time than she would if she did all the screenings herself. New staff members fit into the practice quickly because they are chosen by their new co-workers.

4. Print business cards for each member of your staff: Include on the card your logo (with your practice name, address, and phone number) and the staff member's name and title. Encourage staff to give their cards to friends and wherever they conduct their personal business in your community — banks, stores, health clubs, salons, day-care centers, the pharmacy.

Successful applications: See the examples of staff business cards in Appendix D. Practitioners who provide staff cards report more new clients as a result of getting their names into the community.

Tip: Consider allowing staff members to print both your address and their home addresses on their cards. This sometimes makes the cards easier to use.

5. Run a referral contest for staff: Offer cash or another valuable prize to the staff member who brings in the most referrals (over a specified minimum) in a set time period.

6. Have your logo, practice name, address, and phone number imprinted on ballpoint pens: Use the pens in your office and give them to clients. Encourage staff members to give pens to friends and leave them wherever they can in your community.

Idea in action: They might leave a pen at stores and restaurants when they sign a charge receipt or make out a check. Create a contest for staff with prizes to see who can leave the most pens in the most places. To determine a winner, ask staff members to submit, on their honor, a list of places pens were left.

7. Print personalized practice stationery for each staff member, using name and title: Have staff use it to write notes of thanks and appreciation to clients.

Idea in action: Assign the writing of five or ten appreciation letters to each staff member each week. Schedule letters so no client receives more than one letter at a time.

8. Offer a shopper bonus: Do potential clients call your office frequently to ask about your fees and services? If so, devise a cash bonus or other incentive program to encourage your receptionist to get these "shoppers" to make appointments.

9. Establish a code of dress for your practice: *Successful application:* A health-care practitioner was dissatisfied with the choice of ready-made uniforms for his staff. He and staff custom-designed navy blue uniforms emulating stewardess outfits. The cost was $700 per staff member, including two pairs of pants or two skirts, two pairs of shoes, two vests, three blouses, and two silk bow ties. He feels the uniforms make the practice unique and present a more sophisticated image than the traditional white or pastel medical uniforms. Patients are more relaxed with the staff and the uniforms are a conversation piece.

Tip: If the staff wears uniforms, ask them for *their* preferences. They probably know which styles and colors make them look best. When possible coordinate uniforms with your office decor. Always choose a dress code that reflects your practice's image.

10. Teach staff members to compliment clients whenever they can do so sincerely: An especially good idea is to have staff members compliment the client for something related to *your services.* This isn't always possible, but when it is, it can be a fantastic practice builder. Try these:

Profession	Staff Member's Compliment
Dentistry	"Your smile looks sensational. Dr. Dalton always does terrific dentistry."
Optometry	"You look fabulous wearing contact lenses (no-line bifocals, rimless frames, tinted lenses). I'll bet you're glad you tried them."
Dermatology	"Your skin looks so beautiful."
Veterinary Medicine	"I hardly recognized Rover. Those vitamins the doctor prescribed have made Rover's coat so shiny. He looks like a completely different dog."
Chiropractic	"Those regular adjustments must be helping you. You seem to be getting around much better."
Architecture	"I saw your new building. Wow! Is it ever a knockout!"

11. Introduce new staff: Write a letter of introduction to all clients of record each time you add a new person to your staff. Written on your practice letterhead, such a letter should inform clients of the background and qualifications of your new team member. Stress in your letter any *changes* that the terrific new addition to your practice will bring about, such as new services, expanded hours, or better client service.

12. Include marketing on the agenda of every regular staff meeting: In addition, call special meetings when undertaking major marketing projects that involve staff. Inform them of your plan and goals. Solicit their active participation.

13. Invest in your staff's marketing training: *Successful application:* One practitioner sends every new employee to the Dale Carnegie course to learn how to become a better communicator, and feels the skills they learn are essential for relating to clients well.

TAKE THE ULTIMATE STEP: HIRE A MARKETING COORDINATOR

In most practices, the receptionist is busy answering the telephone, greeting visitors, and scheduling appointments. The business manager is tied up with individual clients' payment plans, insurance forms, and collection duties. The professional and the technical assistants are busy preparing for and providing services for clients. *No one person is responsible for marketing.*

Marketing does take time, a commodity of which you probably have too little already. If you are pressed for time but want to be active in marketing, the answer may be in hiring a *marketing coordinator* for your practice. Such a position could be a major investment in a new full-time employee, or a half-time position, or less. It might even be assigned to a qualified staff member. If you hire a marketing coordinator, consider the following:

1. Qualifications: Look for an assertive, outgoing individual with a college degree in journalism or a related field and work experience in public relations, advertising and/or print or broadcast journalism. A part-time alternative may be a college student majoring in journalism, public relations, marketing, or business who may be looking for hands-on work experience and will be delighted to serve as a part-time or summer marketing coordinator for salary close to minimum wage. Semiretired individuals may also be qualified. Perhaps a gifted former staff member who can't work full time would be interested in part-time work.

2. Duties: Develop a job description for your marketing coordinator. Responsibilities might include

a.   Reading this *Guide* and establishing a marketing plan.

b.   Writing letters to clients (welcome to the practice, thank you, congratulations, and all the others suggested in Appendix B).

c.   Reading the newspaper daily to learn of clients' accomplishments, obituaries, and news.

d.   Establishing a client complaint record (described in Chapter 7).

e.   Conducting internal market research with client feedback surveys and client file studies.

f.   Conducting external market research about potential clients with surveys and by gathering marketing data from other organizations.

g.   Conducting external market research about competitors. Learning about the marketing activities of other practices and their results.

h.   Developing any of the written marketing materials described in this *Guide:* a practice brochure, client newsletter, logo, stationery, signs, letters to the editor, press releases, feature stories, public service announcements, filler articles.

i.   Organizing special events for your practice: open houses, office tours, contests, client appreciation parties, fairs, concerts, fund raisers for charity and the other events described in Chapter 16.

j.   Taking professional-quality photographs of these special events for use in your client newsletter, office bulletin board and press releases.

k.   Serving as the host of your practice: greeting clients, offering to hang their coats for them, serving beverages, escorting clients through the office, seeing them to the door at the end of the appointment.

l.   Booking public speaking engagements, seminars, and appearances for you in schools, in community groups, and on TV and radio shows in your area.

m.   Scheduling and conducting press conferences.

n.   Running staff meetings that focus on marketing and developing a marketing attitude in your staff.

o.   Keeping abreast of the provisions of your professional society's code of ethics and your state practice act regarding practice promotion and publicity. Making sure your marketing efforts do not violate them.

p.   If you advertise: Working independently or with an ad agency to create attractive direct-mail packages, Yellow Pages ads, and newspaper, TV, and radio ads.

3. Successful applications: One successful eight-doctor practice hired two full-time marketing coordinators. Their combined duties were welcoming new patients, helping patients complete get-acquainted forms, giving office tours, escorting patients to the treatment rooms, sending flowers to hospitalized patients, mailing graduation and wedding cards to patients, writing "welcome to the practice" letters, handling other patient communication tasks.

Bottom line: The marketing coordinators act as a liaison between the patient and doctor. If the patient has fears, concerns, or questions, the marketing coordinators relay them to the doctor. Patients are more satisfied and the doctor feels on top of things.

Another practitioner hired a full-time marketing coordinator. Her duties were writing follow-up letters of appreciation to clients after their appointments and producing other written marketing projects, including a practice brochure and client newsletter.

Bottom line: The practitioner pays the marketing coordinator $16,000/ year. He feels that it is an excellent investment in his practice. He sees at least that much back in goodwill and new client referrals.

How to Use Office Policies as Marketing Tools

T hese days clients are likely to see sophisticated professional advertising that tries to entice them with low fees, convenient payment plans, and easy appointment scheduling, and they will be more critical of your policies in these areas. If clients like the way they're treated on the telephone, get convenient appointments, and feel that your fees and financial arrangements are fair, they are likely to stay with you and make referrals. However, if they feel that you fall short in these areas, they may be lured to another practice that offers (and advertises) more client-centered policies.

Office policies are a marketing tool because they affect clients' attitudes about your practice — whether it is convenient or inconvenient, fair or unfair, worth sticking with (and recommending). Many practice management books explain how to organize your appointment book, billing, and insurance claims systems so they are convenient for *you*. The marketing professional's policies must also be convenient for *clients*.

In this chapter we will explore basic office policies from a marketing angle. In each of eight policy areas — telephone, appointment scheduling, case consultations, fees, financial arrangements, insurance, recall, and follow-up/ referrals — we will consider ways to keep both new and established clients satisfied and loyal.

POLICY AREA 1: THE TELEPHONE

How well does your staff handle the telephone? Establish marketing-oriented policies on correct procedure.

1. Fee quotes: Will your receptionist quote fees over the phone? Potential clients may be shopping for the lowest fees or want to know the fee in advance so they can pay in cash. Give callers a *cautious* fee quote that will attract shoppers but not mislead them.

Idea in action: An optometrist's office is typically asked for the price of soft contact lenses. A cautious fee quote might be: "Standard soft contact lenses include a complete eye examination and lens fitting; instructions on insertion, removal, and care of the lenses; all the equipment and a supply of the solutions you will need to care for your lenses; a complimentary pair of nonprescription sunglasses from our optical dispensary; (warranties, trial period, and discounts). The fee for all of that is just $175. There are different types of contact lenses depending upon the prescription and needs of the patient, and the prices do vary. When was your last eye exam?"

2. Interruptions: Which incoming calls can interrupt your work schedule? Return messages during a call-back period blocked out in the appointment book. Make a list of exceptions — those callers who are to be put through right away. Have your receptionist screen callers, take messages, and explain when you will call back.

3. Coverage: How will your phone be covered when you're not in the office? Hire a first-rate telephone answering service. Clients who need to reach you after hours, especially in an emergency, will want to speak to a *person,* not a taped message from a phone answering machine.

4. Evaluation: How will you monitor your receptionist? Call your own office periodically to hear for yourself how your receptionist handles the phone. Does your receptionist: (1) Answer the phone with a smile? (2) Answer within three rings? (3) Start with a sincere "Good morning" (afternoon, evening)? (4) Identify your office? (5) Identify herself? (6) Ask the caller's name early on and address him by name at least once during the conversation? (7) Speak directly into the mouthpiece? (8) Give the caller her full attention? (9) Control the conversation? (10) Thank the person for calling? (11) Speak clearly and distinctly? (12) Communicate a positive and professional image of your practice? (13) Provide an adequate reason if you can't come to the phone right away? (14) Screen callers properly to reduce interruptions of your work? (15) Tell the caller when his call will be returned? (16) Have a thorough knowledge of your practice? (17) Transfer calls to the correct people in your practice? (18) Get back to persons on hold within thirty seconds? (19) Take complete telephone messages? (20) Wait for the caller to hang up first? (21) Return the receiver gently to the cradle at the end of the transfer or call?

POLICY AREA 2: APPOINTMENT SCHEDULING

Clients often leave practitioners because they feel they cannot get convenient appointments. Some good policies are

1. Offer clients a choice of appointments so they feel in control. Ask them, "Do you prefer a morning or afternoon appointment?" "Which is better for you, Thursday or Friday morning?" "The doctor can see you at 10:45 Thursday or Wednesday at 3:15. Which appointment is better for you?"

2. Save evening, weekend, and other premium office hours for clients who need them most. If they can't get them they are likely to look for another practitioner with more convenient hours.

Idea in action: After-school hours are usually in great demand for child clients. One practitioner set aside those hours for children who have learning difficulties. They cannot afford to take time from school to see you during the day.

3. Limit advance appointment scheduling to prevent getting booked too far ahead. Clients expect to see you *soon.* If they can't, they may be tempted to go elsewhere, especially if something is concerning them. It is important to remember that clients who can't get an appointment for several weeks or months are less likely to make referrals. They may assume (perhaps correctly) that the practice is already too busy with the clients it has and does not have room or the desire for new clients. To keep from filling your schedule too far in advance:

   a. Set a time limit for advance scheduling.

   b. Create a *call list* when you're booked up. Explain it by saying, "It is not possible to give you an appointment at this time because the doctor schedules only three weeks into the future and is now completing treatment that has already been started. Might I hold your name and telephone number? I should be able to contact you in about ____ days to schedule a definite appointment. Once I call you there won't be any further delay in your appointment. When do you prefer an appointment, in the morning or afternoon?"

   c. Exception: Appoint new clients *immediately.* New clients have no relationship with you yet and no loyalty to your practice. A long wait will invite them to go elsewhere.
      Tip: Leave some appointments open just for new clients. You can always fill them from your call list if you don't use them.

   d. Monitor your call list. If you use it often, explore ways to expand your practice. You might add extra assistants or an office manager to take over more administrative duties. Hire paraprofessionals, interns, associates, or partners to help handle your case load.

4. Are emergencies usual in your practice? If so, schedule emergency

time in your appointment book. Clients with emergencies will appreciate prompt attention. Clients who don't have emergencies will appreciate your staying on schedule. And, *new* clients who receive prompt attention to emergencies are likely to become *regular* clients. Do only what is necessary at the first appointment to relieve the new emergency client's discomfort or concern. Schedule later appointments to provide more complete services and follow-up. Additional meetings are important. They help develop a relationship with the new client, an important factor in keeping her.

5.   Plan appointments carefully. Decide what you will do for the client at each appointment and predict how much time it will take. Clients appreciate knowing how long each appointment will last, and realistic planning will help you stay on schedule.

POLICY AREA 3: CASE CONSULTATIONS

A rich source of new cases may be incomplete work in your current client files.

Idea in action: A lawyer may have clients who need wills or revisions of existing wills. An optometrist probably has eyeglass patients who would be good candidates for multiple pairs or contact lenses (see sample letter 11, Appendix B). Almost every dentist has major restorative work that was recommended to clients but never accepted.

Comb client records monthly to find outstanding work and candidates for new services. In addition, become a master at conducting case consultations. To get clients to accept your recommendations:

1.   Schedule a consultation in your private office. (Health-care practitioners: Patients will feel threatened and vulnerable when they're disrobed or lying down. Don't hold a case consultation in a treatment/examination room.)

2.   Describe what you would see if you were looking at a client who had undergone the services you recommend.

Idea in action: A dentist recommending major restorative work might say: "In a healthy mouth, I'd expect to see clean teeth with no decay and firm pink gums." Use pictures and models to illustrate.

3.   Explain what you found when you examined the client. Start with the good news, review the client's main concern or a condition he already knows exists, and describe the other conditions, lumping similar ones together. Continuing with our dental example: "Your gums are healthy (good news). However, the pain in that tooth is caused by extensive decay (main concern). In addition, two fillings show evidence of breakdown (other conditions).

4.   Describe what will happen if the client doesn't do anything: "The pain in that tooth will worsen if you don't take care of it now."

5.   Outline your recommendations. Present extensive procedures in steps: "I recommend first that we clean out the decay in that tooth and put a crown on it. Next, I recommend replacing those two fillings."

6.   Describe what it will be like when you're done: "When we're done, that tooth won't hurt anymore."

7.   Tell the client how many appointments and months the entire service will take.

8.   Quote your entire fee.

9.   Outline the methods of payment available.

10.   Ask for questions. "Is there anything you would like me to explain better?"

11.   Have your assistant make the financial arrangement.

POLICY AREA 4: FEES

Competitive pricing techniques such as sales and price wars are generally avoided by most professionals. Yet there are other ways to use fees as marketing tools.

1.   Compare your fees with those of other practitioners in your area. Be sure yours reflect your image.

2.   Keep fees for initial appointments low and competitive. High first examination fees may scare new clients away.

3.   Clients tolerate slight frequent fee increases better than sudden sharp ones. Review fees every four to six months and raise them slowly and gradually.

4.   Explain fee increases only if a client asks. Then do so directly, without apology. Link the fee increases to rising costs and explain that they are for the client's benefit. Tell the client, "I could use cheaper materials of less quality or do less thorough examinations, but I insist on only the best for my clients and refuse to compromise. That's why I must raise my fees."

5.   Speak about fees positively. Say that a fee is a substantial *investment* in the client's health, comfort, appearance, or well-being. Avoid words like *expensive* and *costly*.

6. Clients more often object to round-figured fees than to odd ones, according to a recent study. Consider fees such as $17, $33, $165, and $3,300 instead of rounder figures such as $25, $50, $150, and $3,000.

7. List no-charge services on your statements to remind clients of all the things you do *not* bill them for (and that another practitioner might).

Successful application: One practitioner's statements list *dollar values* of no-charge services: "Telephone Consultation. . . . . .$40. . . . . . No Charge."

8. Don't charge for missed appointments. Clients usually feel such charges are not justified, and they may do harm to your image. As an alternative, you can avoid scheduling any more advance appointments for chronic offenders. Put them on a short-notice call list.

POLICY AREA 5: FINANCIAL ARRANGEMENTS

"Buy now, pay later" is a way of life for many clients. Use financial arrangements to make your practice grow.

1. Avoid a cash-only policy and provide as many methods of payment as you can. Today's client expects credit and may go elsewhere if he doesn't get it. Many practices offer these payment options: payment in advance; credit cards; bank plan; three equal payments prior to, halfway through, and upon completion of services; half now and half later; monthly statements issued as work progresses.

2. Publicize new payment plans. Put a sign in your reception area that says, "Ask us about our payment policies." Mail statement stuffers. Include payment information in your practice brochure. Instruct your assistant to discuss new payment options with every client at his next appointment.

3. Make fees and payment options clear to clients *before* providing services.

4. Consider discounts. *Successful applications:* Several practices offer a 5 percent fee reduction for payment in advance or cash on the day of the appointment. Others have a "family package" plan with reduced fees for children. Others provide discounts for students and senior citizens.

Tip: Refer to a discount as a "courtesy." The word *discount* may have negative connotations of lower-quality or second-rate service.

5. Make firm financial arrangements with clients who need them. Follow the ten-step procedure:

Step 1: Delegate responsibility for making financial arrangements to your assistant.

Step 2: Hold a case consultation and get the client to accept your recommendations.

Step 3: Briefly outline payment options. Tell the client your financial secretary will make the actual arrangements.

Step 4: Leave your office and acquaint your assistant with the case, including (a) how soon the first appointment (or first several appointments) should be, (b) how much time you will need scheduled for the appointment(s), and (c) the total fee for the services the client has accepted.

Step 5: Let your assistant meet with the client in your office to make the financial arrangement. The assistant should begin by scheduling the first appointment(s) and introducing the topic of finances. A good approach is, "Did the doctor discuss with you the various methods we have for taking care of your fee?"

Step 6: If the client says, "Yes, she told me I could spread it over a couple of months" or something similar, tell your assistant to establish a schedule of payments with dates and amounts. Proceed to Step 9.

Step 7: If the client is not sure what to do, tell your assistant to repeat the methods of payment you've already outlined, illustrating them with dates and amounts.

Step 8: Don't force a client into a hasty decision. If he needs time to review his finances, have your assistant write down the total fee and the methods of payment available. Schedule another conference to complete the financial arrangement.

Step 9: When the client chooses a method of payment, have your assistant summarize the agreement in writing with dates and amounts. Ask the client to sign it. Give him a copy.

Step 10: Have your assistant send a letter to the client after the meeting, congratulating him for going ahead with your services (if appropriate), outlining the financial arrangement again, and offering assistance if he has any questions.

POLICY AREA 6: INSURANCE

How to use insurance to build your practice:

1. Treat clients who have insurance the same way you treat those who do not.

2. Use tact when asking a new client if he has insurance. At the end of

the first phone conversation, have your receptionist ask: "By the way, do you have health-care or dental insurance?" *Caution:* Do *not* ask about insurance first thing. Clients may wonder if you're screening them, going to treat them differently, or concerned mostly about their money.

3.   If a new client has coverage, have your receptionist ask him to bring his insurance identification card and other relevant information to the first appointment.

4.   Process insurance claims for clients. Other practices do and clients expect it. However, don't miss an opportunity to tell clients that this is an *extra* service. Emphasize in your practice brochure that this is an "extra."

5.   Become familiar with clients' most common insurance plans and coverage. Contact personnel managers of major area employers who provide insurance benefits. Volunteer to help interpret insurance coverage. Remember that personnel managers are good referral sources (see sample letter 32, Appendix B).

POLICY AREA 7: RECALL

Do you see clients regularly for recall appointments? If so, recall can have marketing value in two ways. First, recall assures that clients of record return to your practice regularly and remain satisfied. Second, if you keep clients active they will be more likely to make referrals. To motivate clients for recall:

1.   Indicate a specific reason for the recall appointment.
Idea in action: An OBG specialist can tell patients to return for a *Pap smear* and *pelvic examination.* An ophthalmologist can tell patients to return to have their *vision and corrective eyewear checked.* A chiropractor can tell patients to return for *adjustments.*

2.   Watch your language. The word *recall* has a negative connotation. Clients may think of defective merchandise being recalled by manufacturers. Use *reexamination, reevaluation, regular visits* (or *appointments*). Tell the patient he'll *want* to see you, not *have* to see you.

3.   Tell clients the *month* they're due for recall, not just the *number* of months. For instance, say, "You'll want to see us again in *June,*" not "You'll want to see us again in *six months.*" *June* then becomes a mnemonic device for the client.

4.   Similarly, link recall to easy-to-remember dates or events. For example: "You'll want to see us again in June, *right after school lets out,*" or "in May, *right after Mother's Day.*"

5.   When sending *written* recall reminders, tell the client the name of the assistant to call for an appointment, or tell him who will be calling him and when. This makes appointment scheduling seem much more important.

6.   Make recall calls when you're most likely to reach the client. Call after 5:00 P.M. on weekdays or on Saturday morning.

7.   Have your assistant call to schedule the appointment and (a) remind the client that he already knows he needs the appointment by saying, "As the doctor suggested to you at your last appointment, you will want to see him this month"; (b) review the *purpose* of the appointment; (c) give the client a *choice* of two appointments.

8.   Be diligent about follow-up. Your assistant should make every attempt to reach the client by phone and send letters if the phone calls are unsuccessful.

9.   If a client refuses to come in for recall, try to find out why. Perhaps you can remedy something you are doing wrong. Send a letter to all clients who do not come in for recall. Stress the importance of recall and invite them to make an appointment (see sample letters 15, 16, and 17 in Appendix B for letters to inactive clients).

POLICY AREA 8: FOLLOW-UP AND REFERRALS

You are in a terrific position to build your practice after you provide services for a client. You can point out the fine job you did and seek referrals in various ways.

1.   Health-care practitioners: After extensive treatment, make a postoperative call to see how patients are doing. Be brief. Say that you *always* call after such a procedure so you don't alarm the patient. If you delegate postoperative calls to an assistant, provide her with a list of patients to call each evening and the procedures you want her to ask about. She might say, "Hello, Mrs. Martin. This is Marie from Dr. Blake's office. The doctor asked me to call you this evening to see how you are feeling (adjusting) and whether you have any questions." One surgeon even has a nurse from his office go to the patient's home the day after discharge. The whole neighborhood learns about the thoroughness and concern of that doctor.

2.   Send appreciation letters to clients after you complete services (see sample letters 7 and 10 in Appendix B).

3.   Hold a postservice conference to seek referrals.

a.   Schedule five or ten minutes with the client after the last appointment.

b.   Make the client feel important and positive about being in your practice. Thank him for his cooperation, for enduring any discomfort or inconvenience, for being on time, or for being an enjoyable client.

c.   Review where the client was when he came to you and show him the progress you have made. In short, boast about your fine services. If applicable, use before-and-after photographs.

d.   Reinforce the need for follow-up care and regular recall.

e.   Write your home phone number or emergency number on one of your business cards and give it to the client. Reassure him that you will continue to be concerned about him. Ask him to call you any time he or any member of his family has a problem.

f.   Give the client a second card (or several cards). Ask him to keep it in his wallet to give to any neighbor or friend "as nice as he is" who is in need of your services. Ask the client to tell his friend to say who referred him to your practice. This will encourage him to look for an opportunity to use the cards.

g.   If you have provided services for a child, conduct the conference with both the child and the parent. Emphasize how good and cooperative the child was. Give your card to the parent in case one of his acquaintances has a child who needs your services.

4.   Consider giving clients a small gift as part of the follow-up procedure.
Idea in action: After extensive treatment, some practitioners give clients flowers, a bottle of wine, gift certificates, or magazine subscriptions. For added effect, you can send the gift to the client's work place with a card signed by you and your staff. Flowers or plants delivered on a Monday can cause co-workers to talk about it all week long — a very good way to generate new interest in your practice.

5.   Write a thank-you letter or call every client who refers someone to your practice (see sample letter 20 in Appendix B).

6.   Consider an incentive program for clients to make referrals.
Successful applications: One practitioner holds an appreciation party for clients who make a given number of referrals each year. Another sends various gifts for different numbers of referrals. In this practice, five referrals are rewarded with a bottle of wine, eight with an exotic houseplant, and twelve with dinner for two at a local restaurant. One inventive practitioner rewards refer-

rers with a bottle of wine that has the practice's name on the label. He designed and printed the labels himself and arranged with a small local winery to have them adhered to the bottles.

7. Some practices give a free examination or credit to thank clients for referrals. Your assistant can explain it by saying, "Dr. James asked me to mark your statement 'paid in full' for today's appointment to thank you for referring the Johnsons and the Smiths to our practice."

Fifty Ways to Roll Out the Red Carpet for Clients

T he most successful practices are those in which clients are not merely *satisfied and comfortable,* but *enthusiastic* about the way they are treated. In this chapter there are fifty no- and low-budget "red carpet" projects that other practitioners have used to put clients in a referring mood. Try those that best fit your image and profession and watch clients become enthusiastic missionaries for your practice.

1. Remember personal information about clients: When the client mentions something personal, for instance, that his poodle is going to be in a dog show or that his son goes to Yale, *write it down* in his file. Check your notes on his next appointment and ask if Fifi won any blue ribbons or how Billy did on his midterms. The client will be impressed that you "remembered" personal information about him.

Tip: Develop a form like the one below for recording personal notes about clients. Keep one in every client's file. Have staff members date and initial any notes they add to the form so you know who heard the comment and when. Then you can say, "Dorothy tells me that you went to San Francisco last month. . . ."

PERSONAL INFORMATION FORM

Client's Name: *ANDREA MALONE*

Information	Date	Heard By
Plans to vacation in New York in mid-July	5/7/84	R.S.
Daughter, Jennifer, just began nursery school	9/11/84	S.K.
Attending creative writing classes at community college	10/2/85	M.P.

2. Send a tax reminder: Here's a thoughtful idea if clients' trips to and from your office are tax deductible. Each April, send clients a card saying that travel expenses for trips to and from your office are deductible. On the reverse side, provide a trip diary where clients can record the date and mileage of each trip.

3. Use names: Call clients by name often. It shows you remember them.

Tip: To be sure you pronounce names correctly, have your receptionist write a phonetic spelling of the name when the client calls for his first appointment.

4. Take photos: Is your practice so large that you and your staff have trouble connecting names and faces? If so, take a photograph of every client and make it part of her file. Your receptionist can review the photos each morning for the clients you'll see that day and be able to greet clients *by name* and know who's who in a busy reception area. Also, new staff members who study the photos will learn to identify clients before they meet them.

5. Add little touches: Buy expensive hangers for your clients' coat rack. It's a very small investment that shows clients you run a quality practice and care about their comfort.

6. Provide more little touches: Buy a few other small quality client comforts: leather magazine covers, a fancy welcome mat with your practice name on it, an exotic flowering plant, fresh flowers in your restrooms.

7. Avoid unpleasant sounds: Install a telephone in your business office that chimes instead of rings. Install a door bell that chimes instead of buzzes.

8. Offer free parking: Provide free parking for clients. Reimburse them for garage fees or arrange with a garage to pay fees automatically.

9. Provide a babysitter: Are children frequent guests in your office? If so, hire a babysitter for your reception area. Set aside a separate area or room for the sitter and children.

Successful application: One practitioner has a sitter work part-time certain hours each week. Mothers with small children are scheduled during these times. The practitioner believes the cost of the sitter is more than offset by the goodwill he receives, and if there are no children to care for, the sitter also helps with clerical tasks.

10. Send Thanksgiving cards: Send clients a Thanksgiving card or letter to thank them for their continued loyalty to your practice. These are more unusual than Christmas cards and easier to keep track of than birthday or anniversary cards (see sample letter 4 in Appendix B).

11. Write to clients about their news: Have your assistant read the local newspaper each day to see if any of your clients has been promoted, won an award, gotten married, or had a baby. Also have her check the obituary column. Ask her to clip any mention of a client or a client's relative and put it on your desk with that client's full address. Then use your memo paper or a notecard to handwrite a short note to the client to offer congratulations or condolences or send a gift if appropriate.

Successful applications: One practitioner sends a pink or blue corsage to new mothers. Another attends funerals and awards ceremonies whenever possible for clients or members of their families. Another puts newspaper wedding and birth announcements about clients in their files to give to them at their next appointments.

12. Take charge: Stress to all new clients your personal interest in the operation of your practice. Encourage them to inform *you* if anything ever bothers them about you, your staff or policies. You might say, "Mrs. Hunter, I'd like to welcome you to my practice. We always try to provide our clients with the best possible care and service. However, if you ever find that you're unhappy with us for any reason, please don't hesitate to tell me personally."

13. Have transportation schedules available: Have your receptionist maintain a supply of local train and bus schedules at her desk. Post maps of local routes on a bulletin board in your reception area or office entryway.

14. Change the reception area: Rearrange the furniture in your reception area from time to time. Clients will appreciate the change. Some may think you've redecorated.

15. Be ready for the rain: Keep a supply of disposable plastic rain bonnets at your reception desk to give to clients in case of a sudden shower. Better yet — keep loaner umbrellas and raincoats.

16. Be ready for car trouble: Also keep jumper cables, a gasoline can, and other automobile emergency supplies in your office in case one of your clients gets into trouble. Have handy the phone number of a reliable service station near your practice. If you're in the snowbelt, also keep a windshield ice scraper and de-icing solution.

17. Have a practice "host" or "hostess:" Have your receptionist come out from behind her desk to greet clients and offer to hang their coats for them.

18. Provide beverages for visitors: Offer beverages and snacks to visitors in your reception area.

19. Meet clients in the right setting: Health care practitioners: Meet all new patients *in your private office,* not in a treatment/examination room. It is much more comfortable for the patient to meet you in a nonclinical setting. If you treat children, consider coming out to the reception area to meet a new child patient and escort her and her parent back into your office. Squat down and meet the child at her eye level.

20. Improve the get-acquainted process: Do you ask new clients to complete a get-acquainted form for your records? If so, make the task as pleasant as possible. Assign an assistant to complete the form with the client in a comfortable private room while the client has a beverage. Or if the information you need is sensitive, *you* might complete the form as the client answers questions during your first meeting in your private office.

21. Provide an escort: Never leave a client unescorted in your office. An assistant should escort the new client to your private office and introduce him to you at the first appointment. You or an assistant should also escort the client back to the reception area at the end of the appointment.

22. Add a mailbox: Attach a colorful mailbox to the wall of your office area for your outgoing mail. Invite clients to use the box to mail their own stamped letters.

23. Install a night depository: Provide a night depository box on the outside of your building so clients can drop off payments after office hours.

24. Page parents: If you regularly have appointments with children, buy paging devices to lend to their parents. Tell parents they may leave your office to run errands while the child is with you as long as they stay within the pager's range. Have your assistant page parents ten minutes before the end of the appointment to tell them their child's appointment is almost finished.

25. Offer enjoyable gifts for children: Do you give small gifts or prizes to children who visit your office? If so, make the gifts exciting. Wrap each one differently in colorful wrapping paper, bows, and ribbons. Display the packages in a toy box, in a treasure chest, or hanging from a tree. Let each child choose the package he or she likes best.

26. Help newcomers: Give clients new to your town a local map and other materials that tell about your area. (These are available from your chamber of commerce.) Have your assistant volunteer to answer questions about your community. You can also send a welcome letter to all area newcomers. Get names from clients, realtors, or the phone company (see sample letter 31, Appendix B).

27. Supply a photocopy machine: Make your office photocopy machine available to clients.

Idea in action: One practitioner suggests that clients photocopy the contents of their wallets while they are waiting for appointments. (A copy of credit cards and other papers could prove very valuable if a wallet is lost.) You might make photocopies of your newspaper's daily crossword puzzle and put them in your reception area with clipboards, pencils, and a dictionary. Encourage clients to copy magazine articles or puzzles they didn't have time to finish in your reception area.

28. Add a payment "thank you:" Have your financial secretary write or rubber stamp the words "thank you" on the back of clients' checks before endorsement.

29. Install a clients' phone: Install a telephone in your reception area for clients to use. Limit its service to local outgoing calls.

30. Offer a free ride: Ask clients who remain in your office after their appointments if they need a ride home. Provide one if they do. Call a cab if necessary.

31. Always have a firm handshake: Shake hands with all of your clients — men, women, and children. A firm handshake welcomes a client, communicates confidence, and initiates physical contact — all important to the client's feeling of security. Be prepared for a handshake by keeping your right hand free when a client is scheduled to enter your office or room. Keep your hand warm and dry (a few squeezes or rubbing before the client enters should help) and don't wear large rings on your right hand. Always stand to shake hands and try to exert the same squeeze pressure as your client. (If the client offers a limp hand, exert a bit more pressure but not enough to be uncomfortable.)

Idea in action: Have your assistants shake hands with the client, too. Practice shaking hands with them until they can establish eye contact and give a couple of good, firm two- to six-inch shakes.

32. Do more for new clients: When a new client calls to make her first appointment, have your appointment secretary do *more* than is necessary to make her feel welcome. Ask the client if she needs directions to your office. Explain about parking or public transportation. Tell her about your practice brochure and when she will receive it. Explain whether and how appointments will be confirmed.

33. Have a plan for schedule delays: Do everything possible to see clients promptly, but do have a plan in case you fall behind schedule. Have your receptionist call the client to let him know you are running late and by how much. If the client is already in your office, have your receptionist tell him that you have run into an unexpected delay (or emergency, if that is the case) and how late you will be for the appointment. Give him the choice of waiting, running an errand, or rescheduling. After the incident, write a short note to apologize and thank the client for his patience. Assure him that it is unusual for you to be behind schedule.

Successful application: One practitioner reduces his fee if a client has to wait more than ten minutes for his scheduled appointment. He doesn't charge any fee if the client waited more than a half hour.

34. Conduct a tour: Provide a short tour of your office to all new clients.

35. Send an introduction letter: After a new client's first appointment, send a letter that introduces each member of your staff by name, title, and role. Example: "When you paid us a visit recently, you met some but not all of our staff. I'd like to introduce you to our team: Brenda, our receptionist, greets all clients and schedules appointments. Donna, our financial secretary, is at your service if you need help completing insurance forms or making financial arrangements. . . ."

36. Flattery will get you everywhere: Compliment clients whenever you can do so sincerely. Pay at least one deserved compliment to every client you see.

37. Plan holiday giveaways: Plan special giveaways for clients who visit your office on holidays. For example, give red carnations on Valentine's Day, green ones on St. Patrick's Day, daffodils on the first day of spring, and small pumpkins or treats on Halloween.

38. Establish lay advisors: Establish a lay advisory panel to involve clients in your practice. Choose a cross-section of clients whose judgment you value. Ask them to serve on the panel one year. Schedule regular meetings and get their advice about practice policies, community needs, and ways in which you can better serve your area. If appropriate, compensate panel members with a gift, free appointment, or party. Rotate your panel each year to get different viewpoints and more clients involved in your practice.

39. Respect clients' time: When staff members call clients, have them identify themselves and ask, "Do you have a few minutes to discuss. . . ?" or "Is this a good time to talk?" This is considerate and leads to better conversations. Find out the most convenient time to call back if the client can't talk when you call.

40. Start a complaint record: Take client's complaints seriously by starting a complaint record.

    a.   Make one staff member responsible for keeping the record.

    b.   Develop a form for recording complaints. Leave spaces for the client's name, complaint, date and time of the complaint, special circumstances of the complaint (background about the client and the events that led to the complaint), name of the person who heard the complaint, response the client was given, and any later actions.

    c.   Instruct all staff members that any complaint, even those that seem harmless, must be reported to the employee in charge of your complaint record.

    d.   Have your complaint keeper complete a form for each reported complaint and photocopy it. Copies should go to you, to your office manager, and to any staff member directly involved in the complaint. File the original in a looseleaf binder.

    e.   Update the original complaint form to keep track of later developments or actions related to a complaint.

    f.   Review your complaint record monthly or more often. Be sure all complaints in that period have been given satisfactory responses. Pinpoint weak areas in your practice that cause many complaints. Set goals to help you improve in these areas.

41. Write to children: Send letters to child clients whenever possible. Children do not usually receive a great deal of mail so your letter can make quite a hit. The parents will also appreciate the extra interest you take in their child. Write to children before or after the first appointment, to congratulate them for a good check-up, when they win awards or accomplish something special at school or in a club (see sample letter 9, Appendix B).

42. Write to adults: Also send letters to adult clients whenever possible, for example: thank you for referrals, congratulations, new client, treatment confirmation, completion of treatment, inactive client, anniversaries. Study the sample letters in Appendix B for more ideas.

43. Become a good listener: Listen for clients' hidden meanings.
Idea in action: Suppose you quote a fee and the client says, "Wow! That's a lot of money!" His true meaning may be

    •   I can't afford that now.

- I can't afford that ever.
- This must be pretty serious.
- My mother-in-law had it done for less.
- It used to cost half that much.
- I'll have to spread my payments over several months.
- I wonder what my wife will say about this.
- I don't understand. Why does it cost so much?
- Oh well, there goes my trip to Bermuda!

Your best response is, "What do you mean by a 'lot of money'" and a long pause. Let the client explain what he means before giving a further response.

44. Look through clients' eyes: Sit in your own reception area regularly for at least ten minutes per session. Try to see it from the client's point of view. Use your observations to assess strengths and weaknesses and set new goals.

45. Inform as you perform: Clients very often fail to appreciate the good service they get from professionals because they don't know exactly what they're getting. Make clients perceive the value of your services *as you provide them.*

Idea in action: (for health-care practitioners) Tell the patient what you're doing throughout each part of the examination. Talking in the patient's language relieves his anxiety, solidifies your relationship and illustrates that you're thorough. For example, a physician conducting an ophthalmoscopic exam in the dark might say, "The lining of the posterior chamber of the eye is normal. That's the retina. We can sometimes see evidence of hardening of the arteries or diabetes there, even before those conditions can be detected by laboratory tests." Better understanding of what you're doing will make clients more enthusiastic and involved and often more tolerant of your fees.

46. Make referral appointments: If you refer a client to a colleague, offer to make the appointment for him. Follow up by calling the client afterward to show him he's still *your* client.

47. Provide conveniences for the elderly: Make an extra effort with elderly clients — install ramps, get large-print magazines for your reception area. Elderly clients are a growth market. One study predicts that the number of Americans over sixty-five years of age will eventually match and exceed the number of Americans in the work place.

48. Have a client call-in program: Encourage clients to call your office with questions during an established hour or half hour in the early morning or late afternoon. Make it known that you, not an assistant, will be available to answer questions when they call. Clients will appreciate the chance to talk with you. This kind of personal service shows you really care. Publicize your call-in hour in your practice brochure, client newsletter, reception area signs, bulletin board, and letters.

49. Offer multilingual written materials: Print your practice brochure, instruction sheets, and other written materials in languages that are spoken by large numbers of current or potential clients.

50. Have a positive attitude: Enthusiasm is contagious. Smile, be positive, and show clients and staff your own enthusiasm.

C · H · A · P · T · E · R   8

How to Design a One-of-a-Kind Logo for Your Practice

I n the next three chapters, we will explore the various printed materials you can use to market your practice and the steps to produce them. Many successful applications and outstanding examples of these materials are reproduced in Appendix D. Most practitioners rush into these printed marketing projects before they have developed a practice logo. As a result, they end up with a series of unrelated printed pieces, often terribly expensive ones, that project many different images and compete with one another for attention.

Think of a practice logo as your professional face on paper. The public will learn to recognize it and judge you by it. If you do not have a clear logo or if you use a different logo on every printed piece, potential clients will have more trouble recognizing you, just as they would if you wore a different mask over your face each day. Consistency — one good logo on all printed pieces — is the best way to develop visual recognition for your practice through printed marketing materials.

WHAT DISTINGUISHES A GOOD LOGO?

A *logo* refers to the visual elements you will use in all your printed materials to identify your practice. All logos contain a specific typeface that spells out the name of the practice, specialty, address, phone number, and slogan, if you have one. Some logos also contain a symbol that identifies the practice.

It's hard to define what makes a logo appealing, as that is largely a matter of personal taste. However, the best logos generally share these characteristics:

1. A good logo is consistent with the image of the practice: If your image is very modern, your logo should also look modern. It might contain a clean, futuristic typeface and an abstract symbol. On the other hand, if your

77

image is traditional, your logo should also look more traditional, both in type-face and symbol.

2. Good logos are also consistent within themselves: The type-style and the symbol should both convey the same image.

Successful application: A pediatric practitioner uses a child's drawing of him for the symbol of his logo. The typeface looks like a child's handwriting. Old English or elaborate script would be an inconsistent typeface with that symbol.

3. Good logos are crisp and clean: There are exceptions to this, but the most appealing logos seem to be those that contain only two elements — a clean typeface and a clear line drawing that's easy to trace or draw.

4. Good logos are unique and easy to identify: They are different from other logos, especially those that belong to competitors.

Idea in action: The logos reproduced in Appendix D are all unique and easy to remember. (Keep in mind that physicians' logos that use a caduceus as their symbol are common and usually easy to forget.)

5. Good logos are ageless: Remember how popular psychedelic lettering and pop art were in the 1960s? Logos using these design elements are outdated now.

6. Good logos are easy to read: Some logos use overly complicated typefaces that force the reader to struggle to make out the words. Avoid highly stylized typefaces that are elaborate and fussy, too-scrolled scripts, too-detailed versions of Old English, extremely square or slanted typefaces.

7. Good logos function well in a variety of sizes: Some logos look fine when they're large, on a brochure or letterhead, but muddy and overburdened when reduced to business card size. This happens most often when the logo is dark and highly detailed.

Tip: Determine all the sizes you'll want to print your logo. Certainly you'll want to print it as small as your business card, but would you consider something smaller such as a ballpoint pen? How large will you print your logo — on your exterior office sign? Would you ever consider billboard advertising?

8. Good logos reproduce well: If you advertise, good logos are those that reproduce as well in black and white as in color or with embossing. Newspapers, magazines, and the Yellow Pages cannot always give you your choice of colors when they reproduce your logo in an ad.

9. Good logos have one dominant element: Either the symbol dominates the type, or the type dominates the symbol. Both elements cannot have equal emphasis.

GETTING A TOP-NOTCH LOGO DESIGNED IN TEN EASY STEPS

1. Collect examples of logos you like and dislike to get ideas from them: Study the logos reproduced in Appendix D. Also look at product packages in your local supermarket. You may not have realized before how much you are attracted by the logo on a cereal box or shampoo bottle. Take a fresh look at these packages with an eye toward logo design. Note those that appeal to you strongly. Next, take out your Yellow Pages, newspapers, and magazines and look for appealing logos in ads. Finally, walk or drive through your town. Note which storefront and corporate signs appeal to you.

2. Gather the examples of favorite logos you have collected: While you cannot legally copy any of them, study them and make a list of design elements you particularly like. You may find you're drawn to logos that use certain typestyles, shapes, initials, line patterns, colors, or symbols.

3. Gather examples of logos you strongly dislike: Note general design elements that you prefer to avoid in your logo.

4. Prepare notes for your logo designer: The more organized you are, the more you will be able to tell your designer, the more she will have to work with, and the better your final logo will be. Include the following information in your notes:

a.   Examples of logos you like and dislike and notes about your design preferences.

b.   A brief statement of the professional image you want your logo to convey (formal vs. informal, modern vs. traditional).

c.   How you already convey that image in your practice: location; personal appearance; policies; staff; decor (note the color scheme and style of your office).

d.   A brief description of your current and potential clients — age, income, demographic data. Use the market research techniques described in Chapters 1 and 2 to obtain this information.

e.   Do you have a second practice where the logo will be used? Will there ever be one?

f.   A brief profile of you: area of specialization, personal goals, hobbies, philosophy of practice.

g.   How will you use your logo? Possibilities are: business cards, memo paper, postcards, letterhead, appointment reminder cards, envelopes, statements, brochures, newsletters, exterior and interior signs, balloons, name tags, pens, refrigerator magnets, books, pamphlets, billboards, television ads, T-shirts, print ads.

h.   Your practice slogan if you have one.

i.   Examples of all the stationery and other printed pieces you are using now.

j.   If you already have something in mind for your logo, describe and sketch it in your notes.

5. Choose the designer for your logo: The best person for the job will be a free-lance graphic artist or one who works at a design studio, public relations firm, or advertising agency. Follow the advice in Appendix A for choosing a qualified graphic artist or agency.

6. Invite your artist to your office for a meeting: Let her see your location, decor, and staff and get her own impression of the image you are projecting. Review your notes with her, telling her everything you can about the logo you want.

7. Discuss fees: Usually the artist will quote a fee in one of three ways: a flat fee, an hourly rate or a flat fee plus an additional fee or rate for extra revisions. Some artists include the fee for a logo in a package that includes the design of other marketing materials such as a brochure or newsletter.

Tip: It is generally worthwhile to invest as much as is needed to get a quality logo designed; several hundred dollars is the minimum. A top-notch logo is a good reflection of your practice and can last forever.

8. Ask for sketches: When you have agreed on the fee, the artist will usually suggest that you give her a week or two to develop some ideas and work out several black-and-white thumbnail sketches. She will then meet with you again, show you what she has come up with and ask you to choose the one or two sketches you like most. If you don't like any of the sketches, the artist will ask for suggestions and work on another set. Check to see if there is an additional fee for extra revisions.

9. Narrow your choices: Once you say you like a sketch or two, the artist will return to her studio to work these out fully and carefully, with specific typestyles; colored ink; subtle shading; and suggestions for embossing, foil, background colors, textures, and other elements that would be used when printing the finished logo. Following are some tips about these design elements.

a. *Typestyle images.* There are hundreds of typestyles that you can use in your logo, but any typestyle can be classified as either *serif* or *sans serif.* Choose the appropriate category of typestyle according to the image you want to convey:

SERIF TYPESTYLES	**SANS SERIF TYPESTYLES**
Thus	**Thus**

Serif typestyles have little slabs or ''feet'' on the tops and bottoms of the letters. In general, serif typestyles are a little easier to read. They project a warm, traditional image.

Sans serif typestyles do *not* have little slabs on the tops and bottoms of the letters. In general, sans serif typestyles project a modern, somewhat colder image.

b. *Consistency.* Use colors consistently each time you print your logo. Potential clients may have trouble recognizing a logo that's printed in blue one time, red another, and orange a third.

c. *Color images.* Certain colors and combinations of colors project images. Dark brown ink on a tan background usually looks very formal and businesslike. Using two tones of the same color is generally soothing and low-key. Primary colors on a white background give a bold, cheerful, and often modern impression. Silver or gold foil and embossing look expensive and classy.

d. *Background.* For maximum readability, most practitioners will want to choose a light background color for their logos. Good choices are white, off-white, light gray, ivory, buff, light tan, pastels.

e. *Budget.* Colored ink is more expensive to print than black. To save money you can use only one or two ink colors or for variation, print one color in different tones, called ''screens.''

f. *Highlights.* A good, economical color choice is black ink plus one other color or a gold or silver foil. However, a color or foil highlights, so be sure to use them on the most important parts of the logo.

Idea in action: If your logo is black and orange, use the orange ink on your practice name or symbol, *not* on your phone number or ZIP code.

g. *Two tones.* If you use two tones of the same color for the logo and background, be sure the difference between the tones is extreme.

Idea in action: Use dark navy blue ink on a pale blue background. Don't use two shades of medium blue.

h.   *Coordinate.* If possible, choose logo colors to match or coordinate with your office decor or staff uniform. That way *color* becomes an identifiable symbol of your practice.

i.   *Textures.* Your artist may suggest textures for the paper you use for printed pieces. Textures have different qualities and images. They should be consistent on all printed pieces. Felt-finish and embossed-finish papers are heavily textured, convey a quality image, and are well suited for embossing. A laid-finish paper looks ribbed. It can have a watermark, it looks old-fashioned, and it is ideal for reproducing line art. A vellum-finish paper has little texture, but is glare-free and ideal for clear reproduction of photographs.

10. Final revisions: The artist will meet with you to show you the completed logo and get your ideas for final alterations or revisions.

Tip: Ask the artist to show you the logo in the various sizes you will use it — business card size, letterhead size, poster size. This exercise will help you determine how well your logo shrinks and expands.

AFTER YOU HAVE YOUR LOGO

1.   Ask your attorney for advice about registering your logo as a trademark.

2.   Use your logo universally on all printed pieces: stationery, brochures, newsletters, recall reminders, statements, giveaways.

3.   Resist the temptation to change your logo after a few years. You may tire of it because you see it all the time, but a logo is a long-term investment. It can take months or years until potential clients begin to identify you with it. The Coca-Cola logo, for example, is exactly the same as it was when first designed in the late 1890s. Now there's hardly a person who doesn't recognize it; even people who can't read know that logo.

4.   If you must change your logo, try to revise, not discard it. Keep basic design elements the same or similar so potential clients can still identify you with them.

Idea in action: The White Rock girl used as that company's logo symbol has been revised to gain and lose weight over the years according to current fashion. However, she has never been discarded, she has always been their symbol, and she has dressed the same and kept her wings.

Designing Stationery and Signs with Your New Logo

DESIGNING STATIONERY THAT CONVEYS YOUR IMAGE

Throughout this *Guide* you will read about scores of opportunities to send marketing letters to current and potential clients, colleagues, the media, and community groups. The stationery you use for these letters will affect the way your message is received. If you use the correct stationery with your attractive logo on it, the reader will know that your image is like your stationery's — first-rate, modern or traditional, bold or conservative, formal or informal. By the same token, if you use the wrong stationery — inconsistent, poor logo, ugly or dull paper — that, too, tells your reader something about you, perhaps that you're careless about details, sloppy, second-rate, dull, unoriginal, or run-of-the-mill.

You'll need the help of a good graphic artist and printer to create quality stationery for your practice. Suggestions for finding qualified help are offered in Appendix A. In addition, study the examples of outstanding practice stationery that appear in Appendix D and the tips in this chapter for designing and printing first-rate stationery.

How to Design Practice Letterhead

Use letterhead for formal typed correspondence only. Some design tips follow.

Size.   Have letterhead paper cut to $8\frac{1}{2}'' \times 11''$; that is the standard size and is perfect to keep in a file folder or mail in a business envelope.

Logo placement.   Most practitioners place their logos at the top of the letterhead. If you do, limit the logo size to the top fifth of the paper. A larger logo will overpower the letter you type below it. Experiment with other placements for your logo. Some attractive letterheads are designed with the logo running vertically down the left side of the paper. Others print half the logo at the top of the paper (usually the symbol and practice name) and the other half at the bottom (the practice address, phone number, slogan, and office hours).

Paper.   When designing a logo, a graphic artist will suggest a texture and color for the background of the logo (Chapter 8). Use paper in that color and texture for all your stationery. In addition, choose the correct weight paper for each piece. Most letterheads are printed on 20- to 24-pound bond paper, a sturdy weight that folds easily and doesn't rustle.

> **Hint:** Before printing any stationery, take a few pieces of the paper you plan to use back to your office. Try typing and writing on it and fold it just as you will when it is printed as your stationery. This exercise can point out problems with some papers; some may fray on the folds, slip in the typewriter or printer, glare, or be too flimsy.

Blanks.   Order some of the same paper unprinted, also cut to $8\frac{1}{2}'' \times 11''$. You will need this to type the second, third, and subsequent pages of letters. Formal business correspondence does not use letterhead after the first page.

Commemorative letterhead.   Consider designing special letterhead to commemorate a significant practice event or anniversary (such as twenty-five years) and use it throughout that year.

> **Hint:** Design commemorative letterhead just like regular letterhead — same colors, logo, weight, texture — but add an anniversary slogan or banner heading.

How to Design Envelopes for Letterhead

The standard, business-size envelope to accompany $8\frac{1}{2}'' \times 11''$ letterhead is a #10 envelope. It measures $4\frac{1}{8}'' \times 9\frac{1}{2}''$. Design tips:

Coordinate.   Order #10 envelopes that exactly match your letterhead and other pieces — same paper, color, ink colors, texture, and logo.

Weight.   You may not have much choice about the paper weight of #10 envelopes, but be sure your envelopes are not too flimsy. Hold a sample up to the light to test whether you can see through it. Put a typed letter in one to see if you can read it through the envelope. If you can, ask your printer for a heavier stock.

Logo placement.   Your logo should serve as the return address on the front of your envelope. Usually it appears in the upper left-hand corner. As an alternative, some excellent designs run the return address up the whole left side of the envelope.

Information. An envelope's return address may include your slogan. However, it usually does not include a telephone number or office hours.

How to Design Business Cards

Do not underestimate the value of your business cards. They are a versatile marketing tool. Three ways to use them to solicit referrals are: (a) give several cards to clients at a post-service conference (Chapter 6); (b) give cards to local shopkeepers or anyone in your community whose services you use; (c) give cards to any client who pays you a compliment. How? Suppose a client says, "You know, you're the first doctor who has ever seen me on time." You might say, "Thank you. I am so glad you told me that you like what I'm doing in my practice, Mrs. Jensen. And I'd be even happier if you would also tell some of your friends. Here are several of my cards. . . ."

Design tips for business cards follow.

Paper. Use paper in the same color and texture as your letterhead. The weight you will want is heavier than letterhead paper and is called "card" stock.

Size. Standard business card size is $2'' \times 3\frac{1}{2}''$. This is a convenient size that fits easily into a wallet or business card file. Some cards are a fold-over style like a miniature greeting card. These cost more and convey an extremely fancy and expensive image.

Logo placement. A logo can be printed on the business card so the card is held horizontally (most common) or vertically. Examples of both placements are reproduced in Appendix D. Have your graphic artist help you decide which is best for you.

Other information. Simple business cards are most appealing to the eye. However, you may wish to include information in addition to your logo. Office hours are excellent. So is the phrase, "New Clients Always Welcome."

Appointment cards. Some practitioners use a combination business and appointment card. If you do this, also print a straight business card. Use these to solicit referrals in the ways suggested above.

Make cards valuable. Here's an idea that will encourage clients to keep your business cards with them always. On the back of your card, print the step-by-step instructions for handling some sort of emergency.

Successful applications: A lawyer printed instructions for what to do in case of arrest or accident. A dentist listed instructions for what to do if a tooth is knocked out. (See Appendix D.) An optometrist printed instructions for what to do in case a foreign object gets into the eye. To explain it to clients (suppose you're the dentist), say, "Here is a card with the instructions you should follow in the event a tooth is knocked out. Many people don't realize that if they act fast and follow these instructions, there's a chance we can save the tooth. I suggest you keep this card in your wallet so you'll have the instructions with you in case you or someone you know is involved in this sort of accident."

> **Hint:** Offer the client extra copies of your card to give to friends and family members. This is a great way to get your name into the community by providing a valuable service.

Staff cards. When ordering business cards for members of your staff, design them exactly like yours, but with their names and titles. This has two advantages; first, designing cards the same is yet another opportunity to emphasize one consistent image to your clients; second, using one design will reduce your graphic design and printing costs. (Examples of staff cards appear in Appendix D. Suggestions for how to use them are in Chapter 5.)

How to Design Memo Paper and Notecards

Small memo paper and notecards are handy for short handwritten or typed notes. Design tips follow.

Memo size. Most memo paper is a miniature version of the letterhead, same paper, color, texture and weight. A convenient size is $5\frac{1}{2}'' \times 8''$.

Personalizing memos. You might start with some general-purpose memo paper for your practice. Later have memo paper personalized with your name and the names of each member of your staff.

Notecards. Many practices have developed notecards for writing notes of thanks, holiday greetings, and congratulations. Run notecards in the same color and texture as your memo paper, perhaps in a slightly heavier weight. The most popular size for notecards is $5\frac{1}{2}'' \times 8''$ folded in half. Print your logo very large on the front panel and leave the inside of the card blank for your handwritten message. Some practices also print unfolded flat cards that measure $2\frac{3}{4}'' \times 4''$ that look like a miniature of the letterhead. This tiny card is very convenient for extremely brief notes.

Envelopes. Memo paper and notecards the same size ($5\frac{1}{2}'' \times 8''$) and tiny notes half that size ($2\frac{3}{4}'' \times 4''$) will all fit in the same envelope, $4\frac{1}{2}'' \times 5\frac{3}{4}''$. These envelopes should be the same texture and color as all your other stationery. *Do not* use your #10 envelopes for mailing your memos and notecards. They are clearly the wrong size and everyone will know it.

Designing Other Stationery Items with Your Logo

Letterhead, memo paper, notecards, envelopes, and business cards that coordinate and use your logo are the basic items of stationery that you will need for most of your marketing projects. You may also consider the following items:

Appointment cards. As suggested earlier, you may wish to design a combination business and appointment card. If not, design separate appointment cards using the same logo, paper color, and texture.

Recall reminders. Many practitioners design these to match their other pieces. Idea: Print a postcard with your logo large on one side, like a picture postcard. Leave room for the client's address and recall reminder message on the other side.

Stickers. Small stickers printed with the practice logo can be used many ways: as a decorative seal on memo envelopes, on books and pamphlets you give to clients, as a recall reminder for clients to put on their calendars, as an emergency notice for clients to attach to their home telephones, as inexpensive badges for child clients.

Rolodex cards. Lawyers, accountants, and other practitioners who serve businesses and business people sometimes print their logos on telephone index cards. These can be given to clients to put right into their files — a nice reminder of you and your logo.

Get-acquainted forms. Do clients complete get-acquainted forms at the first appointment? If so, you might design a form on your stationery paper with your logo at the top. Benefit: New clients will learn to associate your logo and colors with you right from the start.

Financial papers. Written financial arrangements, monthly statements, payment envelopes, even collection stickers indicating that the account is past due can all be coordinated with your other stationery by using the same logo and colors.

Recipe cards. Some practitioners provide recipe cards in the reception area to keep waiting clients amused (Chapter 7). These cards can be printed with the practice logo and coordinated with your other stationery. The client will then think of you and your logo each time he uses the recipe.

Greeting cards. If you send greeting cards to clients at Thanksgiving or on birthdays, you can have special cards printed with your logo to match your other stationery.

Surveys. Client feedback surveys and surveys of potential clients (Chapters 1 and 2) can be coordinated with other stationery.

Giveaways. There is virtually no limit to the number of giveaways you can buy for clients. These will be most effective if they carry your logo and colors.

Successful applications: Many practitioners use their logos and colors on refrigerator magnets, pens, pencils, wall and pocket calendars, balloons, memo pads, telephone book covers, key chains, T-shirts, buttons, coloring books, and children's story books.

Postage Meter Imprints or Stamps?

Are postage meter imprints appropriate for posting marketing correspondence? Follow these tips:

1.   An attractive postage stamp may call attention to your mail. Many practitioners prefer to use stamps on special personal marketing correspondence, such as thank-you notes, invitations, client appreciation letters, welcome-to-the-practice letters.

2.   Stamps have been shown to increase the rate of return on client feedback surveys. They are particularly effective when put on return mailing envelopes. A stamp seems like money to people (more than a postage meter mark does). They may return the survey just so you won't waste money.

3.   Postage meters do save time and are quite appropriate for large marketing mailings such as client newsletters.

4.   When you use a postage meter, consider using additional imprints to carry special messages and make your envelope stand out. Meter imprints generally measure a maximum of $1\frac{7}{8}'' \times \frac{5}{8}''$. They are printed automatically just to the left of the postage mark as envelopes pass through the postage meter. Check with your meter manufacturer to see if it sells off-the-shelf imprints. In addition, you can usually custom-design your own messages.

Successful applications: Many practitioners imprint holiday greetings and announcements of special events such as open houses, weeks designated by their professional societies, and other activities described in Chapters 15 and 16. Some design imprints that carry a clever or especially inspiring phrase. For instance, some dentists imprint:

— Dental Disease Can Be Cured if Detected in Time
— I Didn't Cry
— A Bright Smile — The Most Convincing Form of Communication
— Flossers Kiss Sweeter
— There Is a Difference

DESIGNING SIGNS THAT CONVEY YOUR IMAGE

Do you have control over the signs outside or inside your office building? If so, they can be extremely valuable marketing tools. Signs not only help your current clients identify and find your office; they also convey your image to potential clients passing by and can tell them a lot about the professional services you offer.

Good signs compare very favorably with other forms of marketing communications. They are:

On the job twenty-four hours a day, seven days a week, every week of every month, all through the year.

Read by nearly everyone. Studies show people read signs and remember the messages they convey.

Oriented to your specific market. Money spent on signs is not wasted reaching market segments outside your geographic area.

Comparatively inexpensive when considering cost-per-thousand exposures (the cost of having your message received by one thousand people — a common measure of cost-effectiveness in advertising media).

Easy to use. Once installed, no resources or professional services are required. You need only operate and maintain your sign.

Diverse. Numerous styles are available. You can custom-design signs with your logo and colors to fit every need.

The graphic artist who designed your logo and stationery will probably be able to help you design signs for your practice. In addition, you will need the help of a reputable sign company (see Appendix A). Study the design tips in this chapter before meeting with an artist or sign company.

Choose the Best Sign Construction Method for Your Needs

Many professionals today are turning away from the standard "shingle" in favor of signs with different construction methods. Each of these five methods is suited to a specific purpose.

1. Wall-mounted or facia signs: These are the most popular signs and are attached directly to buildings, often bolted flat onto the facade. They are used where traffic can see the office building head-on without obstruction.

2. Hanging or projected signs: These are signs attached perpendicularly to the buildings they identify. They are used over storefront offices where traffic travels perpendicularly to building fronts.

3. Post-mounted signs: These are free-standing signs *not* attached to the buildings they identify. The popular "shingle" is one example, although there are many other types available. Post-mounted signs can be mounted perpendicular to or parallel with the building, usually on a lawn or in a parking lot. They are used to identify buildings not easily seen from the road or sidewalk.

4. Ground-mounted or low-profile signs: These signs are also free-standing signs. They are generally used in conjunction with landscaping low to the ground. They are used on the lawn in front of suburban and rural buildings when the building is far from the street and sidewalk and is not easily seen.

5. Window lettering or window-mounted signs: These are signs mounted from the inside of the building identified. They are used in city offices, sometimes in conjunction with other signs. Many storefront offices use them but also attach a projected or facia sign to the building.

Which construction method is right for you? Take this quiz to help you decide.

a. Do signs, trees, or other buildings obstruct view of your building? If so, choose a free-standing sign away from your building or above it on a high post.

b. Do local ordinances restrict your sign's size, height, color, or setback from the road? Does your landlord or professional society place restrictions on signs? Get a list of all restrictions in writing so you'll be assured that your sign does not violate any of them.

c. Do you maintain nighttime hours? Does traffic pass by your office at night? If so, plan on illuminating your exterior signs, either with spot lighting or electrified signs.

d. Does your office environment restrict construction options? In areas with a lot of ground moisture or high vandalism, the best signs are extremely durable and placed high up and out of the reach of vandals. A good choice is a metal sign bolted high into the building's facade.

e. From which direction(s) will clients be approaching your office? If clients can approach you many ways, choose a two-sided perpendicular sign or several signs on different sides of your building.

f. Will traffic be primarily pedestrian, vehicular, or a combination? In general, signs viewed from cars need to be larger than those for pedestrians only. If you have a lot of car traffic, install extra signs to mark all parking lot exits and entrances.

Logo, Color and Other Sign Design Considerations

1. Logo and colors: Design your sign with the same logo and colors as on your printed materials. *Reason:* A sign is a terrific way to develop visual recognition for your practice in your community. As potential clients pass your office, they will begin to identify your sign and logo with *you*. This can only help when the same people also see your business card or brochure, get a letter from you, hear your public service announcement, read your press release or are exposed to any other of your external marketing projects. If people like your sign and remember it, they may call you when they have a problem that you can help them with.

2. Compatibility with your building: What is the architectural style of your office building? This will influence your sign's design.

a.   A rustic-style wooden building would be complemented by a wooden sign. A neon or plastic sign would clash.

b.   A Spanish-style building with an orange terra-cotta roof might suggest that orange should be used in the sign or that certain clashing colors should be avoided.

c.   A practice located in an old stately Colonial house will probably call for a sign that is low-key and old-fashioned. It would be better to illuminate such a sign with hidden spotlights rather than using neon or a modern plastic electrified sign.

d.   Buildings with smooth simple facades can use signs made of individual letters attached directly to the building. However, such a sign might get lost when attached to a building with a complicated facade of intricate brick or marble patterns.

3. Compatibility with neighboring buildings: Obviously, you won't want your sign to cause problems with your neighbors or to be viewed as an eyesore in your community. Stay away from too-commercial signs, especially in a residential or low-key business area. What if you practice in an area where commercial signs abound for fast-food chains, discount stores, and gas stations? While you will want your sign to be noticed, don't resort to any design elements that seem unprofessional to you.

4. Coordinating interior office signs: Don't forget to use your logos and colors on the signs *inside* your building if they are in your control. For example, use your logo on

a.   *Directional signs* that point the way to your reception area, restrooms, and exit.

b.   *Door signs* that identify rooms, saying, "Employees Only," "Examination Room," "Restroom," and "Laboratory."

Tip: Examining room numbers should be on projected signs perpendicular to the wall. If you use a wall-mounted or facia sign, patients have to get to the door to find out what number it is and then go to the next door to see which way the numbers run.

c.   *Desk signs* that indicate your name and the names of your receptionist, financial secretary, marketing coordinator, and appointment secretary.

d.   *Name tags.* Study the name tags worn by employees of airlines, restaurants, hotels, and department stores. These are usually designed in the company's colors with the slogan and logo. Name tags with a logo and colors that coordinate with staff uniforms are best.

e.   *Reception area signs.* Examples are: a list of all the services you offer, requests that clients register with your receptionist, signs about smoking, information about methods of payment.

How to Write, Produce, and Distribute a Practice Brochure

A first-rate practice brochure is a versatile marketing tool that can benefit every practitioner. Other professionals use brochures to

• send to new clients to make a powerful first impression and to established clients to reinforce ties.

• mail to colleagues, area businesses, and personnel officers to encourage referrals.

• display in pharmacies, health and counseling centers, clubs, schools, and other places in the community where potential clients may see them.

• mail directly to newcomers and other potential clients.

• include in press kits and handouts for open houses, speeches, office tours, community fairs, and the other special events described in Chapters 15 and 16.

You'll need a graphic artist and printer to design and print a first-rate practice brochure. Some practitioners will also require writing and editing assistance from a free-lance writer, public relations firm, or advertising agency. Suggestions for finding qualified help appear in Appendix A. In addition, study the fine examples of practice brochures in Appendix D and the guidelines in this chapter for writing and designing a quality brochure.

STEP 1: CHOOSE THE TOPICS FOR YOUR BROCHURE

The first step in producing a brochure is deciding which information you wish to cover. Make a list of the policies and attributes of your practice that clients would find most helpful. Your staff and client feedback surveys may provide good suggestions. Also study this list of topics covered most frequently in practice brochures:

- Practice logo, including name, address, telephone number, area of specialization, and slogan.

- A short welcome message.

- Office hours.

- Directions to the office and/or a map.

- Parking and public transportation information.

- A short history of the practice.

- Credentials.

- Philosophy of practice.

- Telephone policies — after-hours phone numbers, call-back policy.

- Appointment policies — how far in advance clients should schedule appointments, information about missed appointments, emergencies, and confirmation calls.

- Financial policies — billing procedures, when accounts are overdue, methods of payment, finance plans.

- Insurance policies.

- Fee policies (general information only).

- Recalls — what you do at recall appointments, why recall is valuable, length of time between recall appointments.

- Back-up professional support when you're unavailable.

- General functions of auxiliary staff.

Tip: Describe *functions* of the receptionist, office manager, financial secretary, and paraprofessionals, not *individuals.* Staff biographies are better suited to a letter or brochure insert that can be revised inexpensively and easily when turnover occurs.

- Information for new clients — what to expect at the first appointment.

- Information for clients of record — requests for changes in address, phone number, and insurance coverage.

- Description of office facility, especially unique features.

- Requests for referrals.

Pitfall: A practice brochure serves as an *introduction* to the practice. You can't possibly cover every conceivable question or all the topics on the list above. That's more than most people will be willing to take in in one reading. Pare your list so you're down to the best, most important information. Then arrange the topics in logical order. Start and end your brochure with your most motivational topics. Put the driest material in the middle.

Idea in action: Start with an upbeat welcome message; put information about appointments, recall, and insurance in the middle; and end with an inspirational message. An upbeat beginning will encourage the reader to continue; an uplifting closing will make him feel great about your practice.

STEP 2: WRITE BROCHURE COPY THAT SPARKLES

Some practitioners may feel they need to hire a professional writer to produce top-notch brochure copy. If you do, read Appendix A and learn how to find such help in your area. If you will be writing your own brochure, keep the following points in mind:

1. Length: The best brochures are almost always those with the *least* copy. Usually a good brochure has only one to three short paragraphs on each topic and no more than nine or ten lines of copy per paragraph. Don't think in terms of how much you can write; think of the *least* you can get away with.

2. Tact: Tact will be your greatest ally when you describe your policies in a brochure. Compare the authoritarian, "There is no smoking allowed in this office," to the more tactful, "We ask that you do not smoke in our office."

3. Benefits: Emphasize the benefits clients enjoy by being part of your practice and adhering to your policies. Appeal to their natural self-interest.

Successful application: One practitioner requests forty-eight-hour advance notice to cancel an appointment. His brochure explains how ample lead time allows him to reschedule the appointment with another client who is in need of his services. This gets a better result than saying that the lead time makes it possible for him to fill his schedule better or increase production.

4. Editing: Edit all technical jargon and unnecessary or negative words from your brochure copy. Check your final draft against Appendix C, which is a list of words and phrases to use and avoid in marketing communications. In addition, review your draft to be sure it has a consistent point of view. Good brochure copy sounds as though it has been written by one person in one style.

5. Tone: Be serious in your brochure. It will be read by many people and should reflect well on you—always. Avoid sarcasm; some readers may not appreciate it.

6. Headings: Write your headings and subheads last after all your copy. Don't try too hard to be clever or cute. Simple, direct headings and subheads are fine and far better than contrived ones.

7. Title: Finally, write a strong, attention-getting title for the front panel of your brochure. It may be a clever slogan or it may be strictly informational, saying, "Welcome to Our Office," "Client Information Brochure," or "Information for Our Clients." It may also simply be your practice name in your logo.

STEP 3: PREPARE TO MEET WITH YOUR GRAPHIC ARTIST

The graphic artist who designed your logo and stationery will be able to help you choose a format for your brochure. If you do not already have a graphic artist, read the suggestions for finding a qualified individual or studio in Appendix A.

The length of your final brochure copy will determine the way you design it. Once you've got your copy in final form:

1.   Double-space and type it on standard $8\frac{1}{2}'' \times 11''$ paper. Leave a one-inch margin all around.

2.   Count the number of finished pages. The best length for a final typed brochure manuscript is usually between two and six double-spaced pages. That is the amount of text most clients are willing to read in a practice brochure.

3.   It is unlikely that you'll have less than two typed double-spaced pages. However, if you do, think again about your policies and what clients would appreciate knowing about you. Brochures that are too skimpy don't make a strong impression.

4.   On the other hand, clients may be intimidated and bored by a brochure that's too long. If yours is more than six typed double-spaced pages, edit, edit, edit. Remember, your brochure is only an *introduction* to your practice, not the last word.

Once you know how long your brochure manuscript is, make a preliminary decision about an appropriate format. Brochures can be many sizes and lengths, but most practices choose a brochure format that fits into a #10 envelope to save money on printing and postage. There are three preferred formats that fit in a #10 envelope when folded:

FORMAT 1: ONE FOLD, FOUR PANELS

This is the format used for brochure manuscripts that are about two typed, double-spaced pages long. It is printed on $8\frac{1}{2}'' \times 7''$ paper folded in half like a greeting card.

FORMAT 2: TWO FOLDS, SIX PANELS

This is the format used for brochure manuscripts about three or four typed, double-spaced pages long. It is printed on $8\frac{1}{2}'' \times 11''$ paper folded in thirds.

FORMAT 3: THREE FOLDS, EIGHT PANELS

This is the format used for brochure manuscripts about five or six typed, double-spaced pages long. It is printed on $8\frac{1}{2}'' \times 14''$ paper folded three times into four equal sections.

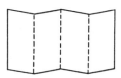

Some cautions about format selections:

1. These format suggestions are general guidelines only. The format you choose will be influenced by the number and size of illustrations and white spaces you use in your brochure. Your artist will direct you to the format that fits your needs exactly.

2. Some practitioners' images may suggest a brochure format other than one that fits in a #10 envelope.

Successful application: An accounting firm designed a brochure that folds to $8\frac{1}{2}'' \times 11''$ and is mailed flat in a $9'' \times 12''$ envelope. They use the larger brochure to attract clients worth at least $10,000 a year in billings. The firm believes the larger brochure looks more expensive, projects its image well, and attracts these kinds of clients better than a smaller more modest brochure.

3. Decide if your brochure will be a self-mailer or if it will be mailed in an envelope. Self-mailers are generally easier and cheaper to mail. If the goal of your image is to serve low- to middle-income clients, self-mailers may be a good option for you. To use a self-mailer, print one of the outer brochure panels with your return address and leave room for the client's name and address and a stamp. (The outer panels are those that show when the brochure is folded up.) On the other hand, if your image is one of high quality and of serving a high-income market, plan on mailing your brochures in envelopes. That's more expensive but it looks it.

STEP 4: WORK WITH YOUR ARTIST TO DESIGN
A QUALITY BROCHURE

Once you've written your brochure manuscript and made preliminary decisions about your format and whether it will be a self-mailer, schedule a meeting with your graphic artist. Prepare notes for your artist about your image, ideas and other printed materials. (See Chapter 8 for a list of the notes to prepare for meeting with an artist.) In addition, consider the following design tips:

1. Typestyle: Professional typesetting will give your brochure a neat, attractive look. For consistency, choose a typestyle for your brochure that is the same as or compatible with the typestyle you used in your logo.

2. Paragraphs: If your typestyle is *serif* (with slabs or feet on the tops and bottoms of the letters), it will look more traditional and generally is used with traditional indented paragraphs. If it is *sans serif* (no slabs), it will look more modern and generally is used with modern block paragraphs with spaces between them. See Chapter 8 for illustrations and a description of serif and sans serif typestyles.

3. Type size: Type is measured in "point" sizes. For any of the three brochure formats described earlier, your text will look best set in nine- or ten-point type, headings in 16-, 18-, or 24-point type. Subheads are normally set the same size as the text (nine or ten points) or a little larger (11 or 12 points). Do not set subheads any larger or they will compete for attention with headings.

4. Thickness: Typestyles come in several thicknesses. Make headings and subheads stand out by having them set in *bold* or *demibold* type (thicker than normal). Set the manuscript in *book* face (regular medium type).

5. Leading: Specify the amount of "leading" or white space you want between lines of type. The standard is two points of leading.

6. Italics and capitals: Use italic typefaces and ALL CAPITALS sparingly if at all. They make your text harder to read.

7. Line length: The consensus among typographers is that the ideal line length is between 39 and 65 characters (counting each letter, punctuation mark, and space as one character). Shorter or longer lines of type are harder to read.

8. Margins: Decide whether to have your brochure text set *justified* or *ragged*. Base this decision on your image.

JUSTIFIED MARGINS	RAGGED MARGINS
This is an example of justified type. All the lines end at the same point in the right margin. In general, justified type projects a formal image and re-quires a great deal of hyphenation. It is commonly used with serif typestyles. Headings are usually centered and para-graphs indented.	This is an example of ragged type. Each line ends at a slightly different point in the right margin. In general, ragged type projects an informal image and requires little if any hyphenation. It is commonly used with sans serif typestyles. Headings are usually set flush left (against the left margin) and paragraphs blocked.

9. Word processing: Most practitioners have their brochures professionally typeset. However, if you are using a word processor to type a brochure, type your headings in all capitals and underline them: <u>OUR STAFF</u>. Type subheads in capitals and lower case letters and underline them: <u>Our Receptionist</u>. You can also buy presstype from an art store and use it for larger bolder headings and subheads.

10. Paper weight: Choose paper for your brochure the same color and texture as your stationery. This will make all your marketing pieces consistent and give each one more impact. However, use a heavier weight paper for your brochure: 70- or 80-pound text paper is a good choice. Avoid flimsier papers or your print may show through from one side of the page to the other. Paper heavier than 80-pound text is not necessary, costs more, and is usually more difficult and expensive to fold.

11. Ink colors: Choose the same ink colors for your brochure as those used on your stationery, again for consistency. As explained in Chapter 8, colors highlight, so they should be used only on the most important parts of your brochure such as your logo, headings, subheads, and artwork. For example, if your logo is black and aqua, use black ink for the bulk of the brochure text and aqua ink on the logo, headings, and artwork only. Color, like perfume, is most effective when you use a little, not a lot. Large areas of text printed in a strong color like aqua are harder to read than text printed in black.

12. Artwork: Good artwork can add quite a lot to almost any brochure. Your graphic artist will be able to suggest many ideas for artwork. Some inexpensive suggestions follow.

a. Clip-art is camera-ready copyright-free professional artwork that you can buy inexpensively at local art supply and book stores. It is usually sold in books on different subjects such as borders, words, faces, animals, vehicles, and buildings.

b. Use thin lines to box in different sections of your brochure. Like spot color, boxes should be used sparingly to be most effective.

c. One good design trick is using a piece of artwork that spans several panels of your brochure when it is opened up.

Successful applications: One practitioner's brochure prints a thick line across the top of all four inside panels of his brochure. Another's has a box around two panels that ties them together. Another uses a sketch of several people that spans four panels. These devices unify the panels and add visual continuity to the brochures. Examples are reproduced in Appendix D.

d. As already suggested, colored ink can add interest to your brochure, but there are other techniques that are less expensive. A reverse can be quite effective and economical. In a reverse, the background is printed in the ink and the letters or artwork are left unprinted (Example A). This is the reverse of the normal printing process in which the letters are printed and the background is left unprinted (Example B).

Example A: Reverse   **Example B: Normal Printing**

e. A screen is another relatively inexpensive printing technique that lets you print shades of a single color.

Idea in action: Using screens of black ink gives you the ability to use *gray* in your brochure. This is far less costly than using a second ink color.

STEP 5: AVOID THESE NINE COMMON BROCHURE DESIGN ERRORS

These nine common brochure design errors distract the reader and make brochures seem amateurish. If you already have a practice brochure, examine it as you read this checklist. Correct mistakes in your next printing:

1. Weak or cluttered front panel: The front panel of your brochure is the most important part. It must invite the reader to open the brochure and see what's inside.

Tip: Think of your front panel as a miniature *poster*. Make it colorful and attention-grabbing and keep it simple. Limit it to a few key elements: a strong title, your logo, and perhaps a dominant piece of artwork.

2. Too many typestyles: Excessive use of typestyles creates a junky, cluttered look. Use the same typestyle for your logo, headings, subheads, and text. For variation, use different point sizes, thicknesses, reverses, screens, boxes, or colors as suggested earlier.

3. Unrelated panels: Brochure panels should look alike. Design them with the same colors, typestyles, margins (ragged or justified), paragraphs (indented or block), and headings (centered or flush left, bold or demibold).

4. Weak art or bad photographs: Bad art destroys a brochure. If you can't come up with good art, use type as a design element to relieve the sameness of blocks of solid text — reverses; screens; different thicknesses, sizes, and colors. Follow the advice in Chapter 13 for composing good journalistic photos. Caption all photos. Do not print photos in colors inappropriate to the subject. Do not print photos of people in blue, green, or purple ink. It makes them look bad, and the photos are hard to distinguish.

5. Misuse of white space: White or blank space in a brochure is not wasted space. On the contrary, it can provide relief to the eye and become a design element itself. Bunch white space so it contrasts with the dark areas of print. Scattered or trapped white space blows the page apart; bunched white space adds a touch of class.

6. Too much or too little text: Too much text intimidates the reader and squeezes out the needed quiet areas of white space and artwork. On the other hand, too little text looks skimpy and gives the impression that you have nothing to say. Two to six typed, double-spaced pages of brochure copy are ideal. Keep each paragraph short, no more than nine or ten lines apiece.

7. Inappropriate type for the message and image: Be sure your typestyle not only looks nice and is easy to read but also fits your image. Review the images conveyed by serif and sans serif typestyles (Chapter 8). Also be sure to use type in the correct point sizes (suggested earlier in this chapter). Type smaller than nine points is generally too small for a practice brochure text. Type larger than twenty-four points for a heading is overpowering.

8. Overuse of spot color: When a strong ink color is used excessively — say, to print *all* the brochure copy — it usually annoys the reader and looks cheap. Use colored ink sparingly, to highlight.

9. Wrong paper: Many practice brochures are printed on paper that's too dark or too flimsy. Use 70- to 80-pound text paper in the same light color as that of your stationery.

STEP 6: PRINT AND DISTRIBUTE YOUR BROCHURE

Most professionals end up revising their brochures after their first printing because of errors, changes, or dissatisfaction with typestyles, text, colors, or artwork. Order the number of brochures you will need for six months of marketing projects. (Estimate the number you'll send to potential and current clients, colleagues, area businesses, and the media.) If your brochure is not a self-mailer, also check your supply of #10 envelopes. Order more if you will need them to mail your brochure over the next six months.

Other practitioners distribute their practice brochures in the following ways:

1.   They mail a copy of the brochure to new clients in advance of the first appointment. The appointment secretary motivates the client to read it by telling him to expect it in the mail. Usually it is mailed with a "Welcome to the practice" letter and appointment card (see sample letter 1 in Appendix B).
    Tip: Sending out welcome packets can be a cumbersome job for a busy appointment secretary; to streamline the system, keep a stack of appointment cards and #10 envelopes on the reception desk. At the time the appointment is made, your secretary can address the envelope to the new client and fill out an appointment card. Later, at her convenience, she can type the welcome letter and place it in the envelope with the appointment card and a practice brochure. Bonus: Studies show that handwritten envelopes get greater attention from the recipient.

2.   They mail a brochure to all clients of record, enclosing a letter explaining that the brochure was printed for their benefit. This mailing sometimes motivates inactive clients to come back to the fold.

3.   They keep a full rack of brochures in their reception areas. A sign on the rack sometimes invites visitors and waiting clients to take extra copies to share with friends.

4.   They send copies of the brochure to area personnel managers and other professionals who may refer clients (see sample letters 32 and 33 in Appendix B).

5.   They use brochures as handouts after speeches, tours, open houses, press conferences, health fairs, classes, career days, and other special events described in Chapters 15 and 16.

6.   They enclose brochures in correspondence with the media seeking publicity for the practice (Chapters 13 and 14).

7.   Some practitioners who advertise use brochures as part of a direct-mail package. Or, they offer them as "free information" viewers and readers of ads can call or write for (usually in conjunction with pamphlets and a client newsletter).

Review your brochure six months after your first printing. Are there any changes you would like to make? Ask clients and staff for feedback and suggestions for improvement. If possible, seek a critique from someone expert in brochure design. Make revisions. Then print enough brochures and #10 envelopes to last you another one or two years.

> **Hint:** Whenever you update your brochure, send the revised edition to all current clients and colleagues again with a letter that points out the changes. It's just one more opportunity to get your name in front of people in a positive way.

C·H·A·P·T·E·R 11

How to Write, Produce, and Distribute a Client Newsletter

A client newsletter has one distinct advantage over most other marketing projects; it reaches *all* potential and current clients *regularly.* A practice newsletter shows clients you care about them year-round, not just when they visit, attend a special event, or receive an occasional letter from you.

Like a good practice brochure, newsletters have many advantages.

- They are highly personal — about you and your practice.
- They promote name recognition and convey your image.
- They reinforce client education programs.
- They provide a forum for your personal philosophy of practice.
- They bring a personal touch to relationships with clients.
- They improve staff morale.
- They invite client participation in your practice.

In light of these advantages, should every practice have a client newsletter? Not necessarily. Unlike other marketing projects, newsletters require substantial investments of time, work, and money *regularly.* The average client newsletter eats up twenty-five man-hours *per issue* and costs more than forty cents a copy (including production and distribution costs). For these reasons, newsletters should *not* be among the first marketing projects you consider. They should come only after you have a strong image, firm policies, and a good staff, as well as an identifying logo, stationery, and practice brochure. These are all higher priority projects.

While all this sounds quite discouraging, newsletters have many advantages that can make them a worthwhile part of some marketing plans. Just be sure that a newsletter is the best marketing project you can undertake with your budget, resources, and time. Do not start a newsletter because you think it would be cute, an ego boost, or the popular thing to do.

THE FOUR QUESTIONS YOU MUST ANSWER FIRST

1. How often should you publish? Once you start, do not stop your newsletter, publish it late, or cut down on the number or size of the issues you produce per year. Readers will expect the next issue and will be disappointed if they don't get it or it is late. Don't overcommit; start your newsletter modestly. You can always upgrade, increase, or expand later.

A good plan is starting with a short, year-end newsletter that contains holiday greetings, a review of the year, and a look ahead. Then if you want to expand, go to a semiannual or quarterly publication schedule. Try going through a quarterly schedule for at least a year before expanding further. More frequent publication is usually not necessary.

2. Who is your audience? No matter how impressive your newsletter is from a journalistic or design point of view, it's a waste of marketing time and money if it doesn't appeal to and reach the right people. There are many possible audiences for a client newsletter.

a.   Current clients, of course. But who among this vast group will your newsletter appeal to most? The *average* client in your practice? If so, who is he? (Your client feedback and file studies should help here.) Will you also try to appeal to specific *segments* of your practice (children, teenagers, career women, housewives, seniors, parents)?

b.   Potential clients. Who are they? Community groups for whom you've held special events? Newcomers? Guests at your open house? Segments of the community targeted through external market research studies?

c.   Referral sources. Pharmacists, realtors, local business people and referring practitioners may all be part of your newsletter audience.

3. What is your purpose or mission? Most publications have a statement of purpose or mission that tells why they exist. Try defining your purpose in a sentence or two to clarify your goals. A sample mission statement might say, "To provide clients with news and information about allergies (taxes, the law, nutrition — whatever subjects are important in your profession). To keep clients informed about changes and events in my practice."

4. What will you call it? Finding a suitable name for your newsletter may be harder than you imagined. Perhaps the tips below will help.

•   Reflect your practice image. *Idea in action:* A dentist with an informal image might call his newsletter *Bridging the Gap;* a more formal dentist might use *Associated Dentists Quarterly Review.*

- Solicit name suggestions from staff and clients. *Idea in action:* Sponsor a *Name the Newsletter* contest. Run the first issue with a large question mark at the top and an article that asks for name suggestions. List prizes for winning and runner-up entries. Put a suggestion box in your reception area.

- Review names of other newsletters. Study the newsletters reproduced in Appendix D. Also check your library's reference section for newsletter directories. All totaled, the *National Directory of Newsletters and Reporting Services* (Gale Research Co.), the *Newsletter Yearbook Directory* (Newsletter Clearinghouse), and the *Working Press of the Nation* (National Research Bureau) list the names of almost 10,000 business and governmental newsletters. These should get your creative juices flowing.

- Study this list of the most commonly used words in newsletter names:

Alert	News
Bulletin	Review
Focus	Report
Guide	Times
Journal	Update

- If you're stuck for name ideas, use your last name or the name of your practice: *The Johnson Letter, The Legal Services Client Bulletin, Jefferson Township Physicians Update.* This is an effective way to build name recognition.

PRELIMINARY DESIGN DECISIONS

1. Size: Most practitioners prefer an $8\frac{1}{2}'' \times 11''$ newsletter because it is the standard size, it is readily available, it is inexpensive, it is easy to read, and it fits into a three-ring binder or file folder for storage.

2. Length: Most newsletters are two pages (front and back of a single $8\frac{1}{2}'' \times 11''$ sheet) or four pages (an $11'' \times 17''$ sheet folded in half, printed on all four panels).

Tip: Don't go longer than four pages. Extra page inserts cost more, usually without great benefit to your practice.

3. Paper: Use paper that matches the color and texture of your stationery and brochure. Most newsletter papers are a sturdy weight such as 50- to 60-pound offset.

Tip: Avoid flimsy papers or print and artwork may show through from one side of the page to the other.

4. Ink: Black ink is easy to read, popular, and cheaper than colored ink.

However, if you used a colored ink in your stationery and brochure, consider using it again as a spot color on your newsletter. Suggestions offered in the last chapter about using spot color also apply to newsletters. (Remember, use colored ink sparingly, only to accent key elements.)

Tip: A fee is charged *each time* you use colored ink. Save money by preprinting: (a) Use your spot color only in your masthead (title); (b) preprint only the colored portion of your masthead on enough newsletter paper for several issues; (c) take only the amount you need for the first issue from your supply of preprints and print the articles in black ink; and (d) save the rest of the preprints for future use. Repeat the process for each issue.

5. Regular features: Will you have features that appear in each issue? If so, decide on them in advance so you can have headings designed. Common features are puzzles, practice news, professional news, joke column, message from the editor, research, recipes, letters to the editor, editorial, book review.

6. Mail: Decide if you will have a self-mailing newsletter (mailed without an envelope). If so, plan to print your return address on the newsletter and leave room to type or write the client's name and address.

DESIGNING YOUR NEWSLETTER WITH A GRAPHIC ARTIST

Make all the preliminary decisions above about your newsletter's frequency, audience, purpose, name, and design. Then choose a graphic artist and arrange a meeting. The artist who designed your logo, stationery, and brochure should be well suited to the job, but if you were dissatisfied, choose another artist according to the guidelines in Appendix A. At your meeting:

1. Review all your basic preliminary decisions: size, paper, ink, name, purpose, frequency, and audience.

2. Discuss your ideas for designing an attractive, attention-grabbing masthead. This is the block of design, usually printed at the top of a newsletter's front page, that consists of the name of the newsletter (and usually the volume and issue numbers), and your name and address.

Tip: Most newsletters have mastheads roughly the size of the top *one-fifth* of the page. Mastheads much larger or smaller seem out of proportion.

3. Review your logo, stationery, and brochure with the artist. Define the image you wish to convey in them and your newsletter.

4. Get fee quotes. Commission the artist to design a masthead that conveys your image.

Tip: For maximum continuity, incorporate your logo in the masthead. Use the same typeface, symbol, and colors.

5. If you've decided to have regular features, ask the artist to design headings for them that coordinate with the masthead.

6. If you've decided to print your mission statement on the newsletter, ask the artist to have it typeset small (six-point type) to be run along the bottom of the front page.

7. If you've decided that your newsletter will be a self-mailer, ask the artist to design your return address on the back page and leave spaces for the client's name and address and a stamp, postage meter mark, or bulk mail permit.

8. Choose a column format. There are three good choices for an $8\frac{1}{2}'' \times 11''$ newsletter; one, two, or three columns per page. Each has advantages and disadvantages:

One Column: Easiest format to type. Projects a formal, businesslike image. Drawbacks: Least visually interesting. Difficult to use artwork. Tip: Create visual interest by framing occasional articles in boxes.

Two Columns: Provides more design flexibility. Greater opportunities to use artwork and photographs. Drawback: A little more difficult to type.

Three Columns: Most interesting visually. Maximum flexibility and the most opportunity for using photos and artwork. Drawback: Very difficult to type. Almost all three-column newsletters are typeset.

> **Hint:** Choose a column format and use it throughout the newsletter in every issue. Consistency makes newsletters look more professional and recognizable.

9. Choose margins. We explored the different images projected by ragged and justified margins in the last chapter. For one- and two-column newsletters, margins may be ragged or justified. Always use justified margins for the three-column format or articles may be hard to read.

10.   Decide about typesetting. Typesetting usually costs more than typing. Its advantages: You can fit more words in the same amount of space and choose from a variety of typestyles and sizes.

> **Hint:** If you have your newsletter typeset, use eight- or ten-point bookface type for the text and 16- or 24-point bold or semibold type for headlines. Use the typestyle used in your logo or one compatible with it. Alternative: Typewritten newsletters generally cost less, can be quite attractive, and sometimes make readers think they contain more personal messages.
>
> *Added Hint:* Use a word processor, not a typewriter. Composing, editing, and laying out pages is much simpler when the typist can edit on a screen. If you don't have a word processor, hire a secretarial service that does. Have the articles word processed and insert larger typeset headlines. Or use presstype to create headlines inexpensively.

EIGHT SECRETS FOR WRITING SUPERB NEWSLETTER ARTICLES

1. Delegate: Some practitioners try to produce their newsletters entirely by themselves. This consumes more time than most of you can afford. What to do:

a.   Proclaim yourself editor-in-chief of your newsletter. That means you contribute some articles and ideas if you wish and that you review, edit, and reject or approve all final copy before it goes to press.

b.   Appoint a managing editor — someone who is creative, efficient, a stickler for details, and a good writer. Choose a managing editor who already knows your practice and newsletter's audience (your marketing coordinator or receptionist?) if you can, but if no one on staff is suitable, hire a free-lance writer. (Instructions for finding a qualified writer are in Appendix A.)
Tip: Pay the writer a set fee for producing each issue of your newsletter. This contains costs and makes it in the writer's interest to be efficient.

c.   Define your managing editor's duties. She can write all the articles in each issue or write some and assign the rest to members of your staff. If this is the case, the managing editor should edit all the articles and understand that *she,* not you, is ultimately responsible for putting each issue together. Typically the managing editor's duties are writing articles and gathering artwork, getting your approval on each issue, establishing a production schedule, typing the newsletter or having it typed or typeset, proofreading, giving the print order and seeing that it is distributed. *Caution:* Be sure your managing editor is competent. You need to have absolute confidence that issues go out as planned without your having to get involved in time-consuming, day-to-day writing, editing, and production tasks. Note: Much of the following information about newsletter content is provided for your managing editor. Share this material with her.

2. Develop sources: The best sources of newsletter material are:

a. Newspaper and magazine articles.

b. Books with inspiring quotations, trivia, amazing facts and statistics, amusing anecdotes.

c. News about your practice: new staff, new equipment, practice milestones, participation in a meeting, involvement in community projects, speeches, open houses, office tours, changes in hours, policies, office decor.

d. Staff news and biographies.

e. News about clients (with their permission): marriages, births, graduations, promotions, awards.

f. Clip-art books (sold in art and book stores). These contain copyright-free, ready-to-use artwork.

g. Transfer tape art. Also called "rub-offs," these are available from most stationery and art supply stores and can be used to add borders and boxes to your newsletter.

h. Original art. Perhaps a staff member or client has artistic talent. You may even hire a cartoonist or graphic artist to draw one of your ideas. *Caution:* Amateurish drawings are the downfall of many newsletters; don't use amateur artwork unless it's good.

i. Photographs. You or a staff member may want to take your own photographs. If so, study suggestions for composing good journalistic photos in Chapter 13. Alternatives: Ask local museums, libraries, corporate public relations offices and newspapers if they can give or sell you photographs, or hire a free-lance photographer.

Tip: To print a photo in a newsletter, you need to convert it into a pattern of dots called a halftone. A printer or commercial photographer should be able to prepare halftones. Suggestion: Always, always print identifying captions beneath all photographs. Photo captions invite your audience to read the accompanying article and help them make more sense of photos.

3. Vary article formats: Some popular ideas:

a.   Question-and-answer column. Solicit clients' questions with a box in your reception area. As an incentive, give a prize to each client whose question is used.

b.   Recipe column — most effective in health-care practices when patients suggest the recipes.

c.   Contests. (See Chapter 16 for good contest ideas.)

d.   Puzzles: crossword, riddles, acrostic, word search. Relate puzzles to your practice and profession.

e.   Book reviews on recommended reading.

f.   "Man on the street" or a "roving reporter." Ask a dozen or more clients to answer one interesting question.

g.   Letters to the editor.

h.   Articles contributed by clients. Put a sign in your reception area to solicit contributions.

i.   Definitions: terms and procedures in your profession.

j.   "A Typical Day in the Life of" each staff member.

4. Vary opening lines of articles: Consider six opening lines or "leads" for the same story about a new aquarium in the reception area of a practice.

a.   Factual: "We are happy to announce that we now have a 30-gallon salt water tropical aquarium in our reception area."

b.   Direct Quotation: " 'It's like a world unto itself.' So says Dr. Wilson of the new salt water tropical aquarium in our reception area."

c.   Famous quotation: " 'Fish gotta swim and birds gotta fly.' At least half of that is now true at Family Chiropractic."

d.   Question: "What's the new wet and bubbly attraction at Family Chiropractic Center? No, it's not champagne but a 30-gallon salt water tropical aquarium in our reception area."

e.   Humorous play on words: "Something's fishy at Family Chiropractic Center" or "Dr. Wilson has a new fish story to tell."

f. Exclamation: "Fish! That's the latest word at Family Chiropractic Center these days."

5. Use attention-grabbing words in headlines: Five of the best:

a. *Now:* "Springfield Podiatry Now Accepts Credit Cards."

b. *At Last:* "At Last: Route 18 Construction Complete."

c. *Announcing:* "Announcing Reduced Fees for Students."

d. *Recent:* "Recent Study Links Diet to Stress."

e. *New:* "New Office Art Exhibit Draws Mixed Reviews."

6. Use action verbs in headlines: For example:

Dull Headlines	Action Headlines
New Staff	Mary Johnson Joins Associated Psychology Staff
Bar Association Meeting	Harold Baker Attends Bar Association Meeting
Change in Hours	Dr. Richard Expands Hours to Friday Evenings
Baby Teeth	It Pays to Save Baby Teeth
Blood Pressure Month Open House	Dr. Woods to Host Open House during Blood Pressure Month

7. Keep articles short: Newsletters are brief publications that should be easily digested in one sitting.

8. Avoid unnecessary words and jargon: Check the final draft of each issue against Appendix C, which is a list of the words and phrases to use and avoid in marketing communications.

DON'T MAKE THESE MISTAKES IN YOUR NEWSLETTER

1. Copyright infringement: A copyright is a monopoly the government grants to people who create literary products. To determine if material you wish to use in your newsletter is copyrighted, look for the symbol © followed by the date and the copyright owner's name. For instance, all comic strips, political cartoons, books, and newspaper and magazine articles are usually copyrighted. To get permission to reproduce copyrighted material in your newsletter

a.   Make a written request to the publisher.

b.   Explain how and why you wish to use the material.

c.   Offer to provide a credit line.

d.   Enclose a copy of your newsletter.

e.   Estimate the number of copies you intend to publish and who will receive your newsletter.

f.   The fair use provision of copyright law may allow you to forego obtaining written permission in some cases. There is no hard-and-fast rule about when it is acceptable to do this and how long excerpts can be. However, one or two excerpts no longer than 100 words and attributed to the source are usually not a problem.

Tip: Most practitioners will *not* want to copyright their own client newsletters, as wide distribution of the contents is in your best interest. However, if you would like to copyright your newsletter, place the copyright symbol, year and your name on each issue. Contact the copyright office of the Library of Congress, Washington, D.C., for more information.

2. Plan for a rainy day: There are, unfortunately, circumstances that can prevent you from publishing your newsletter on time. To plan for the unexpected, have your managing editor write, edit, and type or typeset one spare issue of your client newsletter. Make this issue general enough so it can be used at any time, any season. Then file it away for an emergency. Tell your staff about this spare issue so they can publish it in case you're incapacitated.

3. Ordering too few: It usually costs less to order a few extra hundred newsletters at the time of your initial printing than to run short and do a second printing later. Order all the newsletters you need for one mailing and at least an additional 20–25 percent. These will come in handy for new clients, exchange with other practitioners, and unexpected marketing opportunities.

Tip: If you do run short and need only another 50 or 100 copies, check with a photocopy shop for the second run. It may cost less than going to a commercial printer for such a small quantity.

4. Taking on too much: If starting a newsletter from scratch seems like too much for you to take on right now, you might consider using a professionally prepared newsletter instead. While no newsletter produced outside your office can be as personal as one you do yourself, some offered by outside companies are quite good and may be customized with the name and address of your practice and a personal message in each issue. Some companies also sell just the articles for client newsletters to be mixed in with those you write yourself.

TIPS FOR DISTRIBUTING YOUR NEWSLETTER

1.   Many practices include newsletters with statements or other mailings. As long as the total mailing piece, including the envelope, stays under one ounce and is standard size, it can be mailed first class for no extra postage.

2.   Check with your post office about less costly ways to mail newsletters, such as presorting, bulk rate and third class.

3.   A computerized mailing list is easy to maintain. Consider hiring a secretarial service that specializes in mailing lists if you do not have an office computer.

4.   If you are compiling mailing lists manually, use sheets of peel-off labels photocopied from a master label list. An office supply or stationery store will carry them.

5.   It's quite a job to stuff, seal, and post large mailings. If you need outside help, consider hiring a lettershop (Appendix A).

6.   Make readers perceive value in your newsletter.

a.   Include a statement such as the following along the bottom of your newsletter's first page: "*Family Practice Newsletter* is a quarterly publication provided without charge for the patients of Dr. David Williams."

b.   When you send your newsletter to nonclients, always include this note with the first issue: "I am delighted to provide a complimentary one-year subscription to my client newsletter, *Family Practice Newsletter.*" (See sample letter 14, Appendix B.)

c.   If you display your newsletter in public places such as health-food stores, pharmacies, clinics and other practitioners' offices, also put out reply cards that say: "Yes, please send me a complimentary one-year subscription to your client newsletter, *Family Practice Newsletter.*"

d.   Also send stacks of reply cards to personnel officers and others in your community to whom you send complimentary subscriptions. They might recommend your newsletter (and your practice) to others and share the cards.

e.   Give reply cards to clients to give to their friends.

f.   After a year, if a nonclient reader is still not a client, call or write to see if he wants to continue his subscription or send this note: "I see that your one-year complimentary subscription to my client newsletter *Family Practice Newsletter* is up. I've asked my secretary to extend it for you another year. I hope you are finding it informative."

External Marketing Projects: Making Current Clients and the Public Aware of Your Exceptional Practice

C·H·A·P·T·E·R   12

How External Marketing Builds a Practice

Most of the external marketing projects in the next five chapters will either *publicize* or *promote* your practice:

Publicity occurs when you supply true, interesting and newsworthy information to media not controlled by you and the media use it. For example, publicity occurs when the newspaper publishes your press release or a radio station airs your public service announcement. While publicity does not require a fee, it also does not allow you to control when and how your message will be used.

Promotion, on the other hand, does allow you to control your message. Examples of promotional activities are speeches, posters, external uses of your brochure and newsletter, special events, direct mail, and all forms of advertising.

Many experts believe that publicity has more force than some promotional activities. A publicity message comes from a third party (a newspaper or radio or television station) and is presumed to be more believable. (For example, many people feel that an article about you is more believable than an ad. Anyone can buy an ad.) Don't, however, be afraid of promotional activities. Many practitioners have found that promotional activities such as speeches, open houses, tours, and other special events can be as effective as publicity.

HOW TO BE SUCCESSFUL WITH PUBLICITY AND PROMOTION PROJECTS

To be successful with the publicity and promotion projects described in the next several chapters, you usually have to sell your ideas to someone who has the decision-making authority for an outside group. You must persuade that person to use your speech, public service announcement, or press release. That person has no reason to do so except that it benefits him or his organization.

The person with decision-making authority will differ from group to group. He or she might be an editor, club officer, teacher, or program director. Therefore, try the following when wooing that person:

1. Choose the right media and organizations:

a.   Set specific goals. It is not a satisfactory goal to say you want "exposure" for your practice or to become "well known" in your community. Those are vague goals that will be difficult to measure. Better goals:

— Attract 25 new clients to the practice.

— Attract 150 people to a special event.

— Get information to the public on a specific issue.

— Teach people how to use your profession's services.

— Persuade people to alter their thinking or behavior.

b.   Choose media that are likely to give you coverage. Many publicists make the mistake of assuming that the largest coverage is the best coverage. However, the broader a medium's or organization's audience, the harder it usually is to get coverage. Don't overlook the smaller sources of publicity: weekly and biweekly newspapers and shopper papers, church bulletins, high school football programs, college radio stations, public bulletin boards, newsletters of special interest groups, small clubs, and service organizations. These smaller sources may be more willing to use the information you supply them. They frequently run into difficulty finding enough good material within their limited budgets and staffing.

c.   Choose media to suit your needs. Let's look at some examples of how the right medium can work for you, even if it is a small one. Imagine that five practitioners each have the goal of attracting twenty-five new clients. Each is looking for a different type of new client and chooses a specialized medium or small group that will supply the right audience for his message:

Practitioner 1:   a lawyer looking for new parents. A lawyer thinks new parents would be good clients because they often need wills, trust funds, and representation on real estate transactions. His area health center has an exercise class for expectant mothers and a newsletter for participants. He writes a letter to the editor of the newsletter explaining how a will is a must for new parents and the components of a good will.

Practitioner 2:   an optometrist looking for sports participants. An optometrist thinks people active in sports would be good clients because they need protective eyewear and might be interested in contact lenses. He gets permission to leave brochures on protective eyewear (imprinted with his logo, name, and address) in the lobby of a racquetball and tennis club in his community.

Practitioner 3: an orthodontist looking for children. An orthodontist in a city thinks children in the suburbs would be good clients because they are underserved. He invites scout troups from suburban communities to tour his office and provides the children with literature to share with their parents.

Practitioner 4: an accountant looking for successful business people. An accountant who specializes in investments thinks successful business people in his community would be good clients because they would be likely to have money to invest. He offers to speak to the local Rotary club on an interesting aspect of investments.

Practitioner 5: a podiatrist looking for working adults. A podiatrist thinks that employees of a large department store in his community would be good clients because his practice is located across the street and he could provide his services before and after work and during the lunch hour. He writes a press release to the editor of the store's staff newsletter, offering tips to people who stand on their feet all day.

2. Talk to the right person: Know who makes the decision and has final authority for the medium or group. Don't waste your time trying to persuade the secretary of the local PTA that you've got a great speech if the program chairman is the person who schedules programs and makes the final decision about speakers.

3. Know the group: Do your homework about the group you're trying to sell. What kinds of programs or articles do they usually run? The decision maker of the group won't be interested in you if you don't know what the group is about or what it does.

4. Create a win/win situation: Let the decision maker feel he has come out ahead by using your message. No one will want you to give a speech or write an article about you unless there is something in it for his organization. Develop excellent publicity and promotional materials — things so good that the publication or group will feel it benefited from letting you present them.

EIGHT WAYS TO PREPARE YOUR PRACTICE FOR PUBLICITY AND PROMOTION

1. Account for everything in your budget: You may believe at first glance that the publicity or promotional activities you've planned won't cost you anything or perhaps will require only a small budget. Be sure you're right.

Each of the projects in the next several chapters has expenses tied to it, even projects that seem to be "freebies," such as press releases, public service announcements, and speeches. Your budget should account for all expenses including costs for:

a.   Photocopying and printing.

b.   Postage.

c.   Typewriter and word processor rental, repair or purchase.

d.   The services of a photographer, free-lance writer, graphic artist, secretarial service, or typesetter.

e.   Film and developing costs.

f.   Photography equipment and repair.

g.   Telephone expenses.

h.   Office supplies.

i.   Staff time.

j.   Advice (consultants, attorneys).

k.   Fulfillment (for example, how much it costs to send a brochure or other free material you promise in a public service announcement or speech).

2. Cover yourself:

a.   Establish records to protect yourself. Keep copies of everything you write and your sources for quoted information. That way you'll be able to answer questions that arise about your sources or the accuracy of your information.

b.   Prepare "Plan B" in case of an emergency. Consider in advance every possible mishap or opposition you can think of and how you will handle it. Play the "what if" game: "What if it rains the day of our outdoor reception for clients?" "What if I get sick the day the sixth graders are scheduled to tour our office?" "What if the projector bulb blows out during my slide show?" This isn't negative thinking; it's smart thinking for anyone involved in publicity and promotion. Also consider what you'll do if your response is bigger and better than you anticipated: "What if 400 people come to our open house?" or "What if 75 people call the morning after my letter to the editor runs in the paper?" Could you handle an overwhelmingly *positive* response? Do you have adequate telephone lines? Manpower?

c. Answer legal questions. In some areas, anyone who prepares materials that attempt to influence legislation must register as a lobbyist. Find out about registration requirements if you plan to do anything of this sort. Also get legal advice if you plan to write or say anything that speaks out against someone or something. Know in advance if your remarks could leave you open to accusations of slander or libel. You may also wish to seek legal advice if you plan to use quotations or illustrations from copyrighted material.

3. Define authority: You may delegate the tasks of preparing publicity and promotional materials to a member of your staff or a free-lancer. However, the final authority for any external marketing project that comes from your practice should remain with one person — you. Institute this policy: Any publicity or promotional material or activity from your practice must be reviewed and initialed by you before it is mailed or scheduled. That means that every press release, public service announcement, speaking engagement, open house — every external marketing activity of your practice must get your approval before it goes public.

It's not hard to see why this policy is essential. All of your publicity or promotional activities reflect on you and your practice. You cannot allow a staff member or anyone else to represent your practice without your approval. Mistakes can harm your image seriously and permanently. Retaining final authority is your only way to ensure that your publicity and promotional activities do what you want them to do.

4. Communicate with your staff: Successful external marketing activities will usually evoke questions, comments, or requests for more information from the media and public. It is essential that everyone in your practice is aware of your publicity and promotional activities and that they share the same understanding and enthusiasm for them. Imagine how embarrassing it would be if you wrote a letter to the editor and telephone inquirers were told by your receptionist that you did not write any such letter and they must have you confused with someone else. Or think of the damage a staff member could do if he told clients he thought your upcoming open house was a "dumb idea." Meet regularly with your staff so everyone knows what's going on and is convinced that your efforts are worthwhile. Regular meetings will also help you track progress and pinpoint problems while there is still time to do something about them.

5. Assign a media contact person for your practice: When you seek publicity, one person on your staff should serve as the spokesperson for your practice. That person should be articulate, organized, intelligent, and available to answer questions. You cannot be the spokesperson for your practice because you will be too busy with clients to drop everything for phone calls from inquiring journalists. Your marketing coordinator is the ideal person.

6. Learn about upcoming events to which you can tie publicity and promotional activities: Many activities will have more appeal if you plan them in honor of or in conjunction with a special event such as Good Nutrition Month, Child Health Day, Emergency Care Month, National Nursing Home Week or Law Day. To learn about upcoming events such as these as well as their purposes and sponsors, consult *Chase's Calendar of Annual Events* which is in the reference section of most public libraries (and listed in the Bibliography).

7. Start small: As you plan, start with one small project and work it all the way through from planning to follow-up. Get the experience you need before you launch into major publicity and promotional campaigns.

8. Create a publicity and promotion file for future reference: It should include

a.   All the publicity materials you generate.

b.   A list of sources you use to prepare press releases, speeches, public service announcements, and other materials.

c.   Media requirements — deadlines, format and length preferences.

d.   A list of all the publications and editors that may be, or have been, interested in your practice. Include their phone numbers and preferences.

BE REALISTIC ABOUT WHAT ONE EXTERNAL MARKETING PROJECT CAN DO

You may get your picture on the front page of your newspaper and be elected Citizen of the Year in your town. But that doesn't guarantee that you'll build your practice. There are people who won't look at the paper that night or hear (or care) about your award. And of the people who do receive your message, only some will register it. The others will have their minds busy sorting through a dozen other messages that competed for and won their attention.

Does that mean that you can't succeed with external marketing? Absolutely not! You can get your message heard over the clamor of all the other information as long as it is clear, timely, worthwhile, well placed, and *repeated*. You've probably noticed how many times you will see or hear the same television or radio ad, over and over and over again, until you're absolutely sick of it.

There's a reason for that. People must be exposed to a message repeatedly before they register it.

A realistic external marketer must take this into account. Some people may need to hear only one message from you and they will register and act upon it. Others may need to read about you in the paper two or three times, hear about your open house, and attend a speech you give before they remember who you are, let alone think about you and what you have to offer.

Successful publicity — and promotion — is a process, so don't expect too much from any single project. It may take you a long time before you see the full rewards from your work, but if you choose the right projects and do them frequently and well, you will achieve your marketing goals. Now let's see what kinds of external marketing projects can set your publicity and promotion campaign into motion. Read on to see how you can attract potential clients outside your practice by using publicity and promotion.

C · H · A · P · T · E · R 13

How to Get Publicity for Your Practice with Press Releases

Press releases will be the cornerstone of every practitioner's publicity program. They are the primary means of communicating newsworthy information about a practice to the media and your best tool for getting publicity.

Writing a one- or two-page press release may seem like a simple assignment, yet a press release is a sophisticated, complex writing form that requires you to be both salesperson and storyteller. Your releases must compete — for scarce publication space or broadcast time — with formidable opponents: the wire services, journalists, and other organizations that issue releases at the same time. A large newspaper may receive hundreds of releases each day and have space to publish only a handful.

The press releases that get published are those that best fill the media's needs, wants, and expectations. However, think again if you've decided to call an editor you don't know to ask her what she is looking for or whether she would prefer this press release or that. Some editors will share ideas freely. Others will be annoyed, assuming it's your job to decide how to approach them. Like you, they are busy people with little time to spare.

> **Hint:** Send a few releases to an editor before contacting her for her preferences. She may be more willing to talk once she knows you and the kinds of information you have to offer. Study this chapter's general rules for press releases and sample press releases 41 and 42 in Appendix B. Use these as a guide until you know the editor better. Modify your format or style later if your editor suggests a different approach.

STEP 1: LOOK FOR THE NEWS IN YOUR PRACTICE

You will rarely write a press release about hot news that requires immediate media coverage. Most of your releases will be about less immediate news

—feature or human interest stories. However, any release you write, hard news or feature, must have news content for an editor to take interest in it; it must convey information worth knowing in an objective style and from an interesting angle or *peg:*

1. What's information worth knowing? Pretend you're someone else. If you had no connection with your practice, what would be worth knowing about it? What story about a professional practice would catch your attention in the newspaper or on the radio?

Idea in action: A story about a dentist who uses nitrous oxide to minimize patients' discomfort won't interest most people. The procedure is too widely used. However, a dentist who uses *acupuncture* or *hypnosis* may get more attention.

2. What's an objective style? Objective releases present documented, well-organized facts from the point of view of an unbiased third-person observer. They offer no opinions unless contained in direct quotes.

Idea in action: Here's an example of a *biased* press release:

> This year's Community Health Fair will be held September 22–24 at the convenient Springfield Park Mall. It's sure to be the best fair ever. The special attraction will be an interesting exhibit about the role of computers in health-care research. There will also be many other interesting and informative booths manned by Springfield's finest health-care professionals.
>
> Dr. John Smith is the organizer of this year's fair. He and his capable staff are working day and night to make sure the fair is a huge success. If you'd like to join in on this year's fun, come to the fair this weekend and bring the whole family.

This release lacked vital information—the fair's hours and descriptions of the booths. Opinions such as "the best fair ever" and "Springfield's finest health-care professionals" might persuade an editor not to use the release at all. Now take a look at the same release, rewritten. This version is objective, has news value and is more likely to be published:

> This weekend you'll have the opportunity to go to a single place to find out about diet and nutrition, diabetes, contact lenses, aerobic exercise, cancer research, computers, and heart disease. Just attend the Community Health Fair at Springfield Park Mall September 22–24. Thirty-seven health-care professionals from the greater Springfield area will staff booths and present information.

The organizer of this year's fair is Dr. John Smith, who practices internal medicine at 100 Springfield Boulevard. Dr. Smith told the press he expects this year's fair to be the best ever. "We've added some new and interesting exhibits since we began the fair nine years ago," he said. "We are especially excited this year about our newest exhibit about the increasingly important role computers play in health-care research" (description of exhibit).

The fair will be open from 9 A.M. until 9:30 P.M. each day and admission is free. "I hope parents will bring their children along," Dr. Smith added. "I'm sure the fair will be an enjoyable learning experience for everyone who participates."

3. What's a peg? A peg is a unique angle from which you tell your story. Take a look at the story ideas in the left column, below. These are dull story ideas, the "dogs," as journalists say. Then look at the pegs in the right column. See how they transform the dogs into winners with news value.

The "Dog" Stories	The Pegs That Save Them
1. An accounting practice takes on a new partner.	1. Accounting practice's new tax specialist tells how to build a tax shelter with real estate.
2. An optometrist celebrates Save Your Vision Week.	2. Optometrist holds class about contact lenses that "breathe" during Save Your Vision Week.
3. A dermatologist gets an article published in a professional journal.	3. Dermatologist publishes results of research to find a cure for acne.
4. A periodontist marks 25 years in practice.	4. Periodontist marks 25th year by distributing bumper stickers saying, "I'd rather be having a root canal."
5. A gynecologist attends a medical convention.	5. Gynecologist learns new ways at convention to avoid toxic shock syndrome.

4. What kinds of events have news value?

a.   Contests you sponsor may merit three releases—one to announce the rules and deadlines, one to remind about the deadline as it draws near, and one to announce the winners.

b.   Office exhibits make good news stories. If the exhibit is unique or of community interest, such as a show of original paintings by local artists, the occasion may lend itself to a formal opening ceremony or celebration — good news pegs. (Tips for creating exhibits are in Chapter 16.)

c. *Anniversaries* are especially newsworthy when they mark a milestone such as your tenth or twenty-fifth year in practice, a staff member's employment anniversary, the office building's birthday, welcoming your thousandth new client to your practice, or unusual record setters (perfect attendance, oldest client). To add extra news value; mark the milestone with a luncheon or banquet. Perform a ceremonial act — award a trophy, unveil a plaque.

d. A *local angle* on a national or regional news development makes press releases relevant and timely. *Successful application:* A dentist localized the problem of widespread unemployment. For one day, he treated as many unemployed people in his community as he could for a token fee of one-dollar per visit. The local media gave him fantastic coverage — a one-dollar dental appointment is news.

e. *New office facilities* — construction, expansion, renovation, moving to new quarters — all contain news value. The usual pegs are ceremonies for ground breaking, cornerstone laying, and ribbon cutting. Look for a unique peg; is there something unusual about the building's history, design or technology? Will it take five trucks to move your equipment and furniture?

f. *Civic activities* and charitable events.

g. *New equipment.*

h. *Appointment to a committee* or special projects.

i. *Honors and awards.*

j. *Educational activities:* meetings, conventions.

k. *Unusual office hours,* policies, decor.

l. *Client education events:* open houses, tours, lectures.

m. *New staff.*

n. *Research.* Successful application: An internist read in a medical journal that people who mix bleach and ammonia in cleaning buckets could be overcome by deadly chlorine gas liberated by the reaction. He submitted this information to the editor of the town's weekly newspaper. The result was that the paper printed that article, encouraged another, and eventually asked him to write a regular column, "Doctor in the House," that now appears in that paper and several others.

Bottom line: This doctor averages three or four new patients *per month* who read the column and decide they want him to be their doctor.

STEP 2: WRITE AN ATTENTION-GRABBING LEAD

If an editor isn't intrigued and excited by your press release in the first sentence you can usually forget about seeing it published or broadcast. Picture the editor at his desk. He opens the 315th release of the day and there are still a hundred more in his "in" basket. Here's the kind of first sentence (lead) he'll usually get:

Clinical psychologist Samuel Jones, who practices at 123 Springfield Avenue, announced today that Dr. Deborah Smith of Madison has joined him as a partner in practice.

The editor's mind flashes: "Big deal. Who is Samuel Jones? Who cares if he expanded his practice?" Into the trash it goes. Now suppose the lead read:

Starting today, Springfield has its first clinical psychologist who works only with troubled teenagers and their families. Dr. Deborah Smith announced today that she has joined the clinical psychology practice of Dr. Samuel Jones of 123 Springfield Avenue.

Now the first sentences tell the editor that something has happened, and it may be important to his readers. He'll probably read a little more to find out how this new psychologist will change things in Springfield. Change is news.

An old journalistic myth is that the lead paragraph of a news release should contain the standard "who, what, why, where, when, and how." This style of writing is outdated and often a great bore. A good press release by today's standards will certainly include all this information, but it won't always do so right off the bat. How to write good leads:

1. Write a first sentence that sparks interest and "hooks" the editor.
2. Write the most essential details near the top of the story, in the first few paragraphs.
3. Put less important material at the bottom.

Journalists call this style of writing news stories an "inverted pyramid." The heaviest part of the article (the pyramid's base) is at top and the lighter, less essential detail (the pyramid's point) is at the bottom. Editors prefer the inverted pyramid because it is easier to shorten articles at the end for space limitations.

STEP 3: PREPARE RELEASES THE WAY EDITORS WANT THEM

We're now going to cover the nuts and bolts of preparing press releases. If some of these rules seem arbitrary to you, don't look for something flashier or better. Follow them to the letter; editors expect you to do it this way.

1. Paper and type: Type your release on $8\frac{1}{2}'' \times 11''$, good quality, white, nonerasable paper. Double- or triple-space and type your copy on only one side of the paper. Indent paragraphs ten spaces, not the standard five. Leave wide margins all around, at least an inch and a quarter, so editors have plenty of room to make changes and corrections. Do not hyphenate words at the end of lines.

2. Heading: Do not use your letterhead for a press release. Use blank typing paper and single space this heading in the upper left portion of the page:

    FROM: Your name (or the name of your practice)
               Street Address
               City, State, ZIP Code

    CONTACT: Name and title of marketing coordinator (assistant)
               Telephone number

RELEASE DATE:

    ATTENTION:

        SLUG:

DISTRIBUTION:

3. Release date: Ask the publication or station how far in advance it needs to receive your release. The amount of time will vary, but all editors want some lead time (usually two days minimum) to do needed checking or investigative work. When submitting news not tied to any specific date, type FOR IMMEDIATE RELEASE in the release date slot of your heading. Use specific dates in the text to avoid confusion or the editor may assume incorrectly that he can publish your article months after receiving it. If the release is extremely timely, specify the date and time for publication: RELEASE DATE: TUESDAY, NOVEMBER 15, 3:00 P.M.

4. Attention line: If you are sending your release to a particular editor or department, type and underline an attention line in capitals directly below your release date. Example: <u>ATTENTION: LOCAL NEWS PAGE EDITOR</u> or <u>ATTENTION: DONALD LAMPMAN</u>.

5. Headline: Do not include a headline with your release. Copy editors usually write headlines, so yours will be discarded.

6. Slug line: In lieu of a headline, include a slug line in the heading that will help the editor identify your story. Example: SLUG: Adolescent Psychologist to Practice in Springfield.

7. Distribution line: It is usually not necessary to tell the editor who else will receive your release. However, if you send your story to only one editor, it might improve your chances of being published to tell him so in the heading. Example: DISTRIBUTION: Exclusive to the *Springfield Journal*.

8. Length: Try to limit releases to one page. If you can't, type the word *more* in parentheses at the bottom of each page, except the last. Do not split a word, sentence or paragraph between two pages, even if you must leave extra white space at the bottom of a page.

9. Adds: Leave five lines at the top of the second page and type *first add* and your slug line in the upper left-hand corner. Example: *First add— Adolescent Psychologist to Practice in Springfield*. Skip another four or five lines and continue your story. Use *second add* and *third add* on subsequent pages.

10. End: Indicate the last page with a final *add* line. Example: *Second and final add*. Skip two lines after the last sentence of your story's last paragraph and type the symbol *-30-* in the center of the page. This traditional mark was a telegrapher's signal in former days and is used in releases to tell the editor that your story is complete. If you prefer, use a more modern end-of-story symbol: three number signs (###), three x's (xxx), or three asterisks (***).

11. Other format rules for press releases:

a.   Use paper clips, not staples, to fasten pages.

b.   Use upper and lower case letters to type the story, not all capitals.

c.   Use a clean typewriter and dark black ribbon.

d.   Use a standard typewriter typeface—no script.

e.   Proofread releases for accuracy—correct spelling, dates, and figures.

f.   Send an individually typed release or a good quality photocopy—not a carbon copy.

STEP 4: MODIFY RELEASES FOR
BROADCAST JOURNALISTS

Everything covered so far about press release format and style will apply equally to all releases, whether for print or broadcast media. However, broadcasters appreciate your following these ten steps:

1.   Radio and television programs thrive on brief stories. Limit broadcast releases to absolute minimum length. Many broadcast editors especially like interesting releases of twelve to fifteen lines.

2.   Use the present tense whenever possible for broadcast releases.

3.   Use round figures unless there is a need to be more specific. Example: Write "nearly two-thirds" instead of "sixty-one out of a hundred."

4.   Give phonetic spellings of difficult-to-pronounce names and words. Example: "Dr. Felix Fattahi (feh-TAW-hee)."

5.   Read your release aloud before you mail it. Does it flow easily? How long does it take to read? Some editors prefer stories that are only sixty, thirty, or even twenty seconds long.

6.   Avoid words with hissing sounds whenever possible. They don't come through a microphone well. Examples to avoid are exacerbate, sustain, systematic.

7.   Use picture words to vivify your story. Example: Instead of "Dr. Walter will provide a tour for the children," write, "Dr. Walter will show the children how the dancing dot of light on the EKG monitor can save a patient's life. . . ."

8.   Use punctuation wherever a broadcaster will need to pause for breath. Use dots, dashes, commas, and underlinings for emphasis liberally for scripts intended for the ear, but sparingly for newspaper copy; they slow reading speed.

9.   Use transitional phrases whenever possible to link ideas. Example: "*and that is how* one community today is honoring Dr. Ralph Barton."

10.   Use contractions as you would in speaking.

STEP 5: SUBMIT INTERESTING PHOTOS
TO PUBLICATION EDITORS

A good photograph will often sell a marginal story to a publication editor. When including one with a release, indicate it at the bottom of the last page.

Two lines below your end-of-story symbol and to the left-hand margin, type: *Accompanying material:* and list the photos you are sending.

1. What editors want:

a.   Use of a professional camera — not a self-developing or instant camera. They want only the sharpest photographs.

b.   Photos with strong contrast between light and dark. They reproduce best.

c.   Vertical shots. They can be reduced to fit into one newspaper column.

d.   Photos with a white border all around, large enough for an editor's cropping lines.

e.   Clean photos. Always handle your photographs by the edges so you don't ruin them with fingerprints.

f.   An 8″ × 10″ black and white glossy print. Some papers will accept 5″ × 7″ or 4″ × 5″ prints for simple shots. Check first to see if this is permissible. Color prints are also accepted by some papers, although they generally do not reproduce as well as those in black and white.

2. How to compose the best journalistic photos:

a.   *Action.* The best news photographs usually portray action. If you're submitting a press release about a contest, don't send a static photo of an entry form, the prizes, or you. Photograph the contest judge plowing through a huge pile of entries or a hopeful contestant putting an entry in the box.

b.   *Close-ups.* Close-up photos are usually best, especially for portraits or small objects. If you must use a head shot, check with editors to see if they prefer a light or dark background or if they have other requirements. Typical requirements are: no hands near the face, both shoulders in the shot.

c.   *Few subjects.* Limit the number of subjects — no more than two or three people per photo.

d.   *Relaxed subjects.* Get subjects to loosen up. If they are extremely stiff because of the camera, tell a joke or story to make them relax and look more natural.

e.   *Slenderizing angles.* Arrange subjects at an angle to make them seem more at ease and more slender. Do not ask subjects to face both body and head directly toward the camera. This makes unflattering photos that look like "mug" shots or passport photos. Have subjects keep their heads high to avoid shadows and double chins.

f.   One focal point. Choose only one point of interest in each photograph. Avoid shots with several elements that compete for attention.

g.   Interesting angles. Try photographing subjects from a few different, interesting angles. Crouch down or stand on a step stool. Consider how a shot would look from the floor or a balcony.

h.   No distraction. Avoid clutter, harsh lighting, or other distractions in backgrounds. If you must shoot against a busy background, blur it by using your depth-of-field adjustment. Avoid shots of subjects standing in front of a window.

3. Once you've taken a photo:

a.   Permission. Many publicists recommend getting your subjects' written permission to use a photograph of them. Buy standard release forms at a camera store. These say that the person in the photo gives his permission to use that shot for any and all purposes.

b.   Captions. Photos and other illustrations with press releases should always carry identifying captions. To prepare captions: (1) Repeat your slug line and identify your subjects in a sentence or two, from left to right, including each person's complete name, town of residence, and position. Example: "From left: Anita Gilbert of Springfield, patient; Sarah Williams of Madison, office manager; Dr. John Kilmer of Madison, internist." (2) Do not type or write the caption on back of the photo or attach it with a paper clip. The pressure of a pen, clip, or typewriter keys can indent the photograph's surface and ruin it for reproduction. (3) Type your caption on a separate strip of paper. (4) Use rubber cement or tape to attach it gently to the back of the photograph at the bottom. (5) Fold the caption over the face of the photo. When the editor unfolds it, the caption should be beneath the picture it is describing.

c.   Mailing tips. Prepare your photo for mailing. How: 1. Mail your photographs along with your release in a large padded envelope protected on either side by sturdy cardboard stiffeners. 2. Use only first-class mail. Don't skimp on cardboard or postage. Even a small crack or fold in a photograph can ruin it for reproduction (and frustrate editors). 3. Do not expect or ask editors to return your photographs. Such requests annoy some editors. 4. Don't be surprised if some publications charge a small "engraving" fee when they use one of your publicity photos. While not common practice, it is done occasionally by some small weekly papers on a shoestring budget.

STEP 6: BE COURTEOUS TO EDITORS—ALWAYS

1.   Don't argue when an editor rejects one of your stories. You might see if he would be willing to consider another approach or peg, but if the answer is

still *no*, accept it graciously. You can ask if he would recommend sending your release to another editor in a different department. Caution: Don't try to circumvent the editor or go over his head; that's a sure way to alienate him.

2.   Honor deadline constraints.

3.   Don't conceal vital information from an editor or exaggerate your story. Check releases for accuracy and truth.

4.   Inform the editor of changes in your story. Keep a list of every editor to whom you send a release. Call each one about a change in the time, date, or location of an upcoming event. If you fail to do this, even once, many editors will refuse to work with you again.

5.   Except for changes, stay out of the editor's hair around deadline time. He'll have enough to worry about without interruptions from you to check on your story.

6.   Be sure the person listed as the media contact person in your release heading is available and prepared to answer questions. Editors will be frustrated if they need more information for a story and your contact person can't answer basic questions or is lazy about getting back to them.

7.   Don't talk to journalists "off the record." It puts them and you in an uncomfortable position.

8. Credit sources of facts or figures you quote in a release.

9.   Write in the active voice. For example, write: "Dr. Stephen Weinstein announced" instead of "It was announced by Dr. Stephen Weinstein."

10.   Keep sentences and paragraphs short. Editors love one-page releases that tell the whole story clearly and simply.

11.   Avoid long fancy words when short ones will do as well. Check your final draft against Appendix C, a list of words and phrases to use and avoid in marketing communications.

12.   Let releases incubate before you mail them. You'll edit much better once you've had some distance from your writing.

13.   Proofread releases for spelling errors. You can make one or two clear handwritten corrections per page without upsetting most editors.

14.   Don't try to butter up editors with gifts. Many will be offended by such gestures.

15.   If you buy advertising from the newspaper or station, do not men-

tion this to the editor to whom you send press releases. Advertising dollars will not usually influence an editor's decision to use a story, at least not favorably.

16.   Be familiar with the publication or station and the kinds of stories it runs. Take a tour of the facilities (or send a staff member). Ask the editors for a style sheet or handbook that explains what they want from publicists. Know the various sections of the publication or program — editorial, feature, local news — so you'll have a sense of which editors would be most interested in your releases.

17.   Define the technical terms you use in your releases. Also explain acronyms and abbreviations the first time you use them. Example: "The American Bar Association, hereafter referred to as the ABA. . . ."

STEP 7: BE CAREFUL AFTER YOUR RELEASE IS PUBLISHED OR AIRED

1.   Watch how you thank editors for running or airing your press release. Don't suggest that they have done you a great favor. Say the story was well written or particularly insightful. Describe some of the positive comments you've received about the story.

2.   You will undoubtedly want many copies of any articles a publication runs about you for your office bulletin board and special clients. Do not ask the editors to supply you with these clippings. They may consider it insulting. Get clippings on your own. Exception: If the publication is a magazine, see if you can *buy* article reprints.

3.   If the editor omits something or makes a mistake when publishing or airing your story, discuss the matter calmly. See if you and he can develop a second story to rectify the problem. This will benefit you a lot more than a retraction. If the editor won't correct the error, assess the damage. If it is not serious, it usually pays to let the matter drop for the sake of future releases. However, if the editor's error hurts your reputation, you may have no choice but to go over his head and pursue the matter with higher management. Unfortunately, once you do, that is likely to be the last release the medium ever publishes about you.

C·H·A·P·T·E·R   14

Ten More Projects That Get Publicity for a Practice

W hile press releases will be your primary tool for getting media coverage for your practice, they are not your only avenue for publicity. Here are ten less widely used publicity techniques that can be worthwhile marketing projects:

SUGGEST FEATURE STORIES TO MEDIA EDITORS

A press release is one approach to selling an idea for a feature or human interest story to editors. However, many editors will be happy to receive a letter with suggestions for good feature stories (see sample letters 28 and 29, Appendix B). If you'd like to suggest a story idea:

1. Summarize your idea in one brief paragraph. Don't write the whole story.

2. Explain why the editor's audience would be interested in such a story.

3. Entice the editor further by suggesting possible photographs and pegs.

4. Make the editor regard you as a good, reliable source for stories. You may want to send several press releases before suggesting feature story ideas. You may even try to get to know editors better by calling, meeting with them, or joining organizations to which they belong. *Caution:* There is a fine line between being a good source of story ideas and a tiresome pest. Let each editor set the tone and pace of your relationship.

SUPPLY INTERESTING FILLER MATERIAL ABOUT YOUR PRACTICE

Fillers are short articles many newspapers use to fill small empty spaces after they've completed the layout of major articles. Many papers are so precise they never use fillers while others use only those from wire services, syndicates, and staff journalists, but, some papers will accept good fillers from just about anyone. To write fillers about your practice

1.   Check to see if the editor has an interest in them.

2.   Solicit good filler ideas from staff. They may come up with interesting facts or amusing anecdotes about your practice.

3.   Keep most fillers to approximately fifty to eighty words.

4.   Also write a few very short fillers — twenty-five words each. (See sample fillers 35 to 40, Appendix B.)

5.   Type fillers several to a page in paragraph form, double-spaced with generous margins all around.

6.   Send these to the editor with a brief cover letter on your letterhead. Explain what the enclosed fillers are and remind her that you've already checked to see that she is interested in this sort of material.

7.   Some newspapers and TV stations use unsolicited filler photographs with a feature angle. For example, many TV stations use interesting photos as a backdrop to the evening weather forecast. Check with local stations and papers to see if they can use your photos.

WRITE LETTERS TO THE EDITOR

Letters to the editor are a fabulous form of publicity because they are highly read and can do wonders for your reputation. A good letter from you can establish you as an expert and authority for your profession. Newspaper editors like to publish letters that are

1.   *Brief.* The usual length is 200 to 250 words.
Tip: Count the number of words in the average letter your newspaper publishes. Keep your letters approximately the same length.

2.   *Focused.* Stick to one subject.

3.   *Timely.* Increase your chances of getting published by linking your letter to a current news event or upcoming holiday.

4.   *Signed.* Editors need to know your name, address, phone number, and title. They generally prefer you to use your letterhead and sign your letters yourself.

5.   *Varied.* Some editors limit the frequency with which they will publish

letters from any individual. For example, many won't publish a letter from any author more frequently than once every two months. Idea: Have different people in your practice write letters—partners, associates, staff.

6.   *Original.* Do not send a letter to more than one editor.

7.   *Calm.* Rely on logical arguments and well-documented facts and figures.

Tip: Try writing letters to the editors of smaller publications. They probably receive relatively few letters so your chances of getting published may be quite good (see sample letter 26, Appendix B).

SUPPLY MATERIAL TO EDITORIAL STAFF

Editorial writers often write about the professions or professional news. You may wish to send editorial writers press releases or interesting articles in the hope that they use the information as the basis of an editorial. Although this sort of publicity is usually about a profession, not about a specific practice, you may benefit from it indirectly if potential clients seek your services as the result of an editorial you fueled. When sending material to editorial writers

1.   Send a cover letter with your release or articles suggesting that the enclosed material could be the basis of an editorial.

2.   Do not write the editorial or suggest the stand or angle the writer should take.

3.   Offer to supply additional information.

4.   You may wish to try the same approach with editorial or political cartoonists. Like editorial writers, they will want to come up with their own angles and ideas, so don't suggest them. Just supply interesting, relevant facts that could be the springboard for a good cartoon.

BECOME A LOCAL EXPERT

Journalists often need a local expert in your profession who can answer a quick question, interpret technical information, or give an opinion about how some national trend or event will affect people locally. You may get good publicity by convincing journalists that you're a good person for this job.

1.   Press releases will be a good way to establish credibility with journalists.

2.   Write editors to say you'd be happy to serve as a local spokesperson

or expert in case they ever need someone in your profession to help them in their work (see sample letter 27, Appendix B).

3.   The clincher: Provide editors with a list of hot issues related to your profession along with background information. Send a calendar of upcoming events, meetings, and legislation.

4.   Keep your name in front of editors. Clip and send interesting articles from professional journals. Enclose a brief note giving your opinion of the issue, interpretation, or predictions.

Bottom line: Once editors regard you as a good source of information about your profession, they may quote you in articles or do feature stories — both excellent forms of publicity for your practice.

WRITE ARTICLES FOR IN-HOUSE PUBLICATIONS

In-house publications of large employers in your area may be a good source of publicity for your practice.

1.   Send a brief letter or call large area employers to request copies of their in-house publications for employees. Also ask for the editors' names.

2.   Study the publications; they're usually newsletters.

3.   Contact each editor directly to see if she would be interested in receiving contributions, background material, or story suggestions from you.

4.   Explain how your contributions would be important or relevant to the readers of the publication.

5.   Ask the editor if she would like to be on the list of publications to whom you send press releases.

WRITE PUBLIC SERVICE ANNOUNCEMENTS (PSAs)

Public service announcements (PSAs) are broadcast announcements that serve community interests for which no fee is charged. You may be able to get publicity with a PSA if your message is educational and clearly has importance to the people in your area. To get a PSA aired

1.   Choose the correct format. PSAs fall into four format categories. Policies, lengths, and technical requirements vary from station to station, so you'll want to call the station first to see which format is acceptable.

a.   Live radio: least expensive to produce. Read on the air by the disc jockey (see sample 34, Appendix B).

b. Recorded radio: produced in a sound studio by a professional announcer, sometimes with music and sound effects.

c. Live TV: read on air by announcer, accompanied by slides. Most stations request a dozen slides or more from which they choose two or three.

d. Recorded TV: highest production costs. Videotaped or filmed in a studio, sometimes with actors, props, set, and costumes.

2. If you decide to undertake a recorded PSA, be sure ahead of time that the program director is interested in airing it.

Tip: Ask him to recommend a local production studio where you can have the work done.

3. Writing your own PSA for live broadcast is much simpler. Follow the directions in Chapter 13 for preparing press releases for broadcast, with the following changes:

a. Use this heading:

PUBLIC SERVICE ANNOUNCEMENT

FROM: Your name (or the name of your practice)
Street Address
City, State, ZIP Code

CONTACT: Name of your marketing coordinator (assistant)
Telephone number

DATE: (date you submitted the PSA)

USE UNTIL: (the last date the PSA can run)

READING TIME: (number of seconds it takes to read)

WORD COUNT: (number of words)

b. PSAs should be short, usually ten, twenty, thirty or sixty seconds long. Allow one second of reading time for every two words.

c. Type your copy in a narrow column that is only thirty-five characters long.

HOLD A PRESS CONFERENCE

Call a press conference only when you are about to make an important announcement involving hot news or something that will have a serious, widespread effect on your community. Anything less will not warrant this kind of coverage. If you have a reason to call a press conference

1.   Write a press release on the conference subject. Copies will be distributed to journalists at the end of the conference.

2.   Prepare background material and advance photographs. If you are delivering a prepared speech at the conference, have transcripts of the speech printed for the press.

3.   Choose a convenient location. If your office is far from town, rent a meeting room in a hotel that is closer.

4.   Choose a convenient time. For afternoon papers, eleven o'clock on a weekday morning is a good time. It enables reporters to cover the story and still have plenty of time to return to their desks to write it. For morning papers, a midafternoon conference is generally preferred.

5.   Arrange for refreshments for the press. A buffet-and-open-bar reception is common.

6.   Send written invitations to editors well in advance so they have enough time to make a staff assignment. State who is giving the conference, what will be discussed, where and when it will be, and why it is important (see sample letter 25, Appendix B).

7.   Call editors the day of the conference to remind them about it.

8.   Have staff attend the conference prepared to answer questions.

9.   Keep track of all reporters who attend. Send your press release and other materials to publications that did not send a reporter to attend your conference.

GET LISTINGS IN COMMUNITY CALENDARS

Upcoming promotional activities of your practice—speeches, open houses, and tours—may be worthy of publicity in community calendars.

1.   Check with your local newspapers and radio and television stations for deadline and format requirements for community calendar announcements.

2.   Also investigate other media: local Y's, libraries, churches, special interest groups, community recreation centers. These and other groups use calendars to publicize upcoming events to participants and members.

VOLUNTEER FOR LIVE INTERVIEWS WITH THE BROADCAST MEDIA

Local radio and television talk shows may be another opportunity for publicity for your practice.

1. Familiarize yourself with one show. Find out the name of the program director.

2. Send that person a letter explaining the general topics you wish to discuss on the show. Also submit a few subtopics, a brief biography, and any background information you have on the topic (see sample letter 24, Appendix B).

3. Tell the contact person you will call her in a week to discuss your ideas further.

4. When you call, reiterate your key points and stress the importance of the topics for the listening or viewing audience.

5. Review why *you* are qualified to speak on the subject. Sound confident; the program director will be judging your voice and manner.

6. Ask for a reason if she says she is not interested in having you on the show. If appropriate pursue it just one more time. Then back off.

7. Once you've scheduled an interview appearance, you will have a lot of preparation before you.

a. Don't memorize your whole presentation; rather, anticipate questions and practice answering them. Memorize key facts and figures. Rehearse stories you'd like to tell on the show.

b. Arrange to meet your interviewer before going on the air.

c. Find out beforehand as much as possible about what you will be asked. Make a list of questions you'd like to be asked.

d. If necessary request that specific questions not be asked. Be sure to do this before the interview, not on the air.

e. If the interviewer asks a question you cannot or do not want to answer, decline politely, giving your reasons.

f. You may wish to prepare some notes if you're going to participate in a radio program. If so, put them on sturdy paper or cards so they won't rustle as you turn the pages.

g. Ask your interviewer how far to sit from the microphone. Be aware of your distance from it throughout the program.

h. Keep your voice at the same volume as your interviewer's.

i. Look your best for television interviews: wear eyeglasses on TV if you normally do, avoid hats, highly polished or large jewelry, clothes in black and white, plaid, and checks. These distort on camera.

j.   Be aware of nervous habits or mannerisms you have and make an effort to curb them. Do not gesture too fully or wildly. Keep your hands resting in your lap and legs crossed at the ankle. This looks graceful for both men and women.

k.   Do not look at yourself on the TV monitor in the studio.

l.   Talk to the interviewer, *not* the camera.

m.   Try to give answers to questions in ten- to thirty-second intervals. Then pause so your host can break in with a comment or another question.

n.   Give answers only when you're sure you understand the question. If not, ask your host to rephrase it or give more information, or rephrase it yourself and ask, "Is that what you mean?"

o.   Watch your temper, especially if you're a guest on a show in which listeners or viewers call in to ask questions. Be polite to all callers, even those trying to provoke you. An interviewee rarely looks good on these shows if he's rude to a caller, even if that caller was obnoxious or asked ridiculous questions.

How to Become a Popular Public Speaker in Your Community

G iving speeches to community groups can be a rewarding way to market your practice. Professionals are in an especially good position to be speakers because their expertise overlaps with areas of public concern. Many community groups have small budgets and are anxious to find good speakers like you who will appear without a fee. Speaking is one of the few opportunities you may ever have to market your services to potential clients in person.

THE KEYS TO LINING UP SPEAKING ENGAGEMENTS

1. Interesting topics: The most popular speakers are those who can talk about a lot of interesting things. Choose topics related to your profession that are hot or of particular interest to your community. In general, people like to learn about topics that frighten them, can make them money, or can make their lives easier, healthier, or more fun.

2. Special attractions: A slide show, a demonstration, a movie, or free materials often makes a speaker more appealing.

3. Volunteer: Of course, you can wait for a community group to ask you to speak. However, many practitioners take the initiative and approach groups directly. Learn the name of the person within the group who is responsible for organizing programs. Write a letter volunteering to speak to the group. Suggest a variety of topics you can cover, giving a jazzy title to each and reasons it is important. Provide your credentials and list other places you've spoken. Stress anything special you have to offer.

4. Get the word out: Publicize to clients your availability to speak to their groups. Put a notice in your client newsletter and on your reception area bulletin board. List topics you can cover and special features of your presentation. Also tell staff and colleagues about your desire to launch a speaking career.

5. Do it yourself: If no one seems interested in having you speak, do what many practitioners have done: Get the ball rolling by organizing your own program. Choose a weekday evening — Tuesday, Wednesday, or Thursday is best — or schedule a "brown bag" lunch-time program in a downtown business district. Rent a meeting room in a local hotel or club. Publicize the program heavily — with press releases; public service announcements; community calendars; printed invitations to clients, colleagues, major area employers, or clubs and schools; notices in monthly statements and client newsletters; and on bulletin boards.

Tip: Improve attendance by promoting what participants get for *free:* refreshments, brochures, door prizes. Some professionals also promote self-organized speaking programs in newspaper ads.

6. Reputation: The best way to line up speaking invitations is to become known as a desirable speaker. The remainder of this chapter will describe the ways to develop your speaking reputation in your community.

STEP 1: DO YOUR HOMEWORK ABOUT YOUR AUDIENCE

Once you've been invited to give a speech (or you've decided to organize your own program) and you've chosen a topic, the first thing you must do is find out all you can about your audience and its expectations. You'll need to know

1. *Who they are.* Ask the speech organizer to tell you about the group who has invited you: age of participants, where they live, their interests, occupations, purpose for joining the group.

2. *Time.* Ask the organizer how long the group wants you to speak. If it is more than an hour, plan to take a break midway.

3. *Location.* Where will you present your speech? In a classroom? Lecture hall? Auditorium? Will you have the ability to use a projector and screen? Microphone? Can you rearrange the seating to suit your needs?

4. *Format expectation.* Does the group expect a straight lecture? Audience participation? A little of each?

5. *Publicity.* Will the group be publicizing the speech? If so, how? Will they object to your inviting outsiders to hear you speak (clients)? Will they object to your publicizing the speech on your own?

6. *Purpose.* Why has the group invited you to speak? Are they hoping to get something in particular out of your program? What does the group already know about your topic?

7. *Participant list.* Will the group give you a list of all the people who attend the program (with their names and addresses)? If not, will they allow you to send follow-up materials to the group to be distributed to participants?

STEP 2: OUTLINE YOUR SPEECH ACCORDING TO ITS PURPOSE

Why are you giving your speech? Your purpose will depend not only upon the expectations and needs of your audience but also on your own. The primary purpose of most speeches generally falls into one of two categories. The purpose of the speech is either to *instruct* or impart some information to the audience, or to *persuade* the audience to alter its thinking or behavior. Define your purpose and prepare an outline for your speech accordingly.

1. If your purpose is to instruct, arrange your material logically, with no surprises. Start by giving the audience an outline of your speech — what you will cover and in what order. Then as you go, make sure each segment flows to the next. Use frequent summaries and transitional phrases to link the material and make it easier for the audience to follow. Explain how one piece of information causes or leads to the next. In the end, show the audience that you have indeed covered the material you said you would.

2. If your purpose is to persuade, arrange your material somewhat differently. Start by establishing your own character, credibility, and credentials with your audience. Tell stories about yourself or people who have had experiences with your topic, how you learned about the topic, why it is important. If possible, shock your audience with startling statistics, pictures, or stories. Try to appeal to their emotions. Then, once you've gotten your listeners upset or excited, suggest the precise ways they should change their behavior. Tell them how they can prevent making the mistake others have made or how they can benefit the way others have. Tell them what's in it for them.

STEP 3: PREPARE YOUR SPEECH

Few people can give a good impromptu speech. Preparation is essential for most speakers, even the real pros. Here are some tips for preparing your speech.

Don't Be a Slave to Your Visual Aids

There is no doubt that visual aids can be an invaluable asset to many speeches. However, plan to use visual aids only if you're certain you can do it well and that they actually contribute something to your presentation. If you're relying on a mechanical aid such as a projector, be prepared to go on with the show if it breaks down. Some do's and don'ts for preparing visual aids are:

1.   Don't use visual aids as a crutch. The speech must still be top-notch, well prepared, and interesting.

2.   Make visual aids large and easy to read. For slides and posters, a few key words are usually best.

3.   Prepare your presentation so you keep the visual aids moving. Don't plan to stay on one slide for a long time. Shoot several slides from different angles or show a detail slide. Never leave a slide on the screen when you're not talking about it.

4.   Don't let the visual aids regulate the tempo of the speech. Some speakers let a slide come up, describe or explain it and then pause until the next slide appears, as though they don't know what's coming next. Use visual aids as part of a continuing narrative. Know what comes next and talk as the aid is changing.
Successful application: "So you see that this surgical technique has dramatic effects. Sometimes these effects are most impressive in teenage patients (change slide) as you can see in this photograph of a fifteen-year-old boy who. . . ."

5.   Don't use visual aids at the wrong times. It becomes harder to keep an audience alert when you turn off the lights to show slides or a movie. Get the audience interested first by introducing yourself and your speech. Avoid the common mistake of scheduling a slide show after a lunch break; that's a great way to induce sleep.

6.   Anticipate every possible calamity. If you are using a projector, bring an extension cord, lens paper, and an extra bulb. If you are using an easel and sketch pad or an overhead projector, bring your own markers. Need a pointer? Bring your own; the retractible type is handy.

7.   Don't distribute a handout and talk about it at the same time. People will not listen to you while they're reading your handout or waiting to get it. Provide written materials to the audience *before* the speech so they can look them over and satisfy their curiosity before you begin, or make handouts available *after* the speech.

How to Make Your Notes Foolproof

Expert opinions vary about whether a speaker should use notes. Use them only if they actually help you.

1.   Use neat, organized notes. Have your assistant type them if you have trouble reading your own handwriting.

2.   Prepare notes suitable for the speech you're giving. Almost all speeches you give can be written in skeletal outline form, in topical phrases and key words only. Use a completely written speech only in special instances such as a one- or two-minute thank-you or introduction speech.

3.   Become very familiar with your notes so you don't lose your place during your speech.

4.   Circle all words in your notes that are technical or otherwise unfamiliar to your audience. You'll want to define these during your speech.

5.   If you've got many pages of notes, contact your speech organizer to request a podium. Put the pages of notes in a three-ring binder. That way if you drop your notes they won't scatter and get out of order.

6.   If you use index cards for notes, number them, just in case you drop the whole stack.

Rehearse Your Physical Presentation, Not Only Your Words

Rehearsal is the most important step in preparing a speech. Don't just practice your speech mentally or only in pieces. Rehearse it aloud in its entirety many, many times before you give it. There is no better way to prepare.

1.   Practice in front of a full-length mirror or better, try out your speech on a friend or staff member, especially one who is critical.

2.   Practice walking back and forth on the platform or stage if you plan to do so. Have a friend tell you if you're pacing or distracting from the speech.

3.   Practice making eye contact during the speech. Pick out several focal points in the room and try to give each one your attention during the speech. Turn your whole body to each focal point, not just your head.

Tip: If you find making eye contact difficult, look at people between the eyes, at the bridge of the nose. This is sometimes easier than looking directly into the eyes and no one will be the wiser.

4.   Do not choreograph your speech with lots of exaggerated gestures. Practice gesturing normally as you do in regular conversations. This will seem much more natural when you give your speech.

5.   Practice using any visual aids you have planned for your speech.

6.   If a tape recorder is available, record your rehearsals for self-criticism.

Tip: Some speakers videotape important presentations to study their strengths and weaknesses.

7.   Time your presentation. Honor the time limit given to you by the speech organizer. Cut or slow your speech if you're way off.

8.   Practice keeping your voice volume up. If you're soft-spoken, plan on getting a microphone or saying to your audience in the beginning: "Please raise your hand if you have trouble hearing me at any time during this presentation."

STEP 4: GET ADVANCE PUBLICITY FOR YOUR SPEECH

Find out how your speech is being publicized by the group and how you can help to publicize it further. If the group doesn't object

1.   Invite your clients to attend your speech; include an article in your client newsletter; put notices on your office bulletin board; send printed or handwritten invitations.

2.   Send press releases to media editors (see sample 41, Appendix B). Invite them to attend the speech and take photographs.
Tip: Send an outline of your speech, your credentials, and background material on your topic.

3.   Investigate other avenues for publicity: community calendars, public service announcements, feature articles, letters to the editor, in-house publications.

STEP 5: KEEP YOUR COOL WHEN YOU GIVE YOUR SPEECH — TEN TIPS

There's nothing like experience to help you become a good public speaker. Here are ten down-to-earth suggestions that I've learned from my own experiences giving lectures and seminars:

1.   Pour a glass of water for yourself before the speech and leave it up at the podium. It's amazing how hard it can be to get water from a pitcher to a glass with shaking hands, sweaty palms, and all eyes upon you — and soggy notes are no picnic.

2.   If you begin to get flustered, stop and take a drink of water very slowly and deliberately, as if you're pondering something very deep. Don't start rummaging through your notes. That's a sure tip-off that you don't know what you're doing.

3.   In the beginning, tell your audience three things: how long you're going to speak, when you'll take breaks, and how you plan to handle questions. Example: "I'll be discussing ___ with you during the next hour. Afterwards, we'll take a fifteen-minute break so you can stretch your legs and write down your questions on the cards before you. I will collect your questions when we resume at 8:45 and answer them in the remaining thirty minutes of this evening's program."

Benefits: The audience will not pester you with questions at the wrong time, they will know when the break is and not leave the room earlier, and they will know how long they have to sit still—a real plus if they get fidgety.

4.   Look in a mirror right before you get up to talk. Your audience will not be able to concentrate on what you're saying if you've got ketchup on your face or your hair is sticking up.

5.   Make sure you're introduced well. Take no chances. Send a suggested introduction to your host in advance. Take a copy with you to the speech in case the host loses it.

6.   Arrive early and mingle with the audience. This gets them on your side and helps you think of them as real people with whom you can carry on a conversation.

7.   Check your microphone, projector, flip-charts, posters, screen, and other visual aids in advance. Sit in various seats in the audience to see if you can view your visual aids without obstruction.

8.   If you plan to open the floor for questions at the end of your speech, prepare a few good ones of your own that you can ask and answer. This gets the ball rolling and fills that awkward silence when no one has a question.

9.   Do not try to get a group discussion going with more than twenty participants. That's too many opinions to control.

10.   Smile and tell the audience they've been great at the end of your speech. That will end it on a positive note.

STEP 6: MILK YOUR SPEECH FOR ALL IT'S WORTH

Giving the speeches is only half of their marketing advantage; the other half lies in what you can do afterwards. Check with the group to see what kinds of publicity it is working on and how you can coordinate your efforts with theirs.

1.   Arrange your schedule so you can stay and talk informally with your audience after your speech. Many groups expect you to do this and will organize

a small reception in your honor. If so, great! That's when you're most likely to pick up new clients.

2.   Always send a thank-you note to the group afterwards for giving you the chance to speak to them. Offer to come again whenever they want you (see sample letter 30, Appendix B).

3.   If the group will give you a list of the people in your audience, send individual thank-you notes to each person. Enclose your practice brochure and a complimentary one-year subscription to your client newsletter (see Chapter 11).

4.   If the group will not give you a list of participants, send a package of brochures to the speech organizer to share with the group. Also enclose reply cards for a complimentary one-year newsletter subscription.

5.   Send the group articles, brochures, and other materials to inform them of any new developments in the topic you discussed. This is an excellent way to keep your name before them.

6.   Write an article in your client newsletter that explains what you discussed, where, and when.
    Tip: Write it as a news article from the third person. Pull a couple of the best quotes from your speech.

7.   Send press releases after the speech, again quoting yourself and making it sound as newsy as possible.

8.   Refer to the speech and the group's favorable reaction to it when you contact other groups to volunteer your presentation.

9.   If you give many formal speeches, transcribe tapes of them and print them in booklet form. These make good giveaways for clients and colleagues.

How to Organize Open Houses, Tours and Other Special Events to Promote Your Practice

Practitioners who want more opportunities for practice promotion and publicity may decide to stage special events. For our purposes, a special event will mean anything you do that causes people to gather at a specific time or place to participate in or attend a program. Special events also include new practice activities that are so unusual and interesting that they warrant news coverage and attract community interest.

With your image in mind, consider which of these special events can be a good springboard for publicity and promotion for your practice. Modify these project suggestions or create your own activities to make your special event truly special for you.

SPECIAL EVENT 1: AN OPEN HOUSE

1. Schedule: Open houses generally get a good turnout if they are scheduled for a Saturday or Sunday starting at noon or shortly afterwards. They usually last about three or four hours.

2. Theme: The most successful open houses usually have a theme that ties them to a holiday or event.

Successful applications: A dentist held his open house during National Children's Dental Health Month. An optometrist scheduled his during Save Your Vision Week.

Tip: Check *Chase's Calendar* at your local library for a listing of lesser-known special holidays, weeks, and months that you can use as a peg for your open house (see Chapter 12 and the Bibliography). You can also hold an open house linked to a local festival or chamber of commerce promotion that will attract people to your area, or plan one in honor of a practice anniversary or milestone, new or improved facilities, or any of the reasons for writing press releases (Chapter 13).

3. External publicity: Publicize your open house well in advance. Send press releases to media editors stressing what is newsworthy about your program, and invite reporters, suggesting angles for feature stories and photographs. Plan public service announcements and listings on community calendars, and invite local schools, employers, clubs, and organizations. If you plan to advertise your open house, run six or more ads starting at least two weeks in advance.

4. Internal publicity: Publicize your open house to current clients. Put notices about the upcoming event in your client newsletter and on your office bulletin board. Send printed invitations or letters to clients and colleagues (see sample letter 22, Appendix B). Enclose reminder notices about the open house in monthly statements and other correspondence.

5. Establish the open house program: Your staff can be a tremendous help in planning and running an open house. Hold a staff meeting to set an agenda for the open house and delegate assignments.

a. Traffic signs. If possible, have signs near your office the day of your open house that face oncoming traffic.

b. Equipment signs. Do you have office equipment that will interest open house visitors? If so, design a placard for each piece that states its name and purpose in laymen's terms.

c. Security. Set aside a closet or other small area the day of the open house that is off-limits to visitors. Lock away small items of value. Lock all file cabinets and desk drawers.

d. Tours. If you will be giving tours, organize them so visitors go through your usual traffic patterns. Keep tours brief and repeat them frequently. List the tour schedule in press releases, in invitations and on a sign in your reception area the day of the open house.

e. Other programs. Also publicize and list a schedule of other open house programs: short films, slide shows, demonstrations, lectures.

f. Refreshments. Limit refreshments to neat finger foods. You don't need a great variety of foods, but be sure you have plenty of whatever you serve.

g. Tags. You and your staff should wear name tags the day of the open house.

h. Giveaways. Give your visitors free materials to take with them. A practice brochure and client newsletter are good, but also try to give them other items with your logo on them—balloons, pens, calendars, T-shirts, bumper stickers.

i.   Contests. To spark interest and generate excitement, consider sponsoring a door prize or contest for open house visitors.

Successful application: One practitioner asked visitors to guess the number of jellybeans in a jar.

j.   Press kits. If you anticipate a visit from the press, prepare press kits for reporters. Include copies of press releases, practice brochures, newsletters, photos, and pertinent background information about your practice or the topics you will discuss at your open house.

k.   Guest roster. Have a sign-in book for guests asking for name, address, phone number, and how they heard about the open house—or have a staff member serve as your host and gather this information.

l.   Photographs. Have your marketing coordinator, a staff member or a free-lance photographer take photographs of your open house, following the guidelines for composing good journalistic photographs offered in Chapter 13.

6. After the open house: Get the most out of your open house by publicizing it *afterwards.*

a.   Send a thank-you letter to all open house visitors.

b.   Send all nonclients a complimentary one-year subscription to your newsletter (Chapter 11).

c.   If something newsworthy happened at the open house, send press releases afterwards and enclose photographs.

d.   Write an article about your open house with good photos in the next issue of your client newsletter.

e.   Arrange a display of captioned photographs from your open house on your office bulletin board.

f.   Thank and reward your staff for their participation and hard work.

g.   Send a letter to all clients who did not attend your open house. Express regret that they were unable to attend. Summarize the highlights and enclose the materials that were given away.

SPECIAL EVENT 2: AN OFFICE TOUR

Office tours are usually interesting programs for health-care professionals who have several treatment/examination rooms, equipment, a lab, and other interesting office areas. Other professionals may also wish to give tours if they have enough interesting things to see in their offices.

1. Advantage of tours: Tours are conducted much like an open house except that you will be extending your invitation to a specific group or class. Tours are therefore easier to organize and plan; you will know in advance how many visitors you will have, their ages and their interests.

2. Inviting children: Tours are usually of interest to children, especially if your office is within walking distance or an easy bus ride. Schools, scout troops, 4-H clubs and other children's organizations may be good candidates for tours. To see if they're interested, write to the program leader or teacher and volunteer your tour. Describe your program and estimate the amount of time the whole program will take.

3. Publicity: Once a group accepts your invitation, consider appropriate ways to use the event as a peg for publicity: press releases, feature articles, public service announcements.

4. Establish the program:

a.   When the children arrive, assemble them in your reception area for a brief meeting.

b.   Introduce yourself and your staff and tell what each of you does.

c.   Explain what your visitors will see on their tour. Mention special things they should look for.
Tip: Give your audience a question or something to think about while on the tour. Tell them that you will be waiting to hear their answer when you get back together at the end of the tour.

d.   Break large groups into smaller ones. Staff members can each take a small group.

e.   Children will enjoy your tour all the more if you ask them to participate by sharing information they know about your profession. Ask questions; for instance, ask them to guess what a certain piece of equipment does.

f.   Whenever possible, plan demonstrations and use models, pictures, and funny stories to liven up your tour.

g.   Assemble the group in your reception area again at the end of your tour. Open the floor to questions and opinions. Get back to the question you asked them at the start of your program. Children won't have forgotten it and will be itching to tell you their answer.

h.   Plan healthful refreshments.

i.   Give the children lots of free materials — the more the better. Assemble a packet for each child with literature, puzzles, coloring and activity books, balloons, and badges. The children will probably share these packets with their parents, so be sure to include your practice brochure and client newsletter. Provide a response card so parents can request a one-year complimentary newsletter subscription.

j.   Take a group photograph of you with your visitors. Also have your marketing coordinator, a staff member, or a free-lance photographer take candid shots throughout the tour.

5. After the tour:

a.   Send a copy of your group photograph to the teacher.

b.   The children will no doubt send you thank-you notes or cards. Post these on your office bulletin board along with your group and candid photographs.

c.   Write an article about your tour in the next issue of your client newsletter. Include photographs.

d.   Good candid photographs of your tour may also serve as the basis for a follow-up press release or feature article.

6. Adult tours: Some adult groups may take you up on an offer to tour your office. They may be especially interested if you discuss a hot topic or demonstrate a new technique or piece of equipment that is getting a lot of media attention.

SPECIAL EVENT 3: CLIENT APPRECIATION DAY

A Client Appreciation Day will make your clients feel terrific about you. At the same time, potential clients and colleagues will be impressed by the image you project through such an event.

1. Correspondence: Send personally signed appreciation letters or cards to every client of record. (Use sample letters 2 to 5, Appendix B, as a guide.) Time saver: Print greeting cards for this occasion with a brief message to thank clients for their continued loyalty and trust in you over the years.

2. T-shirts: Give Client Appreciation Day T-shirts to all children in your practice. Imprint them with your practice name, your logo, and a catchy message.

Idea in action: "I'm Appreciated!" then, in smaller letters, "by my pediatrician, Dr. Gerard Wallace and his staff."

3. Party: Hold a party on your Client Appreciation Day.

Successful application: One practitioner gave a breakfast party for his clients and had a huge turnout. Bonus: Breakfast is a relatively inexpensive meal.

4. Superlative awards: Provide awards and gifts to special clients on Appreciation Day. Possibilities: oldest client, youngest client, newest client, largest family group, most recent bride and groom.

5. Publicity: Publicize Client Appreciation Day with press releases and notices in your client newsletter. Take good journalistic-quality photos of all Appreciation Day events for your office bulletin board, releases, and feature articles. Some practitioners may also wish to place an ad in the local newspaper to thank all their clients for their continued trust.

SPECIAL EVENT 4: FAIRS

Practitioners often join together to put on an educational fair for the community. These events provide the opportunity for area residents to learn about the professions and the services they provide. If you're involved in a fair, create a booth for your practice that is a favorite with your audience.

1. Giveaways: Booths that give away good things are always popular. Tasteful giveaways are posters, children's story and coloring books, brochures, subscriptions to your client newsletter — all imprinted with your logo.

2. Appearance: Looks are important when it comes to booths. Make yours attractive with photographs, banners, and colorful signs.

3. Activities: Can you do something for participants? Booths that offer screenings or demonstrations are always favorites. Any professional can come up with a brain-teaser or quiz to test the audience's IQ about a hot topic in his or her field. Display a sign on your booth that challenges participants to take your free test.

4. Fun: You and your staff should look as if you're having fun.

5. Tags: Wear name tags so participants know you belong to the booth.

SPECIAL EVENT 5: AN ART SHOW OR OPENING

The reception area in a busy practice is often a good place to exhibit art works by local talent. Look for qualified artists through area schools, art clubs, and universities, or contact local art galleries. A classified ad or notices on public bulletin boards can also put you in touch with qualified artists.

An artist interested in exhibiting will generally agree to lend you her works without charge. However, make sure she also agrees to the following in writing:

1.   The artist must agree to set up the exhibition herself, prepare necessary handouts, and take down the works on a specified date.

2.   She must agree that she is lending her work to you at her own risk. You will, of course, take reasonable care to see that the work is not stolen or damaged while it is in your office, but you don't want to take full responsibility for it.

3.   Ask all artists who exhibit their work in your office to donate one piece to the permanent collection in your office. This request is common among hospitals, libraries, and restaurants that give local artists the chance to exhibit. Benefit: You will end up with a free collection of original art to exhibit in the rest of your office and when you're not running a temporary show.

4.   Some artists will ask you to make it known that the works are for sale or to have your receptionist keep a price list and handle sales for them. This will usually present no problem as long as visitors to your office feel no pressure to buy.

Of course, an art show in your office can lead to some great external marketing opportunities.

1.   Find out how to get your exhibitions listed in the community arts calendar.

2.   Send press releases to art editors and other media contacts.

3.   Nonclients may visit your reception area to see the art works. These visitors are all potential clients for your practice. Have a sign-in guest book that asks for each visitor's name, address, and comments on the exhibition. Write to these potential clients afterwards to thank them for coming to the show. Enclose a practice brochure and a complimentary one-year subscription to your client newsletter.

4.   If you want to go all-out, hold an art opening at the start of each exhibition. Schedule the opening on a night when you don't have regular appointments. Send invitations to the press, clients, colleagues, art schools, area businesses, and art galleries. Also give the artist a stack of invitations to send to her friends. Invite the media to attend your opening and meet the artist. Serve refreshments. Have all opening guests sign a guest book. Write to them

afterwards to thank them for coming. Enclose a practice brochure and newsletter subscription.

SPECIAL EVENT 6: A MUSIC CONCERT

Along the same lines, some practitioners may wish to organize concerts for their reception areas.

1. Schedule: Schedule music concerts after office hours; Sunday afternoon is usually a good time. You can also ask musicians to play in your reception area during your regular office hours. This makes the most sense for larger group practices that often have many people gathered in the reception area at once.

2. Publicity: Publicize your musical programs with press releases, community arts calendars, and feature articles.

3. Talent: Look for interested musicians at area colleges and high schools. Many of these young musicians will be delighted to give concerts free and will attract their family and friends to hear them.

4. Guests: Have a sign-in guest book for visitors. Write to these people afterwards to thank them for coming. Enclose a practice brochure and complimentary one-year subscription to your client newsletter.

5. Instruments: From a logistics standpoint, you may have to limit your musicians to those who play portable instruments they bring themselves. However, truly ambitious practitioners can go even further.

Successful application: One practitioner has a grand piano on a platform at one end of his reception area. He schedules regular concerts of piano students from local schools.

Tip: Piano rental companies may agree to waive the rental fee if you place a sign near or on the piano that says it is on loan to you as a courtesy of that company.

SPECIAL EVENT 7: BOOK DONATIONS

Donating books to schools and public libraries is a promotional activity that requires a modest budget and a little effort, and it affects only a small audience. However, it is just the kind of special event that can build your image as a caring professional in your community. To make donations

1.   Contact librarians in charge of acquisitions and explain that you'd like to donate a book or books.

2. Make the donation in honor of a holiday, practice anniversary or milestone, or a special day, week, or month designated by your professional association.

3. Suggest books relevant to your profession. Also see if the library needs a particular book or is weak in certain areas. Reference books are always a good choice because they are so widely used.

4. Have dedication labels printed with your logo for the inside cover of each book you donate.

Idea in action: "Donated in Honor of 'Be Kind to Animals Week' (date) by Arthur Hamilton, Doctor of Veterinary Medicine (practice logo, address, and phone number)." You can also hire a calligrapher to inscribe this message inside each book.

5. Some practitioners may prefer to donate equipment, educational aids, or other items to schools and organizations. If so, affix a brass plate engraved with a similar inscription to the base of each donated object.

SPECIAL EVENT 8: DISPLAYS IN PUBLIC PLACES

Public libraries, recreation centers, and schools often have large, attractive display cases in their lobbies and hallways, but many have no budget to create displays. You might help these organizations and get some good exposure for your practice by volunteering to create and donate a display once or twice a year.

1. Write or call the person in charge of the display case. Propose one or more displays you'd be willing to donate.

Tip: Make suggestions of an educational nature. When possible, link the display to a holiday, season, or special event designated by your professional association (such as Child Health Month).

2. Check with your professional association to see if it has posters, models, or other materials suitable for displays.

3. Involve your staff and enlist their help.

4. Solicit clients' suggestions and help. Write an article in your client newsletter asking for suggestions or sponsor a "suggest a display" contest.

5. If you have children in your practice, ask them to draw and paint original posters on an assigned subject for your display. Provide poster paper and crayons in the children's corner of your reception area.

SPECIAL EVENT 9: SCHOLARSHIPS AND AWARDS

Almost every high school holds an annual awards ceremony in which members of the graduating class receive plaques, trophies, savings bonds, certificates, scholarships, and other awards for academic and extracurricular achievements. Sponsoring awards or scholarships is an excellent way to promote a professional practice.

1.   Contact area high schools. Offer to sponsor an award or scholarship on behalf of, and named after, you and your practice.
Idea in action: "The Associated Physicians Award," "The Jones and Jones Legal Services Book Prize."

2.   Work with the awards chairman to establish the criteria for your award and the prize. If possible, arrange it so the student who wins shows excellence in a field related to your discipline. A lawyer might give an award to the most exceptional member of the school's debating team. A healthcare professional might designate a scholarship for the outstanding science student.
Successful application: One dentist awards prizes at each school to the children who prepare the best essays on a subject of dental importance: historic, economic, or cosmetic.

3.   Ask to be the person to present the certificate, plaque, or check at the awards ceremony.

4.   Take precautions that no one accuses you of being unfair about your award.

a.   Let the school officials or awards committee choose the recipient(s) of your award according to your criteria. If you choose them some members of your community may criticize you for your selection.

b.   Offer a separate award or awards to each high school in your area. Otherwise, some clients may feel that you played favorites with certain schools or districts.

c.   Be sure your award is not in direct competition with another award sponsored by another practice or organization. Make your prize and criteria slightly different.

d.   An award or scholarship is a commitment clients will expect you to maintain year after year. Don't discontinue it unless you must.

6.   Most awards are publicized automatically in local newspapers and in the school's graduation programs and yearbooks. In addition, publicize the

awards within your practice with articles and photographs in your client newsletter and on your bulletin board.

SPECIAL EVENT 10: DECLARE YOUR OWN HOLIDAY

Why not declare your own holiday to call attention to a particular problem or accomplishment? The press will probably be interested in such an event, especially if you organize special programs and activities to observe or celebrate your holiday.

Successful application: A dentist proclaimed a certain Wednesday as "Sugarless Wednesday" to call attention to the fact that most of us eat too much sugar in our diets. He asked his patients to cut sugar out of their diets on this day as their form of observance. He got a tremendous amount of good publicity from this event.

SPECIAL EVENT 11: SPONSOR A CHILDREN'S SPORTS TEAM

Sponsoring a children's baseball, hockey, or soccer team is a great way to strengthen relations with clients, get your name out to the public, and have fun at the same time. These benefits can be yours for a relatively small investment.

1.   Contact your city, town, or village recreation or parks department. Find out the local league schedules and age groupings.

2.   Decide which age groups you would like to sponsor.

3.   Publicize your willingness to sponsor a team through your client newsletter, a notice on your bulletin board, and perhaps a special mailing to clients. Have interested children or their parents contact you by a given date.

4.   If the response is very good, consider sponsoring more than one team.

5.   Once you have a group of interested children, hold an organizational meeting for them and their parents. Explain that you will pay the league fee for the team(s) and provide uniforms, team jackets, or T-shirts.

Tip: Your involvement with the team can be limited to financing it. Or you can become more involved by attending games, treating the team to pizza afterwards, publicizing its exploits in your client newsletter, coaching, and giving trophies. It's up to you. Many team sponsors do nothing more than foot the bill.

6.   Decide on a catchy name for your team(s).

Successful applications: "Dr. Sam's Sluggers," "Dr. Albert's All-Stars." Have the name printed on the team's outfits.

SPECIAL EVENT 12: BECOME A SPONSOR OR DONOR IN OTHER WAYS

1.　Local theater groups, concert series, and other art programs often list sponsors or patrons in their printed programs.

2.　High school yearbook sponsors or boosters are usually listed in the back of the book. Other student publications may also be looking for some support: newspapers or literary magazines.

3.　School football teams and other student athletes raise funds by seeking sponsors. They usually credit sponsors in their printed programs and schedules. Bands, choirs, and other clubs also need financial backing and will often thank their sponsors publicly.

4.　Many nonprofit organizations can use your help and will give you a great deal of publicity for your contributions.

Successful applications: One organization runs an annual radio auction to raise funds, auctioning theater tickets, restaurant vouchers, and car tune-ups donated by local merchants. A dentist and a lawyer in the town also donate their services to be auctioned (an initial examination and a set of reciprocal wills, respectively). Both practitioners get their names and addresses mentioned repeatedly on the air and it costs them only a little bit of their time — far less than the same amount of advertising would cost.

Bonus: The people who buy their services at the auction will usually become new clients. Public television and radio stations often run fund-raising auctions of this sort. See if they would like to have your services put on the block.

5.　Practitioners may wish to provide their services without charge to nonprofit organizations, as a form of donation. Most often the group will thank you for your valuable contribution in a printed program, in its newsletter, and at meetings.

Successful application: A dentist donated his time to fit mouthpieces to high school athletes.

Bottom line: He expanded his practice to include sports dentistry. Many physicians have established enviable reputations for themselves as team physicians.

6.　If nonprofit organizations are not interested in having you donate your services, perhaps you can get good exposure for your practice by donating them directly to the public.

Successful applications: Many practitioners provide free screenings or examinations in schools and as part of a community fair. One lawyer provides free legal advice to the public on weekends from noon until sundown. He sets up a few lawn chairs and an orange crate table under a tree near the town's beach. From the tree he hangs his certificate of admission from the state bar and a sign that says, "The Lawyer Is In."

Bottom line: He sees about 100 clients each day who ask mostly about landlord-tenant law, family law, and criminal law. Many become regular paying clients — especially those whose problems require further work and whom he invites to his regular office during business hours. Bonus: The lawyer gets great publicity about his unusual community service, including an article and photograph in a national magazine.

SPECIAL EVENT 13: RAISE FUNDS FOR CHARITY

The media will be likely to cover special events you organize to raise funds for charity.

Successful applications: A large group practice got great publicity when it challenged all other professionals in the city to a road race to see who had the fastest practice. (They raised money for charity by charging a substantial entry fee for all race participants.) Another practitioner donated fees from one day to an organization that grants wishes to dying children, and also got good publicity. Other fund-raising events: auctions, raffles, benefit concerts, lectures, or films that you organize with proceeds going to the charity.

1.   Check with the charity before you go ahead with any fund-raiser on its behalf. It may have some restrictions about the kinds of programs it can participate in.

2.   Also discuss ways you and the charity can work together to put on a program. Chances are the charity already has a volunteer staff, media contacts, and printed materials that can be helpful to you as you plan and carry out your fund-raising event.

SPECIAL EVENT 14: SEND COLORING AND ACTIVITY BOOKS TO TEACHERS

Some professional associations have developed educational coloring and activity books for children that explain some aspects of the profession or treatment, such as what it's like to visit the dentist, optometrist, or physician; and how to eat right or take care of your eyesight. If such materials are available to you and appropriate for your practice, consider sending sets of them to elementary school teachers in your area.

1.   Imprint your practice logo, name, address, and phone number on the books before you distribute them. That way parents will know you have provided these materials for their children.

2.   Send sets of the books to the grade school teachers in your area. Enclose a letter that explains why the material is important. Offer to supply additional copies if they are needed (see sample letter 19, Appendix B).

3.   As an alternative, offer the teacher the use of films or programs from your professional organization.

Successful application: One practitioner sends a travelling puppet show to area schools.

SPECIAL EVENT 15: A CAREER PROGRAM

High school guidance counselors often advise students about careers and will appreciate it if you will answer questions for students who are interested in a career in your profession. Some will organize a seminar for you to talk with an interested group. Others will ask if you might allow the students to visit you in your office to spend a day or half day observing and talking with you. These are excellent opportunities for you to get some good publicity. Contact guidance counselors to volunteer your services.

Tip: Send press releases to media editors. If possible, invite reporters to attend the program and take photographs.

SPECIAL EVENT 16: CONTESTS

1.   Publicize contests with three press releases: one to announce the contest, another to give a progress report, a third to remind people about the deadline for entries.

2.   Come up with some unusual and imaginative contests.

a.   Trivia contests.

b.   Joke contests.

c.   Contests to suggest something you'll use: a practice slogan, a name for your practice mascot (pet or stuffed animal), or a name for your client newsletter.

d.   Essay contests. Consider sponsoring a contest in which participants submit essays explaining the best way your community could use $500 (or however much you wish to donate). Use the winner's suggestion.

Successful application: A company that ran this contest decided the winner was an elementary school teacher who suggested the money be used to improve the playground at the public school. The media gave the company a huge amount of publicity for this community service and unique contest idea.

e.   Contests to write a caption for a particular photograph or cartoon.

f.   Photo contests.

Successful application: A dentist held a contest for his patients, asking them to submit a photo of the most unusual place they had flossed their teeth during the summer. He got some great photo entries of patients flossing on a mountain top, under water, and on the Eiffel Tower. These are naturals for good publicity.

g.   Treasure hunts. Have participants find an object you have hidden in plain sight in your town. Give clues.

h.   Poster contests.

i.   Word contests. Offer a prize to the entrant who comes up with the most words using only the letters in the name of your practice (or if the name is short, the slogan). That will get people talking about you.

j.   Smallest handwriting contest. Offer a prize to the person who writes the name of your practice the greatest number of times on an ordinary postcard (specify the card's size and that the words cannot overlap). Display all entries on a bulletin board in your reception area.

Successful application: A dental practice asked contestants to write "Visit Your Dentist Every Six Moons" as many times as possible on a standard postcard. The winner wrote the phrase 335 times.

k.   Contests to make something.

Successful application: To amuse the children in the reception area, one practitioner conducted a castle-building contest. He invited the children to use building blocks to build a castle in the reception area. As the children finished their masterpieces, each castle was photographed. On deadline day the practitioner invited a local architect to the office for an impartial judging. Result: A local newspaper photographer came to take a picture of the winner receiving the prize. A feature story publicized the contest and the innovative practitioner who sponsored it.

l.   Drawings. Many practitioners sponsor a monthly drawing for a large stuffed animal or other toy for the children in the practice. Here's an even better idea: One practitioner sponsors a monthly Birthday Club drawing. The winner gets to take twenty friends to a birthday party in a fast-food restaurant.

This is a great way to get people talking about your practice (and photos of kids having fun at the party you provided look great in a client newsletter).

3.   Establish rules for your contest.

a.   Make sure rules are legal and do not violate any lottery laws.

b.   State the rules thoroughly and clearly.

c.   Give contestants a sample of what they are to do. For example, if it's a slogan contest, provide a sample slogan.

d.   Make the entry blank large enough so it can be completed quickly and legibly.

e.   Display the rules prominently in your reception area.

f.   Specify the closing date. Emphasize a postmark requirement for mail contests.

g.   Explain how ties will be decided.

h.   Specify where and how to submit entries.

i.   List prizes clearly, showing first, second, third, and so on, in complete sequence.

j.   Indicate that judges' decisions will be final and entries are nonreturnable.

k.   State when and how winners will be announced.

SPECIAL EVENT 17: UNUSUAL OFFICE DECOR
AND ATTRACTIONS

Your office itself can be the basis of some good publicity. Unusual attractions often merit a press release or feature story with a photo spread. Successful applications are:

1.   A charismatic office mascot can draw a lot of attention from clients and the media. Ask your local pet store to recommend an appropriate animal for your office.

Tip: Keep your mascot safe from clients who may unintentionally frighten, upset, or harm it.

2.   Some practitioners have gotten media attention because they decorated their offices in an unusual, photographable theme.

Idea in action: One practitioner uses a circus theme with lots of murals and old circus posters lining the walls. Another, who loves trains, had his office built entirely of old railway cars. Another chose a disco theme and installed a lighted dance floor and stereo system in the reception area. Another has an international motif with each room decorated with the arts, crafts, and music of a different country. Another chose a space theme and uses photographs taken in space and models of spacecraft.

3.   Unusual amusements for waiting clients can spark media interest. We've already explored earlier in this chapter the idea of live concerts and art shows in the reception area, and these can be publicized with press releases. In addition, consider these amusements that have gotten a lot of publicity: Several offices have installed video games, some are using video recorders to show short films and cartoons. One practitioner installed a hot tub in his reception area.

4.   Personal collections displayed in your reception area can be very interesting to clients and the media. To add news value, collect things relevant to your profession.

Successful application: Several eye care professionals display collections of antique spectacles in their offices.

5.   Other personal hobbies can lead to interesting in-office displays with news appeal.

Successful application: One practitioner built a greenhouse in his office and raises magnificent plants, featured in a newspaper article. Another draws many clients because of his expertise and display on magic.

C·H·A·P·T·E·R   17

Proven Techniques for Building and Tracking Referrals

We have already explored the ways to build referrals internally through existing clients and staff. Now let's consider proven techniques for getting referrals *externally* through colleagues, through other professionals, and in your community

1. Insurance: Do you provide professional services that are covered by insurance? If so, you may be able to get referrals from personnel officers and insurance managers of large area employers that provide insurance for their employees. Write a letter explaining that you are already serving a number of the firm's employees. Offer to help them answer questions about coverage and completing and filing insurance forms (see sample letter 32, Appendix B).

Successful application: One practitioner encloses copies of his practice brochure and says that a gift of appreciation for referrals is not out of the question as long as you don't overdo it.

Tip: Provide personnel and insurance officers with complimentary subscriptions to your client newsletter and subscription reply cards to share with employees.

2. Pharmacies: Here's an idea for health-care practitioners: Send a letter to area pharmacists. Explain that you and the pharmacist already serve a number of the same people. Offer to handle any emergencies that arise among his or her clients. Provide copies of your brochure and a complimentary subscription to your client newsletter. See if the pharmacist is willing to display free copies of these materials in the pharmacy. That way pharmacy clients waiting for their prescriptions can pick up a copy, and possibly become new patients (see sample letter 33, Appendix B).

3. Prevention: Do you treat emergencies that stem from work-related injuries? If so, write a letter to local manufacturers and construction companies to provide them with preventive and first-aid information about injuries at work. An ophthalmologist can provide information about safety eyewear and eye injuries. A dentist can offer information about mouth injuries. A dermatologist can suggest immediate first-aid for chemical burns. For added mileage, include information about your availability in emergencies and any pertinent printed materials available from your professional association. Enclose copies of your practice brochure and subscriptions to your client newsletter. Also send copies of your business card, especially if you print emergency information on back (see Chapter 9).

4. Educators: If appropriate, send similar emergency or injury information to school nurses, physical education teachers, and coaches.

5. New Businesses: To all new businesses in your area send a "Congratulations on Your New Venture" letter and perhaps a houseplant or other small gift. Enclose information about your emergency services, your practice brochure, complimentary subscriptions to your client newsletter, and business cards for employees in need of your services.

6. Realtors: Send area realtors subscriptions to your client newsletter and copies of your business card and practice brochure. Encourage them to give these to homeowners new to your area who are in need of your services.

7. Displays: Approach appropriate retail stores, clinics, recreation centers, and other outlets in your community where you might display copies of your business card, practice brochure, and client newsletter (with the subscription cards described in Chapter 11).

Successful application: One dentist who stresses prevention in his practice placed his newsletter in area health-food stores, as people who are interested in nutrition would be good candidates for his practice. At least five stores now carry the newsletter and store customers are taking it home with them. Another practitioner places free copies of his client newsletter in the lounge of his local Y. Other places to consider leaving your materials (with permission, of course, and depending on your profession and area of practice) are

a.   Staff lounges and cafeterias in local companies.

b.   Teachers' lounges and cafeterias in area schools.

c.   Health and tennis clubs.

d.   College dining halls, student unions, dorm lounges.

e.   Senior citizen centers.

f.   Community clubs (Elks, Lions, Kiwanis, the area business association).

g.   The reception area of other practitioners related to your field. A pediatrician might arrange to leave copies of his patient newsletter in the reception area of a nearby OBG specialist or with a Lamaze instructor. An accountant and lawyer who work with similar clients might display brochures and newsletters belonging to each other. Two professionals practicing in the same building may produce a newsletter jointly. (A dentist and optometrist doing this have reported good results.)

8. Letters to colleagues: Consider writing to colleagues who also serve your clients to provide useful information.

Successful application: One dentist writes to physicians who treat his patients to tell when he saw the patient and the conditions he found and treated at that time (restorations, condition of the gums, blood pressure reading). Such a letter may also prove useful for optometrists, dermatologists, chiropractors, or OBG specialists to demonstrate concern and provide a common ground between you and the primary-care physician, who may be a potential source of referrals.

Tip: When a new patient first registers at your office, request the name of his physician. When writing to the physician for the first time, introduce yourself, enclose your practice brochure and ask to be informed of any medical history information which the physician feels is relevant to your concerns (see sample letter 13, Appendix B).

9. Colleague newsletter subscriptions: Send a complimentary subscription to your client newsletter and your practice brochure to all area practitioners who could be a source of referrals to your practice.

10. Cooperation: Start a local multiprofessions marketing cooperative with other practitioners in your area. Share marketing ideas and experiences. Organize joint external marketing activities — health fairs, career days, and other events described in Chapter 16. Getting to know one another often leads to referrals.

11. New practitioners: Write a "Congratulations and Welcome to the Area" letter to all new practitioners in your area, especially if they have the potential to be referral sources.

12. Stores: Shop and conduct private business in the stores nearest your practice. Leave your card and a subscription to your client newsletter with store owners and clerks. The nearby dry cleaner or restaurateur may reciprocate by referring a client in need of your service, or may become a client himself.

13. Post names: One practitioner publishes the names of specialists to whom she refers her clients. In return, she requests that these specialists post a list of their referring practitioners where clients may see it.

14. Specialists' newsletter: If you are in a specialty practice, consider publishing a quarterly newsletter for general practitioners who are or could be referral sources.

Successful application: A periodontist sends a two-page letter to general dentists, with each issue focusing on one important topic.

TWO MANUAL SYSTEMS FOR TRACKING REFERRALS

A successful marketer never fails to give credit for a referral, regardless of the source. That is why it is essential for you to establish systems for tracking referrals.

Tip: Tracking referrals with a computer is relatively quick and many programs are designed to do this easily. Manual tracking, on the other hand, takes time and requires follow-through. If your practice is not on a computer, delegate responsibility for the manual tracking systems described below to your business assistant or marketing coordinator.

System 1: Track Referrals by Kind

1.   Your new client registration form, receptionist, business assistant, or marketing coordinator should ask this question of every new client: "Can you tell us who referred you to this office or how you happened to come here?"

2.   Record the client's answer in his or her permanent record.

NEW CLIENT SOURCE ANALYSIS SHEET

Week/Month of __FEBRUARY__, 19 __86__

Source of New Clients	Tally Workspace	Number
Client Referrals	~~HHt~~ ~~HHt~~ //	12
Staff Referrals	~~HHt~~ //	7
Professional Referrals	////	4
Other Referrals	////	4
Advertising (if any). List separately: Yellow Pages, radio, newspaper	~~HHt~~ ~~HHt~~ //	12
Other. List each external marketing activity separately: press release, open house, speeches, office tour	~~HHt~~ ~~HHt~~ ///	13
TOTAL		52

3.   Have the person tracking referrals prepare a new client source analysis. Conduct a weekly analysis if you have a high volume of new clients, a monthly analysis if you have fewer new clients. Set up a tally sheet with categories for the *types* of persons, organizations, and events that are responsible for referring clients to you. Use the sample on page 176 as a guide.

4.   Review your analysis sheet each week or month to determine the sources for the bulk of your referrals. Decide which sources are worth developing further and which are not.

System 2: Track Referrals by Person or Organization

In addition to knowing the types of referral sources you are getting, you will also need to know the names of the specific people who make referrals each week so you can thank them. To track referrals by person or organization

1.   Create an alphabetical index card file for tracking referral sources.

2.   Each week, have the person tracking referrals gather all the names of that week's new clients and the people or organizations they say are responsible for referring them to you.

3.   Next, create a referral history card for each referral source:

REFERRAL HISTORY

SYLVESTER, JOHN   *CLIENT*
(Name)   (Relationship)

Referred	Date	Acknowledgment
1. SANDY ROSEMAN	12/9/84	LETTER
2. CINDY JORDAN	3/15/85	LETTER AND CALL
3.		

In the upper left-hand corner, write the referrer's name, last name first. In the upper right, his relationship to your practice: client, staff member, former staff member, other practitioner, pharmacist, local businessperson, personnel manager of an area employer, realtor, etc. Under "Referred" and "Date" list the name of the new client who was referred to your practice and the date of that client's first appointment. The "Acknowledgment" column is where you will record the way you acknowledged the referral (telephone call, letter, and/or gift).

4.   Do not refile the referrer's card until the referral has been noted as acknowledged.

5.   Maintain the index card tracking system weekly so acknowledgments are prompt and cards are refiled quickly.

Tip: Some practitioners duplicate clients' referral histories into their permanent files. That way they can thank a client for the referral again in person at the next appointment.

ACKNOWLEDGING AND REWARDING REFERRALS

We've already considered in Chapter 5 the ways to reward *staff* for referrals: cash incentives and referral contests. In Chapter 6 we explored the ways to thank *clients* for referrals: handwritten thank-you notes, phone calls, and gifts. How should you acknowledge and reward colleagues, other professionals, and others in your community for referrals?

This is obviously a delicate area where your own philosophy and image are extremely important. Rule of thumb: Acknowledge external referrals in the nicest way you can that you feel is appropriate. Perhaps for you that will mean a personal phone call or visit. It may mean a nice, handwritten note of heartfelt thanks. For some, it may even mean a gift.

The important thing to remember about referrals: Whether or not you give gifts, acknowledge *every* referral you get from any source. That is the surest way to motivate future referrals and one of the essentials of building any professional practice.

P·A·R·T 4

Developing and Implementing A Marketing Plan

C · H · A · P · T · E · R   18

How to Develop Your Three-Year Marketing Plan

T he potential for building your practice is enormous. You have just studied the array of marketing projects that have worked for others. Learning about these projects and how to implement them is the first step to building the kind of practice you've always wanted.

But beware! This is the point at which many practitioners make their biggest mistake. So often a practitioner reads or hears about a project that has worked for someone else. Motivated and enthusiastic, he plunges ahead on it before mapping out the big picture. Later he finds that it didn't work out as well as he had hoped.

Sure you can pick marketing projects at random or on a whim. You can jump into a project because it sounds good or because a colleague swears by it. Maybe luck will be on your side and you'll achieve the kinds of results you want. But why leave marketing to luck when you can put the odds in your favor? Bet on a sure thing. Plan and coordinate your marketing efforts.

Practitioners often ask which projects they should do first, how many they should tackle at once, and how much they should spend on each project. There is no one answer to these questions. The first priority is to assess your current situation, to see what you have now. Next, you must set long-term personal goals for yourself and your practice. Finally, consider specific marketing projects that would help you attain those goals. This chapter leads you through this three-stage planning process.

STEP 1: ASSESS YOUR CURRENT PRACTICE

The first step in creating a successful marketing plan is to assess your current situation. If you don't know what you've already got, how can you know what you want or what is possible?

The kinds of things you need to know about your current practice are

1. Financial health: What are your current gross and net incomes? What is the breakdown of your overhead? What are your current debts? Do you anticipate any substantial necessary expenses in the next year?

2. Current clients: How many clients do you now see per week? Who are they? How satisfied are they with your current practice? How do they perceive your image? How successful is your current recall system? (Internal market research can answer these questions.)

3. Potential clients: Who are they? Where are they? What kinds of services do they need and want? (External market research can answer these questions.)

4. Competition: Who are your competitors? Where are their practices? What kinds of marketing projects are they currently using? (Again, external market research can answer these questions.)

5. Current referral sources: Who are they? How many clients do they now refer? Who else could be a source of referrals? (A referral source analysis can answer these questions.)

6. Staff: How many staff members do you currently employ? How much do you pay them? How many hours do they work? How do they spend their time? What are their strengths and weaknesses?

7. Time: How many hours per week do you now work? How much of that time is spent with clients? Doing what? How much of your time now goes to administrative duties? To marketing? To continuing education? To waste?

STEP 2: DETERMINE YOUR LONG-TERM PERSONAL GOALS

What do you really want from your practice? It's difficult for some practitioners to answer this question honestly because external pressures are so strong. But honest goals will be the underlying strength of your marketing plan. Try to ignore society's expectations of you — what others tell you about how hard you should work, how much money you should make, what you should do with your time. Set goals for your practice that will really make you happy. Be honest as you answer these questions.

1. How much money do you want to make?

2. How many hours per week do you want to work?

3. What kind of work do you want to do and what do you not want to do in your practice?

4. What types of clients do you really want to have?

5. How large a practice do you want?

6. What kind of physical office do you want?

7. Do you want to be in solo or group practice?

8. How much personal control do you want over your practice? Can you be happy delegating control over major decisions to others?

9. Do you want to be in the limelight?

10. How important is peer approval to you?

STEP 3: CREATE A PLAN TO HELP YOU ATTAIN YOUR GOALS

A good marketing plan will take your practice from what it is now to what you would like it to be. It has the following characteristics:

1. A good plan is specific: It accounts for specific budgets and time-frames.

2. A good plan is realistic: It relies on the truth of your situation and resources.

3. A good plan is aimed at your goals: A plan that brings you *more* clients, hours, money, and work is not successful unless it brings you the *kinds* of clients, hours, money, and work you truly want.

4. A good plan is flexible enough to meet your changing needs: For instance, today's goal may be to attract more clients of any kind. Tomorrow you may want only certain types of clients. A good plan will account for this change.

5. A good plan fits your management style: Some people like to tackle one project at a time from beginning to end. Others are happier working on several projects at once in phases. Either approach can be successful. A good plan will allow you to work the way that makes you most comfortable.

6. A good plan is comprehensive: The individual projects described in this *Guide* are the components of a marketing plan, but a plan is much more. A good plan accounts for a budget, coordinated efforts, timing, prerequisites, phases of major projects, generating funds for more expensive projects, and methods of monitoring progress.

Narrow Your Choice of Projects

With your current practice analysis and your goals in mind, your next step will be to consider which projects from the many described in this *Guide* can best help you achieve your goals. To begin this process:

1. Review this list of the major projects we've studied.

    - Conduct a client feedback survey.
    - Conduct a client file analysis.
    - Establish a client complaint record.
    - Gather other organizations' external market research.
    - Survey potential clients.
    - Learn about competitors.
    - Choose a practice name.
    - Choose a practice slogan.
    - Choose a new practice location.
    - Choose new areas of specialty or special services.
    - Establish new office hours.
    - Change your appearance.
    - Redecorate your office.
    - Add new, unusual attractions to your reception area.
    - Set new telephone policies.
    - Set new appointment policies.
    - Conduct better case consultations.
    - Set new fee policies.
    - Make better financial arrangements.
    - Set new insurance policies.
    - Increase recall effectiveness.
    - Establish new follow-up procedures.
    - Hire good marketing people for your staff.
    - Create marketing incentives for your staff.
    - Hire a marketing coordinator.

- Roll out the red carpet for clients (fifty ways).
- Design a practice logo.
- Design new practice stationery.
- Design new office signs.
- Create a practice brochure.
- Create a client newsletter.
- Encourage and reinforce referrals from clients.
- Encourage and reinforce referrals from staff.
- Encourage and reinforce referrals from colleagues.
- Conduct a referral source analysis.
- Write press releases to publicize your practice.
- Suggest feature articles to newspaper editors.
- Write fillers for newspapers.
- Write letters to the editor.
- Supply material to editorial staff.
- Become a local expert for the media.
- Write articles for in-house publications.
- Write public service announcements.
- Hold a press conference.
- Publicize events through community calendars.
- Schedule live media interviews.
- Become a popular public speaker in your community.
- Sponsor your own client seminars.
- Hold an open house.
- Give office tours.
- Hold client appreciation events.
- Put on an educational fair.
- Hold an art show or opening in your office.
- Arrange a music concert in your reception area.
- Donate books to libraries and schools.
- Create displays for public places.
- Sponsor scholarships and awards.
- Declare your own holiday.

- Sponsor a children's sports team and other groups.
- Raise funds for charity.
- Send materials to teachers.
- Participate in career programs.
- Run contests for current and potential clients.
- Develop unusual office decor.

2.   List priority projects from this list — the ones that seem to you to be must-do's.

3.   List the projects you'd like to do in the next three years but that are not essential.

4.   Include all the prerequisites for these projects if they are not already on your lists. For example, if a logo is on your list, be sure to include a name and slogan for your practice. These will be part of your new logo.

5.   Important: If you have any doubts about a project, check with your state board or professional association for its opinions or guidelines.

6.   Now using the system below, evaluate the resources you need for each of these projects and the project's priority. Try to limit your analysis to no more than ten top-priority projects.

Evaluate Individual Projects with an Analysis Worksheet

1.   Anticipate the kinds of finished results you expect from your top ten projects. There may be great differences in the time and money a project requires, depending on your expectations. For instance, the budget required for a complete office remodeling will be greater than that for a simple paint job; a slick eight-panel brochure will cost more than a modest four-panel one; a full-time marketing coordinator will cost more than one who works part-time.

2.   Investigate the time and money you will need to invest in each of your top ten projects. Some of this information may require digging and meeting with outside help to get estimates (graphic artists, printers, interior decorators, and other sources of help described in Appendix A). Delegate as much of this investigative work as possible.

3.   For each project, referring back to the previous chapters for information, complete a *Project Analysis Worksheet.*

PROJECT ANALYSIS WORKSHEET

PROJECT:_____

Steps/ Phases/ Tasks	Person in Charge & Estimated Man-Hours	Estimated Amount of Your Time	Add'l Staff & Time	Weeks to Complete	Estimated Budget
TOTAL					

Establish Annual Budgets for Time and Money

Now that you know approximately how much money and time it will take to accomplish your top ten projects, see what kinds of time and money you have to work with.

1. Money: It is usually a good general rule of thumb to budget approximately 4 percent to 6 percent of your gross income from the practice for marketing projects. This is only a guideline. You must decide for yourself what you think is a reasonable amount.

2. Time: There is no rule of thumb about how much time per week you and your staff should spend on marketing. The best way to decide how much time you have to spare is to analyze what you're doing now. Use time logs if you're in doubt about the way you and your staff spend your time. Consider how much time you would like to spend on marketing and on other activities. Allot enough time to handle your success. For instance, if people come in the door as the result of a press release or newsletter, be sure you have the time to see them. Consider shifting staff duties to free the right person for the right project.

Eleven Down-to-Earth Tips for Reconciling Your Budget and Projects

Creating a three-year marketing plan is more art than science. No one scheme will work for everyone, but there are eleven basic principles.

1.   Maintain your priorities. Schedule and budget for the most important projects first.

2.   Make conservative cost estimates. Don't underbudget so you can't finish a project you've already started.

3.   Be prepared for success. Have the time and staff to handle new clients and inquiries that result from projects.

4.   Make compromises but only those you really want to live with. If you must have a deluxe practice brochure, don't settle for anything less, even if you must wait another six months before you can afford it.

5.   Consider splitting projects into phases. For instance, redecorating, stationery, and staff changes can be accomplished over time. In some cases you may need to generate more money before tackling the expensive projects.

6.   Tackle projects in order if they require it. For instance, be sure you don't redecorate your office and print new stationery and then decide your location is all wrong for you.

7.   Be realistic about your talents. Plan to get outside professional help if you lack needed skills.

8.   Anticipate seasonal variations in your time and money. For instance, accounting practices will need to plan a marketing schedule around the busy tax season.

9.   Consider optimal times for the projects you undertake. You may achieve a better turnout if you schedule your open house the weekend of a community festival or link it to a holiday.

10.   Don't paint yourself into a corner. Give yourself breathing space for projects that have firm ending dates. Don't plan down to the wire if you need certain projects completed by certain dates.

11.   Seek staff input on your plan. They can be very helpful if you are having trouble deciding between two projects. Staff participation in the decision will motivate them to be more involved in the project.

Map Out a Three-Year Marketing Plan

Using your list of top-priority projects, worksheets, budget and time considerations, and situation analysis, map out a three-year plan. It should include

1.   Specific starting and ending dates for each project.

2.   The person responsible for each project, phase by phase, if needed.

3.   Support inside and outside the practice for each project.

4.   Budget estimates and restrictions.

Depending on your situation, projects may be scheduled to overlap or you can schedule them in a chain, one after the other. If you have trouble formulating your plan

1.   Review your must-do projects. Are they all top priorities or can some wait?

2.   Where are you hung up? Is the problem with your time? Staff time? Money? Setting priorities?

3.   Look for flexibility. For example, can you be satisfied with a more modest result? Can you hire outsiders to help? Can you delay projects or undertake them in phases?

4.   When there is no choice, delay one or more projects until you have more time or money. If you succeed with a few projects this year and increase your practice gross, you'll have more money for marketing next year. Maybe you can undertake more costly projects then.

How to Put Your Plan into Action

1.   Tell your staff about your plan. Make your goals their goals. Hold meetings regularly to keep them involved. Devise incentive programs that will encourage a marketing attitude. If a staff member takes on additional marketing duties, be sure to change the job description and salary accordingly.

2.   Periodically review your progress with your staff. Discuss marketing duties at regular performance review sessions. Also discuss progress at staff meetings and in memos.

3.   Keep records of the money and time spent on each project as you go.

4.   Review the effectiveness of projects and revise your marketing plan. Although you will be planning marketing activities for three years, you will need to take a situation analysis every three months and revise the plan. Your goals and budget may change as you succeed — or don't — with earlier projects.

5.   Get client feedback on projects. Plan to conduct a client feedback survey at least annually. Also pay attention to informal comments from clients about the marketing projects you undertake.

6.   Whatever happens, maintain your own enthusiasm. A positive attitude will help your marketing plan succeed.

SOME FINAL THOUGHTS ABOUT MARKETING

1.   Marketing can help you build the kind of practice you've always wanted, but it's the means, not the end. Although successful marketing has its rewards and pleasures, your ultimate objective is to practice your profession. Remember this, even when you are in the midst of a challenging and time-consuming marketing project.

2.   Analyze marketing problems from all viewpoints. Be open-minded and seek input from staff and clients.

3.   Don't be afraid to be unique. Expressing your personality through your practice, particularly in your marketing efforts, can be fun and fulfilling.

4.   Successful marketing may bring about many changes in your practice, but even positive changes can be stressful. Minimize stress by anticipating and planning for change. Take steps to avoid burnout in you and your staff. Enjoy your successes and plan rewards.

5.   Provide quality services and present an honest picture of your practice in your marketing. There is no substitute for the truth.

6.   The road to success, like love and most New York City streets, has its bumps. Be patient and take the long view. Everyone makes mistakes, so don't dwell on them. Just learn from them and keep going.

A·P·P·E·N·D·I·X   A

Employing Others to Carry Out Marketing Projects

You may need to hire the talents and skills of outside individuals to carry out many of the marketing projects in this *Guide*. The best way to find qualified help is through the enthusiastic recommendation of someone you trust who has worked with that individual or firm. However, if such a recommendation is not available, try the following procedure for finding suitable outside help:

1. Be on the lookout: Seek the services of someone whose work you have seen and admired. If you need a sign company, look for signs you like in your town and ask the owners who designed them. If you need a graphic artist, look for logos, ads, and brochures you especially like and ask the owners for the artists' names.

2. Call trade organizations: If you cannot find an individual whose work you admire, contact the trade associations or other organizations to which they would belong (the American Institute of Architects, for example). These organizations are usually listed in the phone book or your librarian can help you find them. If not, call one individual in the field to get the name or number of suitable organizations. Although not as direct as a personal recommendation from a friend, trade associations usually establish qualifications for their membership and will not recommend individuals who are unethical or whose work has been substandard in the past.

3. Pay a critical visit: Visit the office of anyone you consider hiring. Is it organized? Clean? Are you greeted and handled courteously and professionally? If not, look for help elsewhere.

4. Request proof of ability: Ask for: (a) the individual's or firm's credentials, (b) examples of previous work, and (c) the names of at least three previous clients you may call as references.

5. Ask for a clear statement of fees: Ask for a fee schedule or structure (usually an hourly rate, retainer, per project fee, or some combination). For large projects, ask for a cost breakdown separating labor from materials.

6. Check references: Call the references. Ask if they were satisfied with the work they had done and whether cost estimates were accurate.

Tip: If you are given a long list of references, call the last ones. The first few are likely to be the most enthusiastic clients; the last may represent the feelings of *most* clients more accurately.

7. Interview several candidates: If you have any doubts about the individual or firm, repeat the steps above for several more. Choose the best.

8. Have a written agreement: Once you've decided to hire an outside individual or firm, put all your agreements in a written contract. This should include fees, financial arrangements, the work to be done, guarantees and specific due dates or deadlines, and a termination clause in case either party wants to end the relationship.

9. Develop personal contact: When hiring a firm, insist on a particular individual who will be your liaison. Also try to limit the number of people who will perform work for you.

Idea in action: If you were satisfied with the graphic artist who designed your logo, ask for the same artist for your brochure, newsletter, and subsequent graphic design needs.

The remainder of this appendix should help you get a better idea of the available services. Actual firms or individuals in your area may cover several categories or may vary on the degree and type of services provided.

Advertising Agency

Marketing projects: Developing an advertising plan and market analysis, designing and placing ads in the correct media, creating many nonadvertising projects such as a slogan, logo, and press releases.

Seek referrals for an ad agency from media sales representatives, directories, and advertising publications such as the *Agency Red Book* available in most libraries. Most of the larger agencies belong to the American Association of Advertising Agencies, which has a standard of service for its members.

Architect

Marketing projects: Office remodeling and additions, new construction, landscaping.

Seek the names of qualified architects through the local chapter of the American Institute of Architects. Architects specialize, so choose one with experience in professional office design, or if that is not available in your area, small business design.

An architect analyzes your problems, advises you on costs, and supplies you with sketches of your proposed front, the layout of interior space, the designs, and the arrangements of fixtures. Architects' drawings should be so complete that builders will be able to submit bids on all or part of the proposed construction. The architect should assist you in securing, reviewing, and determining bids, and should also check to ensure that the builder is conforming to plans and schedules.

Builders

Marketing projects: Office remodeling and additions, new construction.

On small contracts lasting less than four or five weeks, most builders will not expect payment until after completion of the work. On bigger jobs, a builder is likely to ask for interim payments as the work progresses. Some tips about working with builders:

1. Before remodeling work starts, completely clear the rooms likely to be affected.

2. Agree with the builder on a convenient place where ladders, scaffold boards, and other equipment and materials can be stored during the project.

3. Set aside reasonable accommodations for the crew to have lunch, or to shelter if the weather is bad and they are working outside.

4. Make sure the crew has access to the services they need — water, electricity, a bathroom.

Graphic Artist

Marketing projects: Design of a logo, stationery, brochure, newsletter, posters, T-shirts, signs, displays, giveaways.

Graphic artists may be free-lance, part of a graphic design studio, or employees of a print shop, public relations firm, or ad agency with an in-house graphic arts department. Try to develop a relationship with one artist who will learn about your preferences and situation and can be called upon to help you with all your design needs.

Local art schools and the art departments of universities may be able to recommend qualified graphic artists. Be sure to hire a *graphic* artist (not a watercolorist or sculptor who lacks graphics experience).

Interior Decorators/Designers/Landscapers

Marketing projects: Office decor, lighting design, landscaping.

Most of the top interior designers and landscapers calculate their fees as a percentage of the total job. *Caution:* Many people claim to be designers or landscapers. Some are talented and able; others aren't. Insist on seeing many examples of a decorator's or landscaper's work and a list of references. Find out exactly how much the bill will be and what it includes.

Lettershops

Marketing projects: Stuffing and mailing newsletters, brochures, and other large marketing mailings.

Lettershops will work on a project, or per-piece, basis and can be called upon to help with large mailings. A good lettershop can get a mailing out quickly and inexpensively. Your printer may have an in-house lettershop, or you can look in the Yellow Pages under "Mail," "Fulfillment," or "Lettershop Services."

Management or Marketing Consultant

Marketing projects: New policies and office procedures, staff management and training, client management, market research and activities.

The greatest contribution a management or marketing consultant can make to your marketing plan is experience. The consultant has seen your problem or a variant of it and has devised solutions to it or will know of solutions employed by previous clients. A good consultant should be a living compendium of case studies. Be sure to choose one with lots of experience with others in your profession. The cost of a consulting job depends on its scope, but many consultants charge a per diem rate. Some work on a retainer.

Photographer

Marketing projects: Photographs of special events, you, members of the staff, and clients, for press releases, feature articles, client newsletters, practice brochures, office bulletin boards, displays, calendar giveaways, advertising.

The most convenient way to get photographs is to take them yourself or have one of your assistants take them. Ideally, your marketing coordinator should have skill with a camera. However, if you have no one on staff capable of taking good journalistic-quality photos, consider hiring a moonlighting press photographer. She is likely to have experience taking good publicity shots that will appeal to newspaper editors and your audience. To find and work with the right person

1.   Call your local newspaper directly and ask for the darkroom. Tell the person who answers the phone what you are looking for. Chances are, she will be interested or know someone who is.

2.   Advise the photographer you hire that she will not be able to have credit lines with her work. Most newspapers will not give credit lines to nonstaff photographers.

3.   Unless you specify otherwise in writing, the photographer will own the negative, although she will sell you the actual physical prints. This can work against you if you ever want to use one of her publicity photos in an ad. Technically, you will need the photographer's permission to do so, and often you must pay an additional fee.

Tip: Prepare a written agreement saying that you buy all rights to the photos you commission. Have the photographer sign it when you hire her.

Printer

Marketing projects: Printing of stationery, brochures, newsletters, posters, handouts for speeches, giveaways.

For most marketing projects you will need the services of a commercial printer, not a quick-copy shop. Choose a printer who has the equipment to fold all finished pieces for you. Many print shops have in-house graphic arts departments and lettershops. These are desirable since they can design, print, and mail your marketing materials for you all under one roof.

Public Relations Firm

Marketing projects: Developing a comprehensive public relations program, media publicity, logo and stationery design, practice slogan and brochures, market research, suggestions for improving office appearance, client newsletters, lining up speaking engagements.

Established public relations firms usually shun "one-shot" arrangements such as placing a single newspaper story. Most prefer to develop a comprehensive public relations program for their clients. A common fee arrangement is a one-time start-up fee (for which the firm learns about your practice and develops a plan) followed by a fixed monthly retainer. Some firms may work by the hour or project; few will accept fees based on the success of the publicity they generate.

Sign Company

Marketing projects: Exterior office signs, interior office signs, signs for special events.

Make an appointment for a sign company representative to visit your office and observe first-hand your sign needs and situation. Discuss at that visit your logo, image, proposed designs, sign permit obligations, maintenance and leasing contracts, financial arrangements, your state association and local sign codes, the need for a variance, and the legal proceedings to obtain one.

You may ask for sketches of suggested designs from several companies (although you must expect to pay for this extra service). Most sign companies will provide a written contract and quote a price for each of their designs. Some companies will allow you to purchase a design whether or not they fabricate and install the sign(s).

Writer

Marketing projects: Writing and editing letters, brochures, client newsletters, press releases, letters to the editor, filler articles, public service announcements, special event handouts, speeches, classified ads for new staff — all written materials.

The names of qualified free-lance writers may be obtained from local universities and publications. Look for writers with *business* writing experience (not creative writing only). Writers usually work on a per-project or hourly basis. For a continuing project such as a client newsletter, the per-project fee generally contains costs and encourages the writer to be efficient.

Tip: When structuring a per-project fee arrangement, include the cost of some revision in the initial fee. This will discourage the writer from dashing off your project in a hurry in an attempt to do less work or charge you additional fees for each revision.

A · P · P · E · N · D · I · X   B

Sample Written Materials to Build Your Practice

1: New Client Welcome Letter (with Brochure)

Dear Mrs. Client:

Welcome to Family Practice Associates! We are so pleased that you have chosen us and pledge to provide you with the very best services possible.

We have produced a client information brochure to help answer any questions you may have. Enclosed is your personal copy. Please keep it and refer to it whenever you have a question about our office procedures. And please, if you ever have a question that is not answered in the brochure, give us a call and we'll be happy to answer it for you personally.

Again, welcome to our practice. We look forward to meeting you at your first appointment on Thursday, September 24, at 3:45.

2: Appreciation Letter to an Established Client

Dear Mrs. Client:

Just as old friends are the best friends, so are established clients our best clients.

It is possible that you give little thought to the fact that Family Practice has served you for some time. To us, however, it is vital— indeed it is our entire existence.

In these busy times it seems to us appropriate to stop

occasionally and think of the people in our practice. This prompts us to write you for no other reason than to tell you how much we appreciate and value your continued loyalty throughout the years.

3: Appreciation Letter to an Established Client (from a Physician)

Dear Mrs. Client:

My staff and I would like to thank you sincerely for your continued trust in our ability to maintain your family's health. Loyal patients like you are our most valuable resource. We wouldn't be here without you.

Your continued confidence in us has enabled us to expand our facility and to add another staff member to serve you better. We now have four examination rooms and an additional receptionist at our front desk, Melissa Barton. We have also expanded our hours and are now available by appointment weekday mornings beginning at 7:00 A.M.

Again, we thank you for placing your confidence in us and pledge to do our very best to continue to earn it. It's a pleasure to serve you.

4: Thanksgiving Appreciation Letter to an Established Client (from a Lawyer)

Dear Mrs. Client:

The mail you receive from our office is usually related to appointment scheduling, special announcements, legal matters, or bills. This is a different type of letter.

We feel that we have a lot to be thankful for this Thanksgiving. One of those things is the pleasure we derive from serving nice people like you. Thank you for choosing us for your legal needs; we do appreciate your trust in us.

Happy Thanksgiving to you and your family.

5: Appreciation Letter to a Long-Term Client

Dear Mrs. Client:

The other day I was looking through our records and noticed that you have been our client for nearly twelve years.

The purpose of this letter is to say "thank you." As you know, we have always done our best to provide you and your family with the finest services possible. You, in turn, have rewarded us with your trust and confidence.

It is a pleasure to have loyal clients and I wanted you to know how pleased I am with our longstanding relationship.

6: Handwritten Congratulatory Note to a Client Starting a New Business

Dear Mrs. Client,

I enjoyed hearing about your new business venture. If anyone can succeed I'm sure it's you.

Congratulations and best wishes for success.

7: Handwritten Appreciation Note to a Client Completing a Treatment or Service (from an Optometrist)

Dear Mrs. Client,

Just a note to thank you for being so cooperative and pleasant while we were fitting your contact lenses. We enjoyed serving you and having the opportunity to get to know you better.

We look forward to seeing you again in January for your regular examination.

8: Letter to Parents of a Teenage Client

Dear Mr. and Mrs. Client:

These days it seems that the only time we hear anything, it's bad news. It is indeed a pleasure to give credit where it is due. I'd like to compliment you regarding your son, Joseph.

Joseph is one of the finest teenagers in our practice. He is always courteous and, frankly, I wish I could serve more young people like him.

Congratulations — you have done an extraordinary job!

9: Handwritten Note to a New Child Patient

Dear Johnny,

Thank you so much for your visit to our office the other day. We all enjoyed meeting you and hearing about your activities in the Cub Scouts and your part in your school play.

We are looking forward to seeing you at your next visit on January 27 at 4:45. We hope you will tell us more about the Cub Scouts then.

10: Letter to a Client Who Makes Final Payment at the Completion of Extensive Treatment (from a Dentist)

Dear Mrs. Client:

Thank you very much for your final payment. It has been our pleasure to treat you over the past eight months. We appreciate your promptness and cooperation throughout the treatment and want you to know that you are truly a special patient to us.

We have enclosed several of our business cards and hope that you will feel free to recommend us to any of your friends and acquaintances who are in need of quality dentistry. If you can think of any ways that we can improve upon our services, we hope you will share your ideas with us. We do value your opinion.

Concern for your dental health remains our top priority, and we look forward to seeing you again in August for your periodic examination. We also urge you to continue with the home hygiene program that we have begun. Preventive dentistry is very important, especially for patients who have had previous problems. We want you to continue to enjoy the benefits of a healthy mouth.

11: Letter to Client Suggesting New Services (from an Optometrist)

Dear Mrs. Client:

One of the advantages of having our own in-office computer system is that it allows us to select patients who meet certain criteria. According to the information we obtained from your last visual analysis, you may be a good candidate for either daily or extended-wear contact lenses.

Here is some information regarding contact lenses you may find interesting:

• We inventory over 1,000 contact lenses representing eight different manufacturers. Thus we can fit you quickly and easily.

• Extended-wear lenses are worn 24 hours a day for one month at a time. They are an extremely popular choice of our patients. I have worn these lenses for nearly three years and feel that their recent improvements certainly make them an attractive option.

• I specialize in contact lenses and am a member of the American Optometric Association Section on Contact Lenses.

• Our complimentary trial fitting allows you to experience the sensation of contact lenses at no charge or obligation.

My goal is to provide the best contact lens care and service to my patients. If you would like to become one of the millions of people now wearing contact lenses, call our office or stop by to schedule an appointment.

12: Condolence Letter to a Deceased Client's Family (from an Optometrist)

Dear Mrs. _____:

I was Larry's optometrist for several years, and it is with a real sense of loss that I heard the news. Please do not hesitate to call on me if I may be of assistance. All my sympathy.

13: Letter to a Physician Regarding a Mutual Patient

Dear Dr. _____ :

I am beginning treatment for (patient's name) and would appreciate hearing from you if there is anything in his or her medical history of which I should be aware.

Thank you for your help.

14: Letter to a Nonclient Who Has Requested a Complimentary Subscription to Your Client Newsletter

Dear Mrs. Nonclient:

Thank you for your interest in our practice newsletter, the *Thompkins Associates Review,* which is published quarterly for our clients. It is our pleasure to provide you with a one-year complimentary subscription. As you requested, we are enclosing our most recent issue. The next *Review* is scheduled for publication in early April.

For your information, we are also enclosing a copy of our client information brochure which describes Thompkins Associates' services, philosophy, and facilities. Please refer to it for any questions you may have about our practice. Should you ever have a question that is not answered in the brochure, give us a call and we'll be happy to answer it for you personally.

Again, thank you for your interest in the *Review.* We hope you enjoy your subscription.

15: Letter to an Inactive Client

Dear Mrs. Client:

Nobody wants to lose a valued friend. I like to regard all our patients as friends . . . and treat them as such. So when I realized that it has been two years since we have seen you and that all our attempts to schedule a periodic examination for you have been unsuccessful, I felt disturbed, and sad.

Right now we are offering a special reduced fee to all new patients on their first examination (explain the discount). I would like to extend this same courtesy to you in a final attempt to renew our relationship.

Won't you call Mary today to schedule an examination appointment? We are looking forward to hearing from you, and I hope we will see you again.

16: Letter to an Inactive Client

Dear Mrs. Client:

We'd grown accustomed to your face, your coming in for your appointments . . . and we liked the idea of seeing you regularly.

What happened?

Please let us know if anything about our services has disappointed you. We'll rectify it immediately because we would like to see you back among our clients again.

17: Letter to an Inactive Client (from an Accountant)

Dear Mrs. Client:

The other day, while browsing through our records, I noticed to my dismay that it has been quite a long time since we have heard from you.

Naturally, this would disturb any accounting firm that values established clients and is proud of a reputation for providing the finest service. It certainly bothered me—enough so that I'm sending you this letter.

Have we failed you in any way? Has something gone wrong that I know nothing about? I certainly would like to know the reason our relationship with you has dwindled so. What can we do to renew that relationship?

Few things are more disappointing to us than the loss of a valued client. So if anything is wrong . . . if there is anything I can do to rectify any misunderstanding that has occurred . . . please do not hesitate to tell me about it.

I am looking forward to hearing from you very soon so that we can resume our former friendly relationship.

18: Letter to Publicize Instructional Services (from a Veterinarian)

Dear Mrs. Client:

As part of our celebration of National Pet Week, my staff and I have developed a collection of instructional materials regarding the importance of proper nutrition in support of animal health. We now have a terrific selection of materials on the subject, including some excellent free brochures and booklets. Please feel welcome to stop in, browse our bookshelf, and pick up some free material.

Thank you for entrusting the health-care needs of your pet to me in the past. Please call my office for further information regarding this or any other matter with which we may be of help.

19: Letter to a Local Teacher to Provide Free Materials for the Class (from a Dentist)

Dear Teacher:

As an elementary school teacher, surely you are concerned about the dental health of the children in your class. But did you know that children should make their first visit to the dentist at age two or three? That's right. Studies show that *half of all two-year-olds* have some tooth decay. Yet I'll bet there are some children in your class who have never been to the dentist.

With today's advancements in preventive dental care and the existence of fluoridated water and fluoride treatments, there is really no reason why children cannot keep their teeth all their lives. But we must reach them—and teach them—at an early age to follow good dental habits.

The enclosed coloring books were designed by the American Dental Association as a child educational tool on dental care. I hope you can use them in your classroom as an enjoyable way to teach children good dental habits.

I will be happy to supply you with additional copies if you need them. Good luck!

20: Handwritten Thank-You Note to a Client Who Has Made a Referral to the Practice

Dear Mrs. Client,

I want to thank you for referring _____ to my practice. I always appreciate such referrals and the trust that they imply. Your recommendation means a great deal to me. To show my appreciation, I am enclosing a gift certificate from _____.

P.S. As a growing practice, we would be pleased to serve any other friends or family members you may wish to recommend.

21: Letter to Potential Referrals Sources (Colleagues, Pharmacists, Health-Food Stores) Offering a Complimentary Subscription to Your Client Newsletter

Dear _____:

Every three months, my office publishes an informational newsletter called _____. The newsletter is sent to all our clients and to others like yourself who we think might find it interesting.

If, after reading this issue, you would like to receive a complimentary one-year subscription, just return the enclosed business reply card and we'll add your name to our mailing list. There is no fee or obligation.

22: Letter Inviting a Client to an Open House

Dear Mrs. Client:

You are cordially invited to attend the Family Practice open house on Saturday, June 17, from noon until 4:00 P.M. We have reserved a special gift for you which will be waiting at the door.

And . . . we hope that you will bring a friend along to enjoy the festivities and receive a gift, too.

The occasion? We want to show off our newly remodeled facilities. As you may have noticed if you passed by our office recently, we have been undergoing major reconstruction. At last, all the work is done, the sawdust has settled, and the hammering has ended, and we can enjoy our two new treatment rooms and our redecorated reception area.

So please do come to see our "new" office and join in our celebration. (Describe features of the open house such as live entertainment, special programs, and food.) We'll be looking for you.

P.S. We've enclosed two invitations. The yellow one is for you and the green one is for your friend. Just fill them in and present them to Mary at the door to pick up the gifts we've reserved for you.

23: Letter to Neighbors during Remodeling

Dear Neighbor:

As you probably know, we're remodeling the Family Practice building. We are trying our best to have our work done with as little noise and inconvenience as possible to you who live or work in the immediate vicinity.

We're sure it will come as welcome news that the construction work is proceeding on schedule and is expected to be completed the early part of June. Your neighborly tolerance during this period will be greatly appreciated. After that, we'll be quiet neighbors once again. We sincerely hope that you will make a point of visiting the remodeled Family Practice building when it is completed.

24: Letter to a Talk Show Producer to Make Yourself Available as an Interviewee (from a Lawyer)

Dear Program Director:

As you know, people are talking about the rights of victims of crimes. While the rights of the accused have been solidly protected and vigorously defended in legislatures and courts of law, the victims of crimes have often been forgotten. However, the pendulum is now swinging in the other direction. I think your viewers might be interested in new developments involving the rights of victims.

As a practicing criminal lawyer in Springfield, I have had extensive experience in court, and I have seen what can happen to a victim who is not represented properly. I have also served on Springfield's ad hoc commission investigating the treatment of rape victims by the police department.

I would like to make myself available to you as an interviewee on ''Alive at Five'' to discuss these matters.

I am also qualified to discuss things home and business owners can do to prevent break-ins, and what they can do when their home or place of business is burglarized.

I will phone you in about a week to discuss whether I can be of service to you.

25: Letter to a Media Editor Inviting Participation at a Press Conference (from a Physician)

Dear (Editor's Name):

You've written in your editorial columns about the need for a full-range medical clinic on Belleville's east side to meet the health-care needs of residents there. Belleville Family Physicians, P.C. will announce at a press conference April 3 their plans to construct such a facility. It will be held at 11 A.M. in the George Washington room of Independence Hotel, 1776 Paul Revere Avenue.

Complete details about the construction timetable, staffing of the clinic, facilities, and financing will be discussed.

We invite you or reporters you assign to attend. A luncheon buffet will be served.

26: Letter to the Editor (from an Optometrist)

To the Editor:

With the approach of Independence Day I would like to caution Springfield citizens about the dangers of using fireworks. As a professional in the vision care field, I can tell you from personal experience that seemingly harmless, legal fireworks can cause serious eye injuries — yes, even blindness. Last year in Springfield four persons, three of them children, were treated for eye injuries due to the mishandling of fireworks.

I recommend that no children under age 16 be allowed to use fireworks without adult supervision. And while it's traditional to celebrate the Fourth with picnics and other events at which alcoholic beverages are served, adults should be especially aware that just a drink or two can make one careless with the handling and lighting of fireworks.

Let's leave fireworks displays to trained professionals this July 4th. If we do so, perhaps Springfield citizens can get through the holiday without a single eye injury.

27: Letter to Media Editor Offering to Serve As a Professional Expert or Spokesperson (from a Physician)

Dear (Editor's Name):

Delivery of medical care is undergoing a revolution that will affect every one of your readers. New modes of delivery and new organizational structures are popping up in Springfield as well as the rest of the nation.

For example, a health maintenance organization was formed here just last year. A number of doctors are planning now to form an emergency medical center that will be separate from the local hospital, and at least one major insurance company is approaching doctors to form a preferred provider organization.

Your readers, who are accustomed to the traditional fee-for-service medicine, will have questions about these new developments and how they will influence the kind of medical care they will receive. Chances are your reporters will need help in untangling the web of new terms and structures they face.

As a 1975 graduate of the University of Pennsylvania School of Medicine I would be pleased to offer my help as a spokesperson, providing the information and interpretation your staff may need when they report on local happenings in medicine. Please call me at the phone number on this letterhead at your convenience to discuss how I may be of help.

28: Letter to a Media Editor to Volunteer to Be Interviewed (from a Dentist)

Dear News Director:

Fear, procrastination, lack of funds . . . these are among the reasons that almost 50 percent of the people in the United States don't regularly see a dentist.

I'm trying to do my part to eliminate one of these—fear. People fear me, the dentist, because of pain during previous treatments, apprehension about their dental health, lack of knowledge of dentistry, and a variety of other anxieties. To ease some of this ''dental anxiety'' among children, I'll be appearing at Frost Elementary School at 11:00 on Friday, April 20.

I believe that dental fear is a good topic for your news shows. Besides dental anxiety, I could also discuss recent advancements in dentistry, dental health and hygiene, and what to do in dental emergencies.

Please contact me to schedule a time for an interview.

29: Letter to a Media Editor to Suggest an Article Idea (from a Veterinarian)

Dear (Editor's Name):

Most of your readers have probably been urged to feed the birds during the snowy season. But do they know *what* to feed them, and *when?* Are they aware that birds wintering in this area eat only certain kinds of bird food? Have your readers been told how birds might die if they are not fed regularly, once they become accustomed to being fed from other than their natural sources?

With the winter season upon us, I'd like to suggest that I contribute an article to your newspaper on this subject. As a practicing veterinarian, I feel I can provide information that will not only be helpful to your readers but also help the local bird population.

If you are interested, please call me at 555-1234 during business hours.

30: Thank-You Note to a Group to Whom You Have Spoken

Dear _____,

This is just to tell you how much I enjoyed speaking to you the other night. Thank you for the invitation and your kind reception. I look forward to having the chance to speak to you again sometime soon. (Suggest other topics.)

31: Letter to New Area Residents (with Brochure)

Dear Mrs. _____:

Our mutual friend, Jane Smith, has mentioned that you have just moved to the area. Welcome!

The people of Springfield take pride in being neighborly and helpful to new residents. That goes for our office too. We at Family Practice would like you to know that we are here for you when you need us.

We have prepared an informational brochure to help acquaint you with our practice and services. Enclosed is your personal copy. Please keep it and refer to it whenever you have a question about our office. You will see that it contains a map of our location, office hours, a list of the services we provide, and a telephone number for new patients. (Mention quarterly patient newsletter if you are willing to provide a complimentary subscription.)

Again, welcome to Springfield. Please call us if we can be of any help.

32: Letter to the Personnel Manager of an Area Employer

Dear (Personnel Manager's Name):

When browsing through our records recently, I realized that a significant number of your employees are patients in our practice. If we may ever be of service to you concerning any of your employees' medical insurance claims, benefits, or coverage, please let us know.

For your information, I am enclosing several copies of our patient information brochure, which will help answer any questions you may have about our practice. Please feel free to share these brochures with any of your employees in need of our services. We always welcome new patients in our practice. (Mention quarterly newsletter if you are willing to provide complimentary subscriptions.)

Again, I hope you will call on us should you have any questions about your employees' insurance benefits.

33: Letter to a Pharmacist, Health-Food Store, Recreation Center or Other Potential Source of New Clients

Dear _____ :

Several of our clients tell us that they use your services.

As a growing practice, we want you to know that we are able to accommodate any other customers of yours who are in need of our professional services. We have produced a client information brochure to help answer questions about our practice. Enclosed are several copies for you to share with interested customers. (Mention quarterly client newsletter if you are willing to provide complimentary subscriptions.)

We appreciate your services and hope that you will not hesitate to call on us if we may ever be of help to you or your customers.

34: Sample Public Service Announcement for Live Radio Broadcast (from a Veterinarian)

FROM: Jack Mallard, D.V.M.
CONTACT: Donna Patterson, Marketing Coordinator
PHONE: 555-1234
DATE: April 15, 1985
USE UNTIL: June 1, 1985
READING TIME: 30 Seconds
WORD COUNT: 77 Words

With the approach of National Pet Week, here's a reminder about the importance of having your dog or cat neutered.

During the month of March the Springfield Humane Society was forced to put 34 dogs and 18 cats to sleep. These animals weren't just strays or abandoned pets. Many were from new litters that couldn't be supported by their owners.

When you get a new pet, contact your veterinarian and follow his advice about neutering and shots.

35: Sample Filler Article (from a Podiatrist)

The building that houses the offices of Doctors David Harris and Joan Melzer, local podiatrists, was once a stage coach terminal. The La Crosse–Milwaukee stage stopped there three times per week until it was replaced by the railroad in 1896.

36: Sample Filler Article (from an Accountant)

Taxpayers in Springfield pay less income tax than the average for the State of Oregon, according to John H. Bean, CPA. The average payment last year was $356 for Oregon residents but only $332 for residents of Springfield.

37: Sample Filler Article (from a Physician)

Fifty-five percent of those attending the smokers' clinic conducted by Family Physicians, P.C., quit smoking completely, according to clinic instructor Dr. Fred Anderson.

38: Sample Filler Article (from a Dentist)

Application of sealants is the most effective form of treatment in the dental office to prevent tooth decay, according to Lester Pateau, D.D.S.

39: Sample Filler Article (from a Psychologist)

More than twice as many work days are lost because of mental disease than because of physical ailments, according to clinical psychologist Nancy Stormgate, Ph.D.

40: Sample Filler Article (from an Attorney)

There were ten percent more divorces than marriages in Springfield last year, according to George Ramey, an attorney for Ramey & Associates. While 120 couples were divorced, only 109 entered into marriage.

41: Sample Press Release Publicizing a Speech (from a Dentist)

FROM: Margaret O'Brien, D.D.S.
          111 Route 18
          East Brunswick, NJ 08816

CONTACT: Jane Hart
         (201) 555-1234

FOR IMMEDIATE RELEASE

SLUG: Margaret O'Brien, D.D.S., to meet with second graders.

Margaret O'Brien, D.D.S., will share information on dental health on February 7 at 10:00 with second grade students at Frost Elementary School.

She will explain dental hygiene and demonstrate proper brushing and flossing techniques. She will also talk about preventing tooth decay. Dental equipment will also be demonstrated by Dr. O'Brien's assistant, Susan Hamlin. Students will have the chance to examine the (name of equipment).

"I want to help children understand dental health," explains Dr. O'Brien. "I also want to help eliminate 'dental anxiety' among youngsters. Once they become familiar with a dentist and get a chance to look at the equipment, they'll feel more comfortable. This will help make their trips to the dentist enjoyable."

Dr. O'Brien is willing to talk to other school groups or organizations. Contact Dr. O'Brien, 111 Route 18, East Brunswick, NJ 08816 or call 555-1234.

-30-

Accompanying material: Photo of Margaret O'Brien demonstrating proper brushing techniques.

42: Sample Press Release (from an Accountant)

FROM: Richard Dorsey, CPA
          111 Albany Avenue
          West Hartford, CT 06117

CONTACT: Ms. Celia Adams
          (203) 555-1234

FOR IMMEDIATE RELEASE

SLUG: Property held in joint tenancy can lead to problems.

A married couple who hold all their property in joint tenancy may be courting a serious estate problem, according to George Arnold, CPA, who has joined accountant Richard Dorsey in partnership. "Under certain circumstances this could result in twice the estate tax," Arnold said.

A graduate of Rutgers College, Arnold passed his Certified Public Accounting examination in 1983. He and Dorsey will practice at 111 Albany Avenue in West Hartford.

Arnold explained that each spouse is granted an exemption to the inheritance tax. When the couple's total estate exceeds the amount of one exemption, property should be divided among both so that both the husband's and the wife's exemption are used.

"The federal inheritance tax laws were completely revised recently," Arnold said. "I urge any persons who feel they may be affected by the changes to consult with their attorney about it."

Arnold is a member of both the Connecticut and national societies of Certified Public Accountants. He specializes in financial and estate planning.

###

A·P·P·E·N·D·I·X   C

Marketing Communication Guide

What's in a name? In some cases all the difference in the world. Here are some frequently used words and phrases you should use and some you should avoid.

SAY OR WRITE THIS	INSTEAD OF THIS
My assistant	My girl
Reception area/room	Waiting area/room
We've had a change in schedule	We've had a cancellation
Use	Utilize
Remind you of your appointment	Confirm, verify
Established client	Old client
Consultation appointment	Case presentation
How do you feel about this?	Do you understand?
Provide a service	Do the work
Fee	Price, cost
Take care of, handle	Pay
Investment	Cost
Substantial investment	Expensive
First payment	Down payment
Payments	Installments
Interrupted schedule	Running late, falling behind
Follow-up visit, reexamination	Recall
Complete this form	Fill this out
Conference, postgraduate courses	Convention

SAY OR WRITE THIS	INSTEAD OF THIS
Spouse	Wife, husband
Inconvenience	Trouble
Discomfort	Pain
Injection	Needle, shot
Medication	Drug
Treatment/examination room	Operatory
Follow	Comply
Find out	Ascertain
Help	Cooperate, assist
Home, address	Residence
Your name/signature goes here	Sign on the dotted line
Need	Require
Give, send	Submit
Now	Presently
Expect	Anticipate
Happens	Transpires
Staff	Personnel
End	Terminate
Having	Experiencing
Yes, no	Affirmative, negative
Make easy	Facilitate
First	Initial
Ask	Inquire
Show	Disclose
Try	Endeavor
If	In the event that
Since	Inasmuch as
Car, truck, bus	Vehicle
Won't you please have a seat?	Have a seat
Hello, I'm Tom. You must be Mr. Haney. We've been expecting you.	Yes, can I help you?

SAY OR WRITE THIS	INSTEAD OF THIS
Good morning, Legal Service Center. Sally speaking. May I help you?	Hello, Legal Service
Please help me understand	What do you mean? Huh?
If you'll wait just a moment, I'll be happy to get that information for you. Thank you.	Hold please
No doubt	There is no doubt that
Whether	The question as to whether
We think	We are of the opinion that
Always	In all cases
Now	At this point in time
We realized	We came to the realization
About	Concerning the matter of
Is there anything you'd like me to explain better?	Any questions?
You'll want to see me	You'll have to see me
He's with a patient/client	He's busy
I can appreciate how you feel	You're wrong
Courtesy	Discount

A · P · P · E · N · D · I · X   D

Successful Applications — Examples of Printed Marketing Materials That Have Made Others Successful

The Dentist's Tree

Robert L. Sturkey, D.D.S.
John F. Learner, D.D.S.

®

Wendy Perkins
Hygienist

653 E. Cuyahoga Falls Ave.
Akron, Ohio 44310
24 hour phone 923-8800

whiteside
PREVENTIVE DENTISTRY

wilfred d. whiteside, d.d.s., inc.

2862 south alameda p.o. drawer 3889
office (512) 882-5688 home (512) 855-0764
corpus christi, texas 78404

CHAT

CAT HOSPITAL-AT TOWSON

610 York Road
Towson, Maryland 21204
(301) 821-9140
by appointment

Jane E. Brunt, D.V.M.

PIO NONO EYE CLINIC

LEONARD W. BELL,
O.D.F.A.A.O.

JOSEPH CITRON,
M.D.P.C.

3131 PIO NONO AVE.
912-781-4310
MACON, GA. 31203

JOANN ONDROVIK. PHD

PSYCHOLOGIST

579 DeShong Drive
Paris, Texas 75460
(214) 785-0746 or 785-1801

Joseph Santelli,
D.D.S., P.C.

746-4033

General and
Preventive
Dentistry

Next to the
Jenney Grist Mill
8 Spring Lane
Plymouth
Ma. 02360

©brogin

These outstanding business cards illustrate a variety of practice logos. Each one conveys a different but effective professional image.

Ernie Lavorini D.D.S.

444-4334

8 a.m. to 10 p.m. · Mon. thru Sat.

426 17th St. #700 Oakland CA 94612

John R. Kelly, D.D.S.
Pediatric Dentistry

240 Elmwood Street
State College, PA 16801
(814) 238-7120

Office Hours by Appointment

Norman Margolies, D.M.D.
FELLOW ACADEMY OF GENERAL DENTISTRY

New Patients always Welcome
257 MAPLE AVENUE
MAPLE PROFESSIONAL BUILDING
RED BANK, NJ 07701
201-842-6370

donald r. sutton   d.d.s.

General Dentistry

norman Mills D.D.S., M.S., LTD
Practice limited to children
and adolescents
845 South Main Street
LOMBARD, Illinois
60148-3397
312-620-8304

All successful dental practices are not alike, as these five logos demonstrate.

CLIFFORD R. TYM, D.D.S., M.P.H.
RES. 886-5544

Innisfail Dental Centre
(C.R. Tym Professional Corporation)

4935 - 49th Street, Innisfail, Alta., T0M 1A0
Phone (403) **227-3011**

Helping <u>you</u> achieve total oral health

PAULINE E. HARRISON, B. Sc., D.D.S., Associate
RES. 252-8088

Innisfail Dental Centre
(C.R. Tym Professional Corporation)

4935 - 49th Street, Innisfail, Alta., T0M 1A0
Phone (403) **227-3011**

Helping <u>you</u> achieve total oral health

DR. C.A. ROLAND LIND, Associate
RES. 343-0407

Innisfail Dental Centre
(C.R. Tym Professional Corporation)

4935 - 49th Street, Innisfail, Alta., T0M 1A0
Phone (403) **227-3011**

Helping <u>you</u> achieve total oral health

BERNADETTE HICKOX
Dental Hygienist

Innisfail Dental Centre
(C.R. Tym Professional Corporation)

4935 - 49th Street, Innisfail, Alta., T0M 1A0
Phone (403) **227-3011**

Helping <u>you</u> achieve total oral health

A good logo is a powerful marketing tool that is most effective when used consistently on all practice marketing tools. Note how the Innisfail Dental Centre personalizes the same business card for each member of the practice.

WHAT TO DO IN CASE OF
A DENTAL EMERGENCY

1. If a tooth is knocked out, handle it by the crown, **not the root.** If it's dirty, rinse it in cool water and if possible place it back into its hole. If not, place the tooth under the tongue; otherwise bring the tooth in water.
2. If a denture or bridge breaks, save all the pieces. Do not repair with glue, as this ruins dental materials.
3. Use cold packs to relieve swelling. Do not use hot packs, they will increase swelling.
4. If you have a toothache, place cotton soaked in oil of cloves into the area. **Do not** put aspirin on the tooth or gum.
5. Call your dentist immediately at **227-3011** (24 hour answering service).

Innisfail Dental Centre

(C.R. Tym Professional Corporation)

4935 - 49th Street, P.O. Box 339, **INNISFAIL, ALBERTA   T0M 1A0**

Phone (403) **227-3011**

CLIFFORD R. TYM, D.D.S., M.P.H.   Res. Phone 886-5544
C.A. ROLAND LIND, B. Odont., Leg. tandl., Sweden · Associate
Res. Phone 343-0407
PAULINE E. HARRISON, B. Sc. D.D.S. · Associate   Res. Phone 252-8088

NAME _____   AGE _____

ADDRESS _____

℞   _____ , ALBERTA

            DATE _____   198 ____

☐ LABEL   _____
                         DENTIST

REFILL _____ TIMES

Helping you achieve total oral health

The instructions for handling a dental emergency appear on the back of all Innisfail Dental Centre business cards. This encourages patients to retain the cards and give them to others. Also note how the logo is repeated on the practice's prescription blanks.

Innisfail Dental Centre

(C.R. Tym Professional Corporation)

4935 - 49th Street, P.O. Box 339
INNISFAIL, ALBERTA T0M 1A0
Phone (403) **227-3011**

Date _____ , 19 ___

To whom it may concern,

_____ had a dental appointment at

_____ A.M.
_____ P.M. _____ on _____ , 19 ___ .

Please excuse from (school, work).

Innisfail Dental Centre

_____

Helping you achieve total oral health

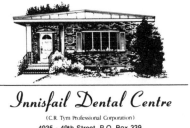

Innisfail Dental Centre

(C.R. Tym Professional Corporation)

4935 - 49th Street, P.O. Box 339
INNISFAIL, ALBERTA   T0M 1A0

Helping you achieve total oral health

The Innisfail Dental Centre logo is also used on the practice's other stationery items, including the excuse card and #10 envelope.

MEDINA EYE ASSOCIATES, INC.

Eye Physician & Surgeon

MEDINA EYE ASSOCIATES, INC.

Eye Physician & Surgeon

Allow me to thank you for having referred

M_____

to me for professional services.

H. Linn Mast, M.D.

We care for people, not just eyes.

Medina Medical Center, Suite 201 / 970 East Washington Street / Medina, Ohio 44256
Telephone (216) 725-7748

H. Linn Mast, M.D.
Diplomate, American Board of Ophthalmology
Medina Medical Center, Suite 201 / 970 East Washington Street / Medina, Ohio 44256 / Telephone (216) 725-7748

Medina Eye Associates also uses its logo consistently on all printed pieces. Note how the logo appears in the same location on the practice letterhead and referral thank-you cards.

MEDINA EYE ASSOCIATES, INC.
Eye Physician & Surgeon

H. Linn Mast, M.D.
Diplomate, American Board of Ophthalmology

We care for people, not just eyes.
Medina Medical Center, Suite 201 / 970 East Washington Street
Medina, Ohio 44256 / Telephone (216) 725-7748

MEDINA EYE ASSOCIATES, INC.
Eye Physician & Surgeon

Medina Medical Center, Suite 201
970 East Washington Street / Medina, Ohio 44256

MEDINA EYE ASSOCIATES, INC.

H. LINN MAST, M.D.
Eye Physician & Surgeon

Please take a few minutes to fill out this Survey.

We care for people, not just eyes.

We care for people,
not just eyes.

Medina Eye Associates uses its practice logo again on the practice business card, #10 envelope and survey questionnaire. Note how the slogan, "We Care For People, Not Just Eyes" ties the practice's printed pieces together and conveys a warm and caring image.

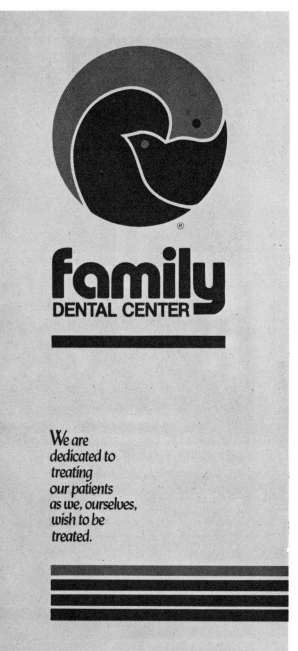

The front panel of a practice brochure is one of the best opportunities to showcase a practice logo. The Family Dental Center brochure (left) uses strong primary colors on white paper. Dr. Roy's brochure (right) is printed in green and black ink on tan paper.

Welcome to Our Office

Medical and Surgical Treatment of the Foot

Dr. Evan Meltzer
Dr. Andrew Chernow

West End Professional Building
612 West Green Street
Ithaca, New York 14850
607-272-6232

The cover of the Downtown Dental Centre brochure (left) is printed in a *reverse*. The words and drawing are *not* printed, but are actually the white paper; the background is what is printed, in this case in blue ink. By contrast, Dr. Meltzer and Chernow's brochure (right) is printed in the conventional manner, with the words and drawing printed with brown ink on tan paper.

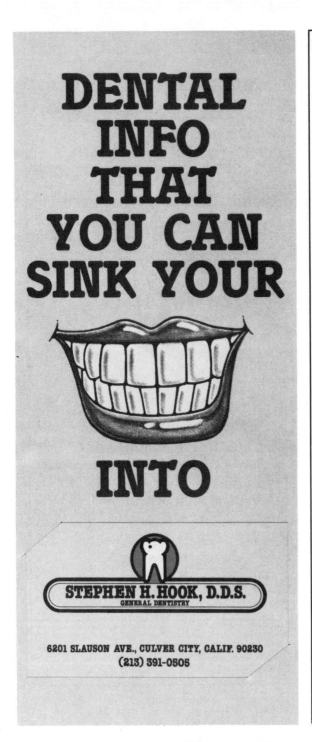

DENTAL INFO THAT YOU CAN SINK YOUR

INTO

STEPHEN H. HOOK, D.D.S.
GENERAL DENTISTRY

6201 SLAUSON AVE., CULVER CITY, CALIF. 90230
(213) 391-0505

PATIENT INFORMATION

Dr. Hook's brochure (left) has been die-cut so his business card can be inserted into the cover. The Little Rock Allergy Clinic's brochure (right) uses white space effectively on its cover to provide graphic relief and invite reading.

These two brochures are printed broadside. They are each 8½″ × 11″ and fold in thirds to fit into a standard #10 envelope. Both brochures use a strong horizontal design on the front panel.

CHOOSE YOUR ACCOUNTING FIRM: FOR ITS ATTENTION TO DETAIL AND A LIBERAL DOSE OF INNOVATIVE THINKING...

Reuschlein, Strickland, Bischoff & Ragsdale, S.C.

This accounting firm has an 8½″ × 11″ booklet-style brochure that is mailed flat. The practice has chosen this larger, more expensive format to attract higher-fee clients.

Patient Information

The Medina Eye Associates brochure (left) uses the practice logo and a strong photograph on the front cover, while Dr. Philip's brochure (right) uses a line drawing. Note how these design elements are repeated *inside* the two brochures on the next two pages.

We care for people, not just eyes.

MEDINA EYE ASSOCIATES, INC.

H. Linn Mast, M.D.
Diplomate, American Board of Ophthalmology

Eye Physician & Surgeon

Welcome To Our Office

Dear Patient,

I appreciate your selection of this office to serve your family eye care needs, and I will do my very best to provide you with quality medical and surgical eye care. I am a medical doctor who has specialized further after medical school in the field of ophthalmology, that branch of medicine concerned with the diagnosis and treatment of diseases of the eyes with medications, lenses, or surgery.

This booklet has been compiled to help you understand the procedures and policies for our office. Please take a few minutes to read it, and then keep it handy, should some question arise later.

Making Appointments

The staff handles the telephone from 9:00 a.m. to 4:00 p.m. daily. It would be helpful for you to know that the staff has been trained to classify appointment requests according to the type of eye problem you are experiencing.

If at any time you feel an emergency has arisen, please tell the appointment secretary so that prompt action may be taken. For a problem which is pressing, but not urgent, your appointment may have to be delayed for a time. For a routine or regular check-up examination, the period of time required to obtain an appointment may vary from several days to several weeks.

Your Appointment

We try our very best to stay on schedule. Sometimes an emergency will arise, causing delays in the schedule. We ask your understanding in this matter.

Please assist us by being on time for your appointment. For your first visit, please come a few minutes early to fill out the necessary forms. If you have been

under the care of another doctor, we may ask you to give us permission to request transfer of some of your records to us.

Since our seating is limited, we would appreciate it if you would limit the number of children, friends and relatives accompanying you to the office to those absolutely necessary. A phone is located in the waiting area, so that you may call a driver upon completion of your examination.

Cancelling Your Appointment

If you are unable to keep your appointment, or are going to be late, please call the office as soon as possible. This allows us to be of service to other patients. A charge may be made for repeated broken appointments.

After-Hours Coverage

If you have an urgent problem, please call the office for recorded instructions. I can usually be reached through the answering service. For any other problems, it is best to contact us during office hours so that we may review your records.

Telephone Calls

Please call the office if you have any questions regarding your condition, medication, or treatment. The assistants are trained to answer your questions, arrange prescription refills, and transmit information to me. If you need to speak to me personally, the assistants will have me return your call as soon as conditions permit.

To save you the time and expense of some follow-up visits, once treatment has begun, I may ask you to call us to report on your condition. The assistants will take this information and give you instructions.

In some cases, optimum medical care cannot be given over the telephone and, therefore, I ask you to accept my judgment regarding the necessity of being seen in the office.

There is generally no charge for phone calls, but we reserve the right to change for unusually long or difficult problems.

Medical Records

Your medical records are held in strictest confidence. Information will not be released unless we have written authorization from you in the office. The only exception to this is when required by law in cases such as industrial injuries, assault, etc.

Should any changes in your medical status, name, address, phone number, or marital status occur, please let us know as soon as possible.

Prescriptions & Refills

We prefer not to refill prescriptions outside office hours when we have no access to your medical records. Please try to anticipate your needs and call the office early in the day to have the refills authorized.

Fees

Charges for office visits and surgery are determined by the time spent and vary with the severity or complexity of the problem. My fees are competitive with other area eye specialists. The receptionist will be happy to discuss charges for services with you. Please do not hesitate to discuss fees if you have any questions. I am concerned with the cost of medical care and appreciate your suggestions.

Billing & Insurance

For each service performed in our office, a "Super

Here is the inside of the Medina Eye Associates brochure, which is a two-fold, six-panel brochure printed on 8½" × 11" paper. Note how the practice logo and slogan are used once again here.

Greetings to All Our Patients

We welcome you to our office, where your dental health, comfort, and convenience is our first priority. This brochure is designed to provide you with information concerning our services and our office. Our highly professional and competent staff are able to serve your many dental needs. Our concern is your dental health. If you have further questions please ask our friendly staff.

About the Office

Because your time is valuable, we want to serve you in the best, most efficient way. To provide you with quality dental care, we recently remodeled and restructured our facility. With four fully equipped dental operatories, two can be devoted to general dentistry, one to dental hygiene, and one exclusively for orthodontic patients.

Our staff of professionals includes a dental hygienist (a Medical College of Virginia graduate) responsible for teeth cleaning, oral hygiene, taking x-rays, and dental care education for patients. Our two full time chairside assistants are trained professionals, with many years of experience.

Our receptionist (also a qualified dental assistant) answers questions, make appointments, and keeps our office running smoothly. Orthodontic appliances and any appliance adjustments are made by a full time lab technician. This saves you time and money.

From complicated dental problems to daily dental maintenance, our office can provide you with the latest in modern dental care. We promise to continue the same quality service that we have been providing for the Washington metropolitan area since 1969.

New Patients

We welcome all new patients. So that we can provide the most effective dental care possible, new patients are asked to fill out a medical history. On your first visit to our office, we will take x-rays, perform a thorough dental examination, and schedule a cleaning with our full-time dental hygienist. The doctor will also have time set aside for a consultation to discuss your dental needs. For your comfort, nitrous oxide is provided upon request. We see all emergency patients on the day our office is contacted.

Long Term Valued Patients

We thank you for your continued patronage. Let us know of any significant changes in your life, like a name or address change. We also are accepting new patients. If you know anyone who is in need of dental care, we will be happy to help.

Advances in Dentistry

While providing routine and preventive services (such as root canals, fillings, and crowns) for our patients, the following new techniques are also available in our office:

Miniaturized Orthodontic Appliances

This new process has revolutionized the cosmetic appearance of orthodontic appliances. In addition, they also provide improvements in oral hygiene and comfort for the patient.

Enamel Bonding

We employ the latest in bonding techniques that allow us to restore color, size, and shape to teeth for a cosmetically pleasing result.

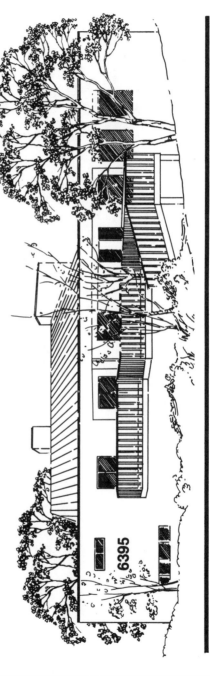

6395

Inside Dr. Philip's brochure, the line drawing from the cover is reduced and repeated. Also an 8½″ × 11″ two-fold, six-panel brochure, the inside panels here are unified by the line at the top and by the drawing of the office at the bottom.

FALL 1983

TOOTH OR CONSEQUENCES
Care

DOCTOR PETER JOINS OUR STAFF

Because of our heretofore limited office hours we realize that there are many of your friends and relatives that have had to put off regular dental care due to their strict work schedules.

In an effort to provide for these patients, we have spent the last several months interviewing several Doctor's, hoping to find one that we feel would be just right to join our practice.

As a result of this effort I am pleased to announce that Dr. Charles A. Peter has joined us and will be working the following hours:

Tuesday - 5:00 P.M. - 9:00 P.M.
Wednesday 8:00 A.M. - 9:00 P.M.
Saturday 8:00 A.M. - 4:00 P.M.

Our entire staff is very excited about Charles' association with our practice. Not only have we found him to be an excellent dentist, we feel he is also a very warm, genuine, and caring human being. We're sure you'll find him to be the same.

While we discourage the shifting of our current patients to these extended hours, we do ask that if you have been pleased with the dental care you've received from our office in the past, please do us the favor of making your friends and relations aware of our additional hours so that we might also serve their dental needs.

A bright smile of tommorrow depends on dental care today!

Dr. Charles A. Peter

Allow Me To Introduce Myself

After receiving my degree in chemistry from Florida Tech. Univ. in Orlando, I left the sand and surf of Florida to come to Dental School at Washington Univ. in St. Louis.

While in dental school I met my wife Beverly and because of the warmth and hospitality of the midwest we've decided to make our home in St. Louis.

In our leisure time we enjoy camping and traveling.

Presently we live in South County but plan to move Oct. 1st to Florissant and look forward to working with Dennis and His Staff.

Doctor S's Message

SWEET DREAMS

Headaches are a plague to modern man and can be traced to many reasons — stress, eyestrain, sinuses. But one reason which you may not think about is when your teeth don't bite together as your jaw intends. The muscles and the joints which connect the jaws, can clench and grind the teeth, usually at night.

Besides causing headaches, there is stress on the jaw joint (TMJ) when the jaws and muscles fight. And it is not a passive fight since our jaws exert pressure of up to 300 pounds per square inch. It may start to melt the bone of the jaw away or cause the teeth to be ground down. Can anything be done? DEFINITELY! Ask Dr. Stovall for further help.

Client newsletters are one of the few marketing tools that allow a practice to be in regular contact with its clients. This one is typeset and makes good use of a strong, two-column format.

EYE TALK

DRS. ANDREOLI & PALERMO, LTD.
Optometrists
1702 W. Campbell Street, Arlington Heights, Illinois 60005
(312) 253-8500

Dr. Mario L. Palermo
Dr. Randall T. Andreoli
Dr. Barbara J. Andreoli

Eye Talk is our quarterly newsletter written to keep our patients informed about current advancements in the eye health care field. Recently we have had a great increase in patients interested in contact lenses and have received so many questions concerning the newest developments in this specialized field that we decided to devote this entire newsletter to contact lenses.

30 DAY EXTENDED WEAR . . .

We are currently fitting the new 30 day extended wear contact lenses that you may have seen on national television. Due to the increased amount of oxygen allowed to pass directly through the lens, you can now leave the lenses in day and night for up to thirty days. Extended wear lenses correct for nearsighted or farsighted people and post-cataract patients. We also have fit the monovision technique for people who require bifocals.

BIFOCAL CONTACT LENSES . . .

Yes, bifocal contact lenses are available! Actually we have been fitting rigid bifocal lenses for many years. Now for the first time we have a soft lens available for use. The lens is designed similar to a spectacle lens, that is, it has a portion for distance vision and a separate portion for reading. The bottoms of the lenses are flattened and weighted to prevent them from rotating. Amazing, isn't it?

CHANGE OR ENHANCE THE COLOR OF YOUR EYES . . .

Tinted soft contact lenses are the newest generation in the evolution of soft contact lenses. These lenses are not just the light blue tint used to see the lens better during handling, but actually come in different colors (sapphire, emerald, topaz, cocoa, and aquamarine) to either subtly enhance or dramatically change the color of your eyes, depending on your natural color. Why should you wear "tinted" soft lenses? For the same reason you wear any soft lens: to look better. The tints are totally safe and beautiful. They in no way interfere with clear vision and when used as directed are guaranteed permanent. These lenses are even available for those people who don't need a vision correction but want to enjoy the cosmetic benefits. To see what these lenses look like on your eyes call our office for a free trial.

THIN LENSES . . .

Soft contact lenses come in not only different curves, powers, sizes, water content, and materials, but also in different thicknesses. In the past all soft contact lenses were a standard thickness. Now we have available super thin and hyper thin contacts. These lenses are usually more comfortable to most people but are harder to handle. If you would like to compare these lenses with the lenses you are currently wearing, please make an appointment for a free trial comparison.

HARD LENSES ARE OUT— OXYGEN PERMEABLE ARE IN . . .

Research shows there is a very good chance that patients fitted with the conventional hard contact lenses will eventually have corneal problems due to lack of oxygen. This may take five, ten or twenty years, depending on the individual. With the new oxygen permeable rigid lenses the cornea gets much more oxygen, keeping it healthy. This is why the conventional (PMMA) contact lens is rarely used. Signs of lack of oxygen are as follows: 1) red eyes; 2) itching/burning after contact lens removal; 3) decreased wearing time for unknown reasons; 4) discomfort after four or five hours of wear. If you experience any of the above symptoms, please call our office for an appointment, as serious damage is possible if prolonged lack of oxygen is present.

SOLUTIONS . . .

Our office can now supply you with the correct replacement solutions needed to keep your contact lenses feeling and looking new. Too often we see patients who have mistakenly purchased the wrong solutions. We hope you will take advantage of this additional service from our office.

SPECIALTY LENSES . . .

Keratoconus—a disease in which the cornea takes on the shape of a cone. In advanced stages vision is extremely poor if contacts are not used. Vision is often improved when contacts are worn.

Cataract—lenses are needed after cataract surgery, and a very high power lens is used. Nowadays, mostly extended wear soft contacts are the lenses of choice.

Cosmetic—as discussed in another part of this newsletter, we can change the color of your eyes. But, more importantly

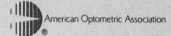

American Optometric Association

Another good example of a typeset, two-column client newsletter.

Dr. Tekavec's Newsletter

A Daily Commitment To Excellence

Produced for the patients of Mel M. Tekavec, D.D.S. ● Fall 1984

OFFICE STAFF— Receptionist (South): Janice Pershin; **Receptionist (North):** Kathy Cusworth; **Patient Relations:** Sue Terrill; **Secretary:** Bev Berge; **Dental Assistants:** Shirley Sanchez, Jeannette Ortiz, Marie Vaughn, Cindy Musso; **Hygienists:** Carol Tekavec, Michelle Layton, Shelly Malouff.

People Hours— Not Office Hours

We have expanded our hours to fit your schedule. In today's hectic world, convenience is essential. Saturdays and evenings upon request can be reserved for you. Call our receptionist for your reserved time.

A "Supplement" for Dental Insurance

Even with dental insurance, comprehensive dental care can mean "out-of-pocket" copayments for you. A "Piggyback" Plan is now available that will eliminate up to 20% of the total fee charged by the dentist. If you have dental insurance that pays 80%, your copayment with this plan is Zero (0). The annual premium is $15 for one person, $25 for two, and $40 for your entire family. Call our receptionist for more details.

A Possible Alternative To "Gum Surgery"

Recent findings have shown that a mixture of sodium bicarbonate, salt, and

Cosmetic Dentistry

Archeological evidence shows that during 3500 B.C. of the Egyptian Empire they replaced missing teeth and ornamented teeth still in the mouth. A definite and continuous history of dentistry begins in the 18th Century. Dentists of that period were artisans, not scholars, and because they were jealous of their craft, they did not keep records. There is ample proof,

however, that Europeans, Arabians, and South Americans worked on teeth. South American Indians practiced operative dentistry, filling teeth through artificial means.

Recently, silver, gold, and new space-age metals have been used to "fill" teeth. In the past few years, tooth-colored synthetic resins have been developed. These materials are now bonded onto the tooth with a light curing wand (a modern "E.T." finger). These tooth-colored fillings can be used to close spaces, repair fractures, and cover stained teeth. Many of these procedures can be accomplished without local anesthesia (no numb lip!).

Your smile is your most important asset. Call us for a smile checkup!

hydrogen peroxide can be used to help prevent gum disease or control moderately active disease. Call us today and have our hygienist explain this "Tooth-Saving" technique.

Golden Age Club

If you are 65 years of age or older and want to keep your teeth, we'd suggest that you join our Dental Plan. For $45 per year ($75 for two persons),

we will professionally clean, x-ray and examine your teeth every six months for no additional charge. Any additional needed dental treatment will be discounted 20% or more. Call our receptionist for more details.

Summer Treat!

Freeze popsicles made from unsweetened fruit juices. Use ice cube trays or other shaped molds to create unusual and healthful treats!

A three-column client newsletter, like this one, offers maximum flexibility for article and artwork layout.

Ask the Veterinarian:

Client: When is the best time to spay or neuter my pet?

Dr. Womer: Both female dogs & cats should be spayed at six months of age. Female dogs spayed before the second heat period will have a much reduced chance of having breast cancer later in life. Male dogs may be neutered soon after reaching sexual maturity - usually 9-12 months of age. Tom cats may be neutered at 9 months of age unless they begin spraying urine & getting into cat fights sooner. In this case the operation may take place as early as six months of age.

Client: How long will my pet need to be hospitalized?

Dr. Womer: Female pets & male dogs spend 2 nights in our Veterinary Clinic while tom cats may go home the afternoon following their surgery.

Client: What changes might I notice in my pets following these operations?

Dr. Womer: In most cases you will probably not notice any changes in your female pet's behavior. Contrary to popular belief, spayed females do not have to become fat & lazy. There may be a decrease in your pet's metabolism and she may not need to eat as much food as before - an economic benefit.

The most notable change is in the tom cat. He will quit carousing at night and thereby decrease his chances of getting into cat fights. A decrease of just one trip to the vet to treat fight wounds will probably pay for the neutering operation!

THE Village Veterinary Clinic NEWSLETTER

Vol. One, Summer 1983

Ralph Womer, D.V.M.
& Associates

205-821-7730

403 Opelika Road
Auburn, AL 36830

Health Maintenance Care

As the weather becomes warmer & sunnier, and we begin to enjoy summertime activities, let's remember to take time to pay special attention to our pet's health.

The summer months are a good time to bring our pet's medical records up to date by getting their annual vaccinations, heartworm checks, and examinations for internal and external parasites. Remember: Preventative veterinary care is much easier & more economical than treating an animal who has developed a disease condition!

Heartworms - A Constant Threat

PREVENTION MAKES SENSE!

Coughing, loss of breath, fatigue upon any physical exertion...

Many of us recognize the above symptoms as those associated with heartworm disease in pets. However, did you know that your pet (esp. young dogs) can have a heartworm infestation and still not exhibit any of the usual signs of chronic heart disease?

Since heartworm disease is prevalent throughout the South, we at the VVC urge pet owners to have their pets checked annually and to keep them on preventative medicine throughout the year.

The heartworm exam is quick and inexpensive. Your pet is special in your heart - let's keep his heart healthy and strong!

Summertime Health Tips

1. Animals are prone to hot weather fatigue & collapse much as we humans are. Make sure your pet has plenty of shade, ventilation, & lots of cool water to drink.
2. NEVER! NEVER! NEVER! Don't ever leave your pet in a parked car with the windows rolled up during hot weather!!
3. During hot days, many pets will cut down on the amount of food that they normally consume. Don't become unneccessarily alarmed, but do take special care to throw out or refrigerate the uneaten portion. This is necessary because pet food can spoil easily in warm weather & is a special "picnic-spot" for unwanted pests such as ants & roaches.
4. Check your pet regularly for fleas & ticks. These pests can make you & your pet miserable if they are not kept under control. The VVC offers a bath & flea dip service and we will be happy to advise you on methods to help keep your pets & home from becoming infested with obnoxious insects.

Drop us a line and let us know what topics concerning animal health you'd like to see in our newsletter, and feel free to send questions in for our Ask the Veterinarian Column!

Note how this client newsletter uses boxes around the articles to provide graphic interest.

CAT CLINIC AND HOSPITAL

5170 LIBERTY AVE.
PITTSBURGH, PA 15224
681-1122

Dear Cat Owner:

April begins outdoor activity for many cats in the Pittsburgh area. Because of the contact your cat will be having with other cats (directly or indirectly), we would like to remind you that if your cat's vaccinations for distemper, rhinotracheitis and calicivirus have not been given within the past year, they are OVERDUE! If you aren't sure, don't hesitate to call us, so that we can check your cat's records. Remember, even if your cat doesn't go outside, these viruses are airborne, and an open window is all it takes for your cat to be exposed to them. And because of the increased incidence of rabies in Pennsylvania last year, it is highly recommended that your cat be vaccinated and protected from this DEADLY virus, also. As Dr. Fox states in his cartoon, "Love is having regular shots and check-ups, ..."

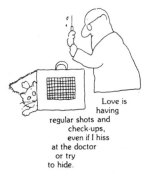

Love is having regular shots and check-ups, even if I hiss at the doctor or try to hide.

From *Love is a Happy Cat* by Dr. Michael W. Fox
Reprinted by permission of Newmarket Press

Text copyright by Michael W. Fox (1982)
Illustration copyright by Harry Gans (1982)

If case you didn't know, the Cat Clinic has the lowest fees in town for feline vaccinations, at our regular Monday evening vaccination clinic. If your cat is healthy and does not need a physical examination, vaccination for Distemper, Rhinotracheitis, and Calicivirus is only $8, and for Rabies, only $6. Money should not be a reason for not having your cat vaccinated.

BOARDING YOUR CAT

Although the best place for your cat while you're on vacation is home (with a daily check by a responsible person), sometimes this is not possible and boarding becomes a necessity. The Cat Clinic has boarding facilities and a new BOARDING SUITE with large, fiberglass cages with a built-in cat perch. The suite has heating/air conditioning, is quiet and clean/clean/clean! We cater to your cat, with 9-Lives® canned cat food (all 25 flavors available), dry food, and vittles. Personal attention is given to your cat by our trained staff (graduate Animal Health Technicians), and our veterinarian, Dr. Bebko, is on call 24 hours a day. Because stress is such a big factor in feline illnesses, we do everything possible to insure your cat is at ease and eating well. So, please, when boarding your cat at a facility other than the Cat Clinic, check for these *minimum* standards: heating/air conditioning, foods your cat loves, and gentle hands. If you are boarding your cat with us, please give us at least 2 weeks' notice.

SUMMER GROOMING

Most of us have been faced with an ever-growing problem with fleas this past year—fleas on Kitty, fleas in the carpeting, and fleas in the furniture!!! We highly recommend flea powdering your cat every 5 days throughout the flea season and flea combing (yes, there is such a comb) on a daily basis. These products can be purchased at the Cat Clinic (powder $3/flea comb $4) and at most pet stores, but make sure they are specifically for cats!! Flea products for dogs are highly toxic to cats!! The 3M Company has released an area spray for your house (Sectrol) which is non-toxic to humans and pets and kills fleas and flea eggs!! This is a new breakthrough, and everyone who has used it is highly satisfied. As you may not know, most area sprays do not kill the flea eggs—and so, a few weeks later, fleas are hatched in your house. The Cat Clinic carries this spray, also, along with a complete line of the finest flea products for your cat at reasonable prices.

Another successful client newsletter, with inviting articles and graphics.

FAMILY MEDICAL CENTER

110 Fields Drive
Post Office Box 1860
Sanford, North Carolina 27330

EDITION 1   SUMMER 1984

ROBERT W. PATTERSON, M.D., P.A.

STEPHEN H. COX, M. D.

FROM OUR FAMILY

· TO YOURS ·

This is the first edition of our newsletter which we feel is appropriately titled, From Our Family To Yours. This will be the first in what we hope to be a long series of such publications from our office that have as their main objective, to inform you, our patient family of ways to better your health. Some call it preventative medicine, others say it borders on holistic medicine. We hope that you will agree that it is just plain old GOOD medicine.

Over the next few months we hope you will watch as our dream unfolds. Our plans have long been to have our primary emphasis on "wellness care" and preventative medicine, as well as patient education. Our dream has begun with this our inaugural issue. Starting in August, we will explore a different theme each month by way of group lectures, seminars, and classes as well as by use of the "printed word" here in this newsletter. We hope to also place added importance to not only treating what ails you, but also "educate" you about it too.

Joan Watson, R.N., will serve as our Director of Patient Education, and in this capacity serve as coordinator for our night classes and for this newsletter. She will also be responsible for teaching all of us, staff and patients alike. The classes that she organizes will be held in our classroom in the early evenings, and as we grow, we will expand to larger facilities, though our present classroom holds about 75 persons.

I want to make sure that you know that YOU are the most important person in the world to us and if there is anything that we are doing wrong or could do it better to help you or yours, please let us know. The only way we can grow and improve is with your help.

We look forward to your comments. Happy reading!!!!

WHAT'S NEW?

IBM 36, AMES SERALYZER, MED TECH, CLASSROOM, MED LIBRARY, DR. C, PT, SAT. HRS. NIGHT SHIFT!!!!!! What does this all mean? Is it a vocabulary drill? No, these are just a few of the new things we are offering at the **FAMILY MEDICAL CENTER.** All of these are being added to add to the convenience and quality of care that is available to you, our patient family.

May 1984 saw our office computerize. What good does that do you? BUNCHES! Now we will file ALL of your insurance for you at each visit. This should also aid in the promptness by which you are refunded for your expenses for medical care.

We feel that laboratory work forms a very important part of any medical practice, and that's why we have updated all of our equipment adding the "top of the line" equipment as well as Cheryl Voss, who is a licensed medical technician who performs all of our laboratory procedures, guaranteeing you the patient, the most accurate, effecient and least inexpensive testing.

NEXT PAGE...

The best client newsletters have a variety of interesting, informative articles, like this one.

Bibliography

Books

Adler, Mortimer J. *How to Speak, How to Listen.* New York: Macmillan Publishing Co., 1983.

Carlson, Linda. *The Publicity and Promotion Handbook.* Boston: CBI Publishing Co., 1982.

Chase's Calendar of Annual Events. Flint, MI: Apple Tree Press, Inc., annual.

Conran, Terrance. *The House Book.* New York: Crown Publishers, Inc., 1983.

Cook, Marshall, Rosella Howe, and Blake R. Kellogg. *The Newsletter: How to Design, Write, and Edit It.* Madison, WI: Cook, Howe and Kellogg, 1980.

Graphic Arts Manual. New York: Arno Press, Musarts Publishing Corp., 1980.

Levoy, Robert P. *The $100,000 Practice and How to Build It.* Englewood Cliffs, NJ: Prentice-Hall, Inc., 1966.

Margolis, Bernard S. *The Growth and Development of the Wisdom Tooth.* El Paso, TX: Kan Chu Enterprises, Inc., 1981.

Marketing Your Law Firm's Services. Harrisburg, PA: Pennsylvania Bar Institute, 1984.

Melcher, Daniel and Nancy Larrick. *Printing and Promotion Handbook.* McGraw-Hill, Inc., 1966.

Milone, Charles L., W. Charles Blair, and James E. Littlefield. *Marketing For The Dental Practice.* Philadelphia, PA: W. B. Saunders Company, 1982.

O'Brien, Richard. *Publicity, How to Get It.* New York: Harper and Row, 1977.

Producing Your Own Practice Newsletter. Madison, WI: Professional Communications, Inc., 1984.

Price, Judith. *Executive Style: Achieving Success through Good Taste and Design.* New York: The Linden Press/Simon & Schuster, 1980.

Public Relations Idea Book. New York: Printers' Ink Publishing Co., Inc., 1953.

Seltz, David D. *Handbook of Innovative Marketing Techniques.* Reading, MA: Addison-Wesley Publishing Company, 1981.

Stephenson, Howard. *Publicity for Prestige and Profit.* New York: McGraw-Hill, Inc., 1953.

Yale, David R. *The Publicity Handbook.* New York: Bantam Books, 1982.

Periodicals

The ADA News. Chicago: The American Dental Association.

The AMA News. Chicago: American Medical Association.

The AOA News. St. Louis: The American Optometric Association.

DDS Alert. Fairburn, GA: Bonner Communications Co.

Dental Care Marketing. Madison, WI: Professional Communications, Inc.

Dental Economics. Tulsa, OK: PennWell Publishing Co.

Dental Management. Cleveland: Harcourt Brace Jovanovich.

Journal of the AOA. St. Louis: American Optometric Association.

Management Consultant's Advisory. Bala-Cynwyd, PA: MCA Publications.

Medical Economics. Oradell, NJ: Medical Economics Co., Inc.

The Mittleman Letter. New York: The Once Daily, Inc.

Money. New York: Time-Life Publications.

Office Administration and Automation. New York: Geyer-McAllister Publications.

Optical Management. White Plains, NY: Advisory Enterprises, Inc.

Optometric Management. White Plains, NY: Advisory Enterprises, Inc.

The Office. Philadelphia: Office Publications, Inc.

PC Advisor. New York: PC Advisor Newsletter.

Personnel Journal. Costa Mesa, CA: A.C. Croft, Inc.

The Practical Accountant. New York: Institute for Accounting Professional Development, Inc.

Practice Management Briefs. Champaign, IL: Colwell Systems, Inc.

Practice Marketing and Management. Madison, WI: Professional Communications, Inc.

The Professional Report. Scarsdale, NY: TPR Publishing Co., Inc.

Small Business Report. Monterrey, CA: Small Business Monitoring and Research Company.

Supervisory Management. Saranac Lake, NY: American Management Association, Periodical Division.

Update. Madison, WI: Professional Communications, Inc.

Index